Dedication

This book is dedicated to Tessa, who brilliantly combines unstinting, uncomplaining support with incisive critiques which have improved so much of my work, and to Dan, Oliver and India.

John Clare's Guide to Media Handling

John Clare's Guide to Media Handling

JOHN CLARE

Gower

Published by
Gower Publishing Limited
Gower House
Croft Road
Aldershot
Hampshire GU11 3HR
England

Gower Publishing Company
131 Main Street
Burlington, VT 05401-5600 USA

John Clare has asserted his right under the Copyright, Designs and Patents Act 1988 to be identified as the author of this work.

British Library Cataloguing in Publication Data
Clare, John
    John Clare's guide to media handling
    1. Mass media. 2. Journalism
    I. Title II. Guide to media handling
    302.2´3

ISBN 0 566 08298 5

Library of Congress Cataloging-in-Publication Data
Clare, John, 1955–.
    John Clare's guide to media handling / John Clare
        p. cm.
    Includes index.
    ISBN 0-566-08298-5 (hardcover)
    1. Public relations. 2. Mass media and business. 3. Industrial publicity. I. Title: Guide to media handling. II. Title.

HD59.C53 2001
659.2–dc21   00-060979

Typeset in 9/12 Utopia by IML Typographers, Birkenhead and printed in Great Britain by MPG Books Ltd, Bodmin.

Contents

*   (handwritten mark)

b oleh include.   (handwritten note)

About the Author

John Clare had nearly 20 years experience as a journalist when he became a media consultant in 1992, and has since worked extensively with some of Europe's biggest companies.

During his journalistic career he held senior positions in print and broadcast journalism. In television he was a producer at ITN and editor of two TV news programmes. He has also been a reporter on publications including the *Yorkshire Post* and two national newspapers including the *Daily Mail*.

He is now the managing director of LionsDen Communications, one of the country's leading media and crisis consultancies. He works regularly with senior executives and opinion leaders across a wide range of sectors, including pharmaceuticals, finance, leisure, travel and IT.

Figures

Figures

Preface

The media is the most important influence on how businesses are perceived. Whether through analysis in the financial pages, news reports of important developments, or TV and radio interviews with company spokespeople, the way a company is portrayed in the media is a significant element in the development of a corporate reputation.

Reputation is a primary corporate asset, and its construction, maintenance and defence is a serious matter demanding senior executive input. The relationship between the headline and the bottom line has never been clearer. For today's executives, knowing how to play their part in that relationship by successful media management is an essential skill.

'Getting it right' has individual benefits too – like a good presenter, a good media manager will always prevail over a similarly qualified colleague who is seen as a media liability.

Yet even for senior executives with years of experience of the corporate world, entering the media world means stepping outside their comfort zone. For them, becoming involved in a media campaign or giving an interview can seem like playing a game without having seen the rule book – they don't know what's permitted or expected, how to score or even how long it will last.

I don't believe this is fair to either party. A well-prepared interviewee will always be worth more to a journalist than one who does not know the ropes. My objective in writing this book is to put the rules of the media game in your hands, and level the playing field. I show you what needs to be done to achieve media success, and give you the tools to do it. Throughout the book I strive to introduce you to the journalist's mindset. If you can understand how journalists think, you can anticipate their reaction to you and your company.

Much of the advice contained in these pages comes from nearly 20 years as a journalist in print and broadcasting, working for some of the biggest media organizations in the UK including ITN and the *Daily Mail*. The rest comes from my years as a 'poacher turned gamekeeper' – as a media and crisis consultant to some of Europe's biggest companies. That period has given me a great insight into senior executives' understanding, fears and misconceptions about the media.

This combination of external and internal perspectives of how corporations are portrayed in the media puts me in a position to guide you through the media world, showing you the routes to a fair press, explaining what journalists want and how you can take advantage of that. Notice I say 'a fair press' rather than 'a good press' – you have a right to the former but have to earn the latter. However good your reputation, journalists are not there to give you free publicity.

Part of a journalist's role is as a watchdog. So if things go wrong in your company you will probably find yourself on the receiving end of negative publicity. I deal with this, too, in the book. My aim there is to equip you to identify issues before they become serious problems, and to help you to deal with a crisis if you do find yourself in the eye of a media storm.

I hope you find this book useful and stimulating.

JOHN CLARE

Acknowledgements

Journalism can be the best job in the world, and attracts individualists and great characters. I've been privileged to work with more than my fair share of both, and this book would not have been possible without the knowledge and experience I picked up from them. They include bosses, colleagues, employees and rivals.

Among the 'poachers' are senior executives in some of Britain's most successful media organizations. Included in the 'gamekeepers' are senior figures in the corporate communications field as well as fellow media and crisis consultants. Then there are the many senior executives who've left me in no doubt just how daunting facing the media can be.

Singling out individuals would either produce a very long list or be unfair, so they must remain unacknowledged in print. They do, however, know who they are.

JC

Introduction: About this Book

MEDIA IMAGE – A VITAL CORPORATE ASSET

Every day in the UK, nearly 30 million of us read a newspaper. We each listen to the radio for an average of 21 hours a week and spend even more time in front of the TV. If you're involved in running a business, then we – as readers, viewers and listeners – are also your customers, investors, competitors, employees, suppliers and financial analysts. Any idea that these two groups of people are different is a fiction. What we read, hear and see about you and your company in the media – its media image – is a major component of your corporate reputation. This in turn influences what we say, think and do about you. It influences the way we regard you, and the way we do business with you – if at all.

In today's business world, defined as it is by the twin Cs of competition and communications, corporate reputation is an increasingly important asset. Measuring it is difficult, but a *Management Today* report in 1998 suggested a positive reputation was worth around one year's turnover. The evidence for the importance of corporate reputation is compelling, and the realization that this is the case is becoming increasingly common among business leaders. The same survey found that two-thirds of business managers agreed that there was a correlation between corporate reputation and financial results.

Just as your customers, investors and employees wear many hats, so do journalists. They are members of the public too, and what they read, see and hear about your company also makes an impression on them, and influences their own articles. The snowball effect of a media image cannot be overestimated – and for you this can be either the start of an exciting ride to the end of the rainbow, or the softening-up for a knockout punch. Consider the contrasting images of two leading British retailers in the summer of 1999 – Marks & Spencer and ASDA. The hammering M&S was taking in the press was only equalled by the beating its share price was taking on the Stock Exchange. ASDA, meanwhile, was enjoying a media honeymoon period after jilting British retail giant Kingsfisher at the altar to leap into bed with the American suitor Wal-Mart. ASDA's share price soared as the British public looked forward to a 'Revolution at the check-out' as the *Daily Mail* front page put it.

Less than a year earlier we had seen more evidence of the importance of good publicity. In autumn 1998 five new names appeared in the FTSE 100 list of companies: Colt Telecom, Securicor, Sema, Southern Electric and Telewest. Their combined market capitalization was £13.8 billion. Yet their total profits were just £1.8 *million*. In sharp contrast, the five they replaced (British Steel, Blue Circle, Enterprise Oil, Rank and RMC) had combined profits of £1.4 *billion*. Besides the bottom lines, there was another stark difference between the newcomers and the leavers – their media image. The new boys had all enjoyed positive media publicity which was reflected in their ever-rising share prices and market capitalizations. They were regarded as exciting, innovative companies with enormous potential – Stock Market darlings. The leavers, meanwhile, were portrayed as either outdated or badly run businesses.

Nobody would claim that a good media image alone is the key to business success – it has to be backed up by sound corporate practices and if you are a plc, equally sound financial management. But a good reputation is the cornerstone of so much in the business world.

A good reputation is far more than just a fair weather friend – it's also a tremendous asset in times of need. A study by New York University's Stern School of Business showed that companies with a good reputation have a rate of profitability in excess of the industry average. During the US Stock Market crash of 1987, shares in the ten most admired companies recovered faster and suffered less, while shares in the ten least admired companies fell three times as far.

If you have a disaster which destroys your HQ or a key production site, you can rebuild it. Rebuilding a good reputation, however, will take longer – indeed it may never happen. In business today, there is a clear connection between the media headline and the company's bottom line. Watch a company's share price rise in the hours and days after favourable media reports of a new contract or other business deal, or fall after criticism of the Board in the financial pages.

That's why putting your message across accurately in the media is so important. Whenever you give a media interview, you are playing for high stakes. Being inadequately prepared is at best risky, at worst verging on negligent if you have shareholders' investments at stake. But the benefits of being a skilled media performer can accrue to you personally as well as your company. In June 1999, soon after Kingfisher's bid for ASDA had been trumped by Wal-Mart, Michael Hingston resigned as Kingfisher's Director of Corporate Communications. *The Financial Times* warned of the threat to the business:

> Kingfisher has been keen to stress that its strategy of expanding its DIY and electricals business internationally and continuing to expand general merchandise in the UK remains intact. However, losing key communicators at such a crucial time could threaten to destabilise the message, suggested analysts, and further erode the share price, which has fallen 10 per cent since the ASDA deal fell apart.
>
> 'It would leave them really bereft at a time when they really do need someone to hold the fort' said one.
>
> (*Financial Times*, 17 June 1999)

THE MEDIA'S IMAGE

Yet the media, ironically, get a bad press among many executives. When I ask executives on training courses how they regard journalists, they tend to adopt what we call the 'wagons in a circle' stance – they assume a defensive position and wait for the Cheyenne to come over the hill and shoot them. I have worked regularly with senior people across a wide range of industries – pharmaceuticals, financials, leisure, transport – and many of them were convinced that their sector or business had been subject to a vendetta by a wide range of media.

It's rarely true. Of course, if the government or the Competition Commission (formerly the Monopolies and Mergers Commission) points the finger at you, then you will find yourself – quite rightly – in the media spotlight. Being a watchdog is part of the media's role. But for the majority of businesses, most media publicity is generally favourable. As an example, take a look at today's papers, or make a mental note the next time you watch or listen to the TV or radio news. Note how many stories are promotional 'plugs' for businesses, ranging from the great beasts of the high street to small start-up companies. The approaches from journalists which led to these items were recognized by the businesses concerned as opportunities for favourable publicity with millions of people.

In the UK media there is a tremendous hunger for business stories as more people own shares and other investments and become interested in how business works. The majority of stories are positive. The next time your public relations people give you a digest of cuttings about your company, take a good look at the coverage over a period. If you're running a successful, ethical business delivering good returns, most of the cuttings will report good news and raise your positive profile.

Sometimes the effect of just a small amount of positive coverage can be dramatic on companies of any size. When Prince Harry was photographed ski-jumping at Klosters on a pair of revolutionary mini-skis, the small company which made them was overwhelmed by the demand. When TV chef Delia Smith recommended a type of omelette pan, the manufacturers took orders for 90 000 within four months, compared to the normal 200 a year. They had to take on extra staff to meet the demand when just a few months earlier they had laid people off.

SOUNDBITES AND SUBSTANCE

A word of warning, here: image-building, PR and media relations only succeed if they are backed up by actions and a well-run company. As American PR guru W. Page put it, 'Public perception of an organization is determined 90% by doing and 10% by talking.' Because society is now so complex, most of us have little firsthand experience of the particular company, organization or person involved in media publicity, so our image of an organization is formed by *perception* rather than *reality*. In the late 1990s Burson-Marsteller, one of the world's biggest PR firms, started describing its business as 'perception management' instead of public relations as an acknowledgement of this. Some critics complained that it sounded too direct and had sinister overtones, but the fact remains that perception and reality are the twin rocks on which business success is built. If your company is perceived as a good employer, responsive to customer needs, ethical in its dealings and delivering good value to shareholders and customers, it is likely to reap bigger benefits than if it does all this but keeps the good news to itself.

Many big company cultures are risk-averse, and naturally cautious about the media. There is nothing wrong in that, but as a consequence they miss opportunities for positive publicity. This cautious outlook is often reflected in the attitude of their senior executives, who feel uncomfortable when I advise them to blow their own trumpet occasionally. Some of them, however, are so publicity-shy that I'm reminded of the words of Blackadder, Rowan Atkinson's TV character, 'It would have at least been good to know that you've got a trumpet, Baldrick.' Trumpet-blowing is at the heart of most media campaigns though as we shall see, you can sometimes create more noise if you get other people to blow it for you.

While you may not have the Midas touch of Michael Heseltine or Sir John Harvey-Jones, you can use the media as a force for good in your company's profile – and you must use a variety of media outlets to get your message across. The reason is that everyone concerned with your business hears about it from a variety of sources

– they all wear sever[...]
ceuticals, for examp[...]
doctors or pharmac[...]
directly through me[...]
also form an impress[...]
via national newsp[...]
their patients, thei[...]
own customers. Tha[...] campaign is far more successful than a few tactical 'hits' – you have to tell people something many times in many different ways to get them to change behaviour, which is the ultimate objective of communications campaigns.

PREPARATION: THE KEY TO SUCCESS

Understanding the media and knowing how to get the most out of it is a crucial skill for today's and tomorrow's executive. To succeed in business, it is no longer enough to be able to read a balance sheet and P&L account, be a dynamic manager and spot market trends offering opportunities or threats. All these are important, but having a positive media image will increase the returns for you and your company. You can actively promote that image by proactively seeking the right type of coverage. When times are good, this is easier and more enjoyable. But that's not all – when your business is under pressure, your investors, partners, customers and City analysts will expect you to defend it in the media.

Dealing confidently with the media will also raise your own profile inside and outside the company. Confident media spokespeople, like confident presenters, will always score over similarly qualified colleagues who don't come across so well. A confident performance will help your image in your own industry sector, because once you've shown yourself to be a good media performer, journalists will come back to you again and again. This gives you and your company 'opinion-former' status. Justin Urquhart-Stuart is a good example. As a senior executive at Barclays Stockbrokers, he was occasionally asked by journalists to comment on City issues. The reporters realized that he had an unusual gift for simplifying complex matters, making them understandable and interesting to the

they approached him more often. By
had regular slots on Radio 4, in the *Inde-*
nt and a number of other media outlets.
rclays Stockbrokers is credited whenever he
appears – it's a win-win for both he and his
employers.

Even if you don't aspire to that level of exposure, to deal confidently with the media you
need to be prepared. That means understanding
what the media is, how it works, and what journalists want. It means understanding about the
different types of media, the relationships
between them, and the pressures on them to
deliver the goods. It means understanding where
stories come from, and the process which turns
events into news and features, so you can anticipate which events and issues will attract media
attention, and which will be ignored.

Then you will be in a position to drive your
image and reputation, steering a course in the
direction you want to travel. Without this capability, your corporate reputation is like a small
boat in a stormy sea, constantly buffeted in one
direction then another – and not knowing how to
forecast when a big wave may appear and
threaten to wash the crew overboard.

HOW THIS BOOK WILL HELP

Setting a course and sticking to it is what this
book will teach you. It will open your eyes to how
the media work, so that you understand what
drives them, and how journalists perceive companies like yours. It will take you behind the
scenes of newspapers, radio and TV programmes to demystify 'the newsmaking
process'. It will introduce you to different types
of news, features and other editorial content. It
will show you how the media are the ultimate
customer-focused business, how well they
target their audience, and how to exploit that
knowledge to your advantage.

It will also give you practical advice in the
shape of 'do's and don'ts' and back up that
advice with real-life, recent examples. Once you
have read this book, whenever you are faced
with the opportunity to talk to journalists, you
will feel confident that you can enhance your
own profile – and that of your business.

When you are invited to take part in a media
interview, or comment on a story, you need to
ask yourself one big question, 'Can I make things
better by doing this interview than by refusing
it?' The answer must be 'yes' to make the interview worth while. This book will leave you
equipped to answer the question correctly and
confidently.

But the benefits of this book are far wider
than preparing for formal media interviews.
Your new skills will benefit you in all aspects of a
media/company interface, from how press
releases are written to knowing when an exclusive deal with one journalist is likely to deliver
better results than calling a press conference.

Increasingly, large businesses recognize the
importance of managing their media image
and dedicate significant budgets to it. They
have their own departments to answer press
inquiries, employ public relations agencies to
plan campaigns which will portray them in a
favourable light, and hire media consultants
with direct access to the chief executive. They
also spend millions on advertising, which is
another form of media exposure, though not a
focus of this book. It is worth noting, however,
that coverage in the editorial columns has far
higher credibility than in the advertising pages
because the readers perceive journalists as gatekeepers who have filtered the information for
them.

It may be, however, that once you or your
colleagues have approved the budget, your attitude is 'let them get on with it', primarily
because you don't understand their world. This
is a mistake, and leads to underperformance and
demotivation on both sides. You wouldn't do
that with the finance, sales or research departments, and shouldn't with communications.
Your business will work more efficiently if you
understand the broad principles of handling the
media, so that you can take informed decisions
about it. This book will enable you to do that.

But I'm not offering a rose-tinted view of the
media. This book is about getting a fair press,
which is the best you can expect. Even in the best
businesses, however, it's clear that things can go
wrong, with disastrous consequences. So this
book also looks at what happens when it does. It

gives you practical advice on how to spot a potential problem before it becomes a crisis, and tells you what to do if you find yourself in the eye of a media storm. It also shows you how coverage of a crisis typically develops, and how the media role in such circumstances changes from its normal, day-to-day behaviour.

The likely outcome of every company/media interface is based on what we may call the 3 Cs – chance, challenge and confidence. It's a great chance to put your company's messages across. The challenge is to achieve that, and make sure you stick to your agenda rather than the journalist's. And, as in so many aspects of business life, confidence plays its part in determining success or failure. This book will give you that confidence, so that you will feel you really understand the media, and are equipped to take part in campaigns on equal terms. Once you understand something, you can start to take advantage of it, and spot the opportunities or pitfalls on the path ahead.

In the words of Machiavelli, 'Information is power.' That is what this book will give you.

CHAPTER SUMMARY

- The media is the most important influence on your corporate reputation.
- The value of a positive reputation has been estimated at up to one year's turnover.
- Increasingly business managers agree that there is a strong correlation between corporate reputation and financial results.
- The headline and the bottom line are inextricably linked.
- A positive media image alone will not guarantee financial success – it needs to be supported by sound corporate practices.
- A good media image can be a great asset when times are hard.
- Becoming a good media performer can benefit your career.
- Too many executives are defensive about the media, and miss opportunities for positive publicity.
- There is a great hunger for business stories in the UK media.
- Understanding how to make the most of the media is a crucial management tool.
- To deal with the media confidently you need to be prepared.
- Information is power. That is what this book will give you.

CHAPTER ONE

What's in the News?

The most common question posed by executives I meet is starkly simple: 'What is news, and how can we get our company on it or in it?' It's a perfectly good question, and the rationale behind it is clear. They feel that if they can learn what a news mould looks like, they can squeeze their own media activities into it, and so make favourable publicity easier to achieve. Unfortunately, this is only true, in the words of Evelyn Waugh in *Scoop*, 'Up to a point, Lord Copper.' In reality, the answer is fiendishly complicated. It depends on who's answering – there is no 'one size fits all' description of news.

Quite apart from that, 'the news' includes many types of articles which are not 'news' in the traditional sense, but are features, which are less time-sensitive and event-driven than news. But even within the traditional 'news' definition, there are two types: breaking news, that is things that happen out of the blue, such as train crashes, earthquakes and unexpected political events, and 'diary stories' which are planned in advance. As an executive you will be largely concerned with 'diary stories' so that is where this chapter will focus. Diary stories offer greater opportunities for media publicity than the 'hold the front page' type of news of folklore, which tends to be almost exclusively the preserve of breaking news.

Despite the great variation, news tends to be made in a systematic way and follows a set process. This chapter explains that process, and gives you the tools to take advantage of it. It will enable you to create the very best chance of publicity for your own stories, and outline the most common traps.

To return to the question, what is news? Every journalist worth their pay cheque understands their own organization's answer, though when asked, they often talk about it being 'instinctive' or a 'gut feeling' and claim that 'having a good news sense' – a highly praised talent in journalistic circles – cannot be taught. This chapter will endeavour to prove them wrong, to enable you to recognize what's news and what's not. 'Having a good news sense' means one that exactly tallies with the newspaper, TV or radio station's own news agenda. If you can recognize this, you will increase your own hit rate of favourable publicity. The extent to which that tallies with the readers', viewers' or listeners' own idea of what should be news is often debated. We comfort ourselves, though, with the thought that we must be getting something right, or readers would go elsewhere (they are, over a period of time, but that appears to be because of other calls on their time).

The debate was neatly (and controversially) summed up by the editor of a national newspaper when debating political news values with a cabinet minister, 'People vote for us every day. They only vote for you once every five years.' The words may be 'over the top', but the sentiment is absolutely right. Every day in the UK, more than 13 million people hand over their money to buy the newspaper of their choice. If they don't like their usual offering, there are nine other national newspapers to choose from. On Sunday the choice is even wider. TV and radio operate in a similarly competitive marketplace. Imagine, if you're in cars, clothing or computers for example, being that susceptible to the whim of your customers – they give you 30 pence one day, then give it to your fiercest rival the next.

Yet brand loyalty is still strong in many media outlets – you probably hear people say 'I don't watch ITN' or 'I like the *Independent*, and never buy *The Times*'. So media outlets put a lot of effort into knowing what their customers think and want. In particular, as news has the highest profile and is the cornerstone of their success, they invest time and money working out what type of news the audience want, and how they like it served. This can vary from serious stories where the intention is to change government policy, to showbiz-focused, picture-led items where the interest of the public is obvious, but the public interest is harder to determine. Both examples count as 'news' and are competing for space with your own stories. Between these wide parameters, however, there are some reliable guidelines for pressing the newsmakers' hot buttons.

For many people, a media interview is like playing a game where only the other side knows the rules. You don't know how long it will last, what you have to do to score, what's allowed and what's good. This chapter introduces you to some of the rules. By the end of it you should be able to identify what types of news values your own stories fit, or change the slant to increase your chances of exposure. Either way you will be able to target your stories effectively – the key to all successful media handling.

THE NEWSMAKING PROCESS

The first point to make is that 'news' does not happen. Events happen, and news is produced by reporting some events. For example, if you're in computers and you launch a new type of touch-sensitive screen which solves the problems caused by a mouse-and-keyboard combination, notably repetitive strain injury, that is an event. If it is reported anywhere it becomes news. If two people are slightly hurt in a car crash, that's an event. If the local paper runs a story on it, that's news. The likelihood of the computer screen or the car crash making it from 'event to news' is influenced by a number of other factors.

Figure 1.1 is my own way of illustrating this 'event to news' process in diagrammatic form, and is an attempt to capture what for most journalists is intuitive behaviour. In practice many of these judgements will be made subconsciously, and the whole process will often be completed within seconds. Most journalists could not articulate the mechanism shown here, but many have confirmed to me that it does approximate quite closely to their own thought processes.

LEVEL 1

The first step in the production of news is in the choice of which events to cover. The thought process is illustrated by the three questions in level 1 of the diagram:

1 Is it relevant, important or interesting to the audience?
2 How unusual, new or different is it?
3 Will we get decent quality coverage (in pictures and/or words)?

These are the first questions journalists ask when they hear of a story. As an executive of a large corporation you, aided by your media advisers, can ensure that your story provokes positive answers to all three.

Relevance

This is the big question you must ask yourself before you approach any journalist with a story – how relevant is this to their audience? I often imagine stories as a sprinter about to take part in a hurdles race. The first hurdle is the tallest, and labelled 'relevance'. This is because when anyone reads, sees or hears a story, they ask themselves one initial question:

> What does this mean to me?

Journalists are immensely skilled at answering this question on behalf of the readers, as flicking through any selection of newspapers will illustrate. For example, the day the AOL/Time Warner link-up was announced, just about all the papers ran stories about how the world's biggest merger could affect their readers. The examples ranged from business web sites containing up to the minute stock prices in the broadsheets to faster sport and fashion news in the tabloids. This is a very good example of the relevance to the readers – and is a test you must apply to your own stories. All the examples fit the classic definition of news:

> News is anything that makes people
> say, 'That could be me'.

The above example is an illustration of how successfully newspapers, TV and radio programmes target their audiences – and it doesn't only happen on 'breaking news' stories which come as a surprise (as opposed to 'diary stories' which we know are coming). When an anti-breast cancer drug called Tamoxifen showed promise at treat-

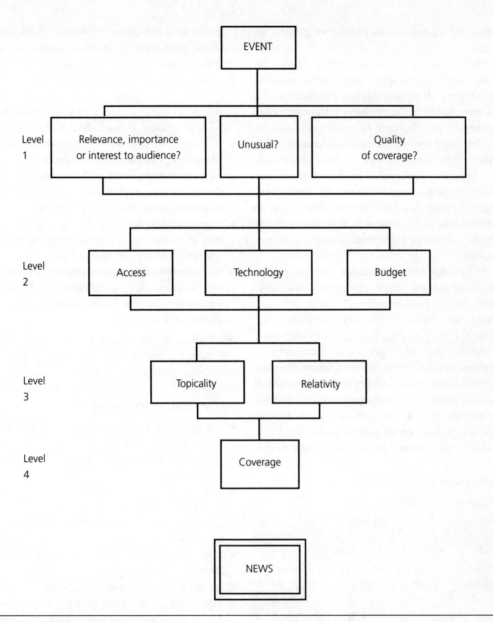

Figure 1.1   How events become news

ing the disease, the story received front page treatment in the *Daily Mail*, giving the makers, pharmaceutical giant Zeneca (now AstraZeneca) hundreds of thousands of pounds worth of favourable publicity. The reason the *Mail* gave this story such prominence is that it is the only national newspaper with a predominantly female readership – a fact you can play on if you're in an area or have a product or service which primarily appeals to women.

The London *Evening Standard* knows that a great percentage of its readers buy the paper as they start their journey home – that's why it gives great prominence to transport stories. So if your company has developed a revolutionary way of digging holes in the road which causes fewer traffic jams, you've got a great chance of publicity in the *Standard*. The *Daily Telegraph* has a large proportion of military people among its readers, so stories with a Services or defence slant stand a good chance of achieving coverage there.

Making people identify with a story can mean many things. Some stories score because they strike a chord and allow us to dream for a moment, such as those about lottery or pools winners, while others are relevant to the way we lead our daily lives, or because they give us information which may be beneficial to our lifestyle. An important point to consider is that your stories are competing for space with these very strong human interest stories. One way to counter this is to ensure that you cover the human angle on your own stories wherever possible.

The National Lottery knows the importance of striking a chord with its customers, as is illustrated by its catchphrase, 'It could be you.' Newspapers, TV and radio programmes are aiming for the same feeling among their customers. Health and finance stories are an excellent way of achieving it – health and wealth being possibly the two longest-lasting subjects under the sun. If you're in either of these sectors, you've probably already had journalists beating a path to your door. If not, don't forget to look for the 'health or wealth' angle – it could be the key to success.

Importance or interest

'Importance or interest to audience' covers many categories of story, including many from the business world. The *Financial Times* carries hundreds of stories a day about the world of business and finance, and is a good example of how far the ripples of importance or interest can spread. Let's assume you are a medium-sized public company announcing a takeover of a smaller plc. The takeover announcement is an event, which will be reported as a news story in the FT, whose journalists know it will be important or interesting at several levels:

- to people who work for either company and their families, who want to know about the possible effect on their jobs
- to suppliers of both companies, who may have to start competing for their existing contracts against other suppliers
- to shareholders and investors in either com-

pany, who are interested in the effect on the share price, dividends and return on their investment

- to people who were considering investing in the larger company's stock, who may now decide to adopt a 'wait and see' approach, or be persuaded that this is the time to buy in
- to customers, who want to know how the deal will affect prices and levels of service
- to competitors, who will see the move as consolidation or expansion, and will see the opportunities or threats it produces
- to people who invest in the Stock Market as a way of earning income, who want to keep up with important developments
- to residents and other businesses in the area where the smaller company was based, as moves like this can have a significant impact on the local economy.

All of the above are important for FT readers, and may also be reported in the financial pages of other national papers. But the story passes the 'importance, relevance or interest' test with a number of other media outlets:

- regional and local newspapers, TV and radio programmes where the businesses are based, as readers, viewers and listeners are employees
- trade magazines specializing in the sector where the two businesses operate. Major names consolidating can have a big effect on one sector
- trade magazines in the sector where the suppliers operate
- national TV and radio programmes such as *The Money Programme* who are always on the lookout for important developments which signify a new trend, or fly in the face of an established one
- if one of the businesses is a well-known name, this will produce another flurry of publicity in the national dailies.

You can see from this discussion the number of media organizations who will regard your story as 'important, relevant or interesting' to their audiences and readers. For all of them, it has cleared the first hurdle, 'What does it mean to me?'

Unusual or different

The next hurdle can be illustrated by another definition of news:

> When a dog bites a man, that's not news.
> When a man bites a dog – that's news.

The event must be out of the ordinary. This leads on to a common complaint from executives I meet in my work: 'Why is it the news only reports things that go wrong?' The answer is that it doesn't. It reports things that are *unusual* or *different*. If you employ thousands of workers who all turn up on time, go about their work quietly and efficiently and nothing untoward happens, that's good news for you. But it's not news for us. Its mundane and routine, and of interest to nobody outside your own human resources or health and safety departments. This might become news, however, if after a long time of ideal behaviour, you receive an award for health and safety at work, but this is something different – it's an event, and your achievement has been recognized by an independent third party. On a daily basis, if something goes wrong, that may be news to us, depending on the other factors discussed in this chapter. As we've already seen, good things which are out of the ordinary can also be news to us. The important thing here is that they're unusual. (There are some occasions when the fact that things keep happening can make news, and we will discuss them later.)

Some years ago the then Chairman of British Rail Richard Marsh was a guest on the Jimmy Young radio programme. At one point, JY said he had some travel news to pass on – including a list of train cancellations. 'Would you like to read them?' he asked Sir Richard. 'No thanks, Jim' he said, digging into his briefcase. 'I've brought a list of all the trains that are running on time this morning – I'll read them out, if I may.' Touché! Of course, they both smiled and JY didn't let him have his way, but the exchange illustrates an important point – daily mundane events don't make news, however unfair it is.

Is it new?

News must be new. That's what the word means. New, however, is a relative concept to journalists. It generally means 'new to me'. If you're an expert in almost any field, it may well not be new to you. Part of the reason is the way news is 'found.' Often stories break in trade journals, which are read by two types of people – experts in the field and journalists. So when there was an argument about bonus payments to electricians working on the tube line extension to the Millennium Dome, it was reported first in *Construction News*. A week later the story was picked up by the London *Standard*, which splashed it on the front page. Readers of *Construction News* had seen it already, but the *Standard* gave it a much wider audience. To its readers, the story was 'new'. This example also illustrates the different ways in which a story can be targeted to different readers. The *Construction News* piece went into detail about bonus payments and how any hold-up might delay other construction projects. The *Standard*, on the other hand, made it relevant to its own readers – and focused on the potential delays to the new line which might prevent it opening in time for the Millennium celebrations.

The relative nature of 'new' can be good or bad news for your company, depending on whether the story concerned is positive or negative to your image. If it's positive, you sometimes find a story gets a 'second wind' when another sector of the media become aware of it – for example it might obtain local or specialist magazine coverage, but nothing nationally, then one national paper runs it, and before you know it you've got ITN and BBC News on the phone. However, the same process can give bad news another airing. One tactic here is to tell the journalist that the story has already been covered, and there's nothing new in it. Whether it works depends on several other factors which we will examine later in Chapter 7 on crisis management.

New – and first

There is another way in which a story idea can be 'new'. That is when you are doing or announcing something which has not been done before. This leads to another very important element of how journalists think:

> All journalists' favourite words end in the letters '-st'.

Look in the newspapers, or listen to the TV or radio news, and see how often you find words like these: first, last, best, worst, fastest, slowest, richest, poorest, cheapest, dearest, biggest, smallest and so on. In particular, the word 'first' tops journalists' polls of the words they like to use most. This is because another definition of news is:

News is change.

Clearly, if something's changed, something is different. So very often you can use the word 'first' – and if it's first, it must be new. If you've got a 'first' in your story you have a great chance of publicity, for example the first mortgage to let you overpay then borrow the money back, the first car which won't let you drive if you're over the drink-driving limit, the first mobile telephone with a built-in Internet connection. These are easy stories for journalists to accept, thanks to the 'first' concept.

When you're discussing your next media story with your media advisers, try this test: complete the sentence, 'For the first time . . .'. If you can complete it with something worthwhile, you've probably got a story which will appeal to journalists. Indeed, when we're stuck for the first few words of a story we'll often ask ourselves, 'What's new, or what's different?' The answer gives us the first sentence. If you do the same with your press releases, you will increase the hit rate. However, there is a crucial phrase in the sentence above: 'If you can complete it *with something worthwhile.*' This is because the definition of news as change is incomplete. In his description, Reuven Frank, one of the pioneers of news television in the USA, went on to say:

News is change . . . as seen by an outsider.

This means that the change must be big enough to be noticeable to someone not closely involved. The size of change required here depends on your intended audience. If you're in pharmaceuticals and you're changing the colour of the packaging of your best-selling painkiller, it's only interesting to *Paper and Packaging News* at best. But if you're in computers and you're launching new machines in pink, purple,

bright green and pillar-box red, you may get wide coverage because they will change the way offices look, with their uniform off-white or grey computers. If you're a small company and you change your logo, it might make a paragraph in your trade magazine during a slow month, but if British Airways changes its logo, it will be on front pages throughout the UK. Size does matter.

Quality of coverage

Having cleared the hurdles marked 'relevance' and 'unusual', there's another obstacle before your story can be truly said to be in contention: what kind of coverage can we expect?

This restriction applies particularly though not exclusively to broadcasters. TV news is about pictures, so without them your story is dead in the water. You and your advisers need to consider this point carefully before you try and obtain coverage. Chapter 3 on TV news examines this in more detail, but suffice to say we want good pictures, sound and interviews, and we want to be able to get them back to the studio or newsroom in time to edit them for the next bulletin. Every story, however, is a trade-off between the perfect and the pragmatic, and the bigger the story the more we'll settle for less than ideal material to illustrate it.

LEVEL 2

You can affect the chances or otherwise of clearing all the level 1 hurdles by the way you shape and announce your story. However, many companies fail to do even this simple thing. The result is that most of the almost infinite number of events available for coverage in a day fall at this first hurdle. For those that are still in the running, the harsh realities of journalism intrude at level 2, and from your point of view these obstacles are not so easily influenced. They concern the way journalists are going to 'get the story' and the likely result. Their main questions are these:

1 How easy is it to get the story?
2 What people and equipment will we need to deploy on it?
3 Will the end result justify the expense in getting it?

Access

Journalists are like anyone else – the easier you can make their life, the more they appreciate it. Unlike some other people, however, their lives are hectic, so access assumes an even higher importance. If you or your PR organization are actively promoting a story, accessibility should prove no obstacle at all – you just need to ensure that it's available in a time and place suitable to the journalists. However, some words of advice here: not so long ago, journalists used to travel quite freely around their own region to cover stories. Today increasingly, they stay in the office. The typical reaction of a news editor when told that a correspondent is going to meet a contact to discuss a story is 'Can't you do it on the phone?' If you're holding a news conference, it's not uncommon for journalists to ring and ask for the press pack to be sent round to their office if they can't physically get to the story. They work at such a pace, it sometimes seems even their own doorstep is not close enough.

An important client once asked if I could help publicize important work being done at their new research plant at Stevenage in Hertford-shire. In particular, they were keen to try and persuade national newspaper correspondents to tour the plant. I rang one correspondent whom I knew well, and put the idea to him. His response was illuminating and a stark illustration of the time constraints on journalists. 'The trouble is,' he said, 'it's in Stevenage. So if I want to do it, it'll take all morning by the time I've been there, had a look round, done a couple of interviews and got back again. Then when I do get back to the office I'll have to do all the stories I would have done on the day anyway, but with less time. I am interested in it, but I'd just be making a rod for my own back.' Stevenage is less than 10 miles north of Greater London, where he was based!

Journalists are like delicate wines – they don't travel well. And that can have serious implications for your story. So what can you do? You may decide to let your story do the travelling, and organize a press conference near their offices. If you're in London, in the days of Fleet Street this was comparatively simple because all the national newspapers were based within a mile of each other. That's why holding press con-ferences in the Press Club was so popular – it minimized the amount of effort required by the journalists. Today, unfortunately, the national press are spread around London, from Canary Wharf and Wapping in the east, to Kensington in the west. Think of this when you're organizing your next media briefing. If you are London-based, central London is the most accessible place for most journalists. Another good tactic is to organize the briefing for around 10 a.m., so journalists will travel from home. This has the extra benefit that they are less likely to be diverted by something more urgent which may crop up if they go into the office first.

'Access' can be difficult if you're a multi-national with operations in many countries, or if you're in the oil or gas industry, where most of your exciting sites are in far-flung parts of the world. In this case, consider commissioning top quality photographs and flying the relevant person into London for media interviews. See Chapter 4 on newspapers for more on the impor-tance of photographs in getting your message across. Another tactic is to take journalists, indi-vidually or in groups, to the plant on a facility trip. If you're dealing with television, consider commissioning a video news release or some broadcast quality core footage to help them illustrate the story. See Chapter 7 on public rela-tions for more on this.

Resources and budget

People and equipment together form the biggest budget lines in any media business. In news-papers, the main resource is the reporter who goes out and covers the story. Fulfilling the criteria for easy access outlined above will ensure that you offer the maximum potential for minimum input on the paper's part. This is generally also true in radio. TV news, however, is ultimately resource-driven. TV news is about pictures – shooting them, and getting them back to base. Moving a TV crew around costs thousands of pounds, so producers will only do it if they're fairly sure they can justify the expense by coming back with a good story.

This means that you have to make your story more appealing than the others around on the day. TV news in particular is like a beauty parade

– the most attractive offering wins. Keep asking yourself, 'What does this mean to the readers?' The readers are also your customers, shareholders and employees anyway so you are gaining a wider benefit from this type of targeting. See Chapter 3 on TV news for more hints on how to make sure it's your head that wears the crown.

LEVEL 3

Topicality

In level 1, relevance was the fence where most potential stories fell. In level 3, *topicality* is the place where most wannabe stories are found wanting. News is the ultimate time-sensitive commodity. It is difficult to overstate the importance of time in a reporter's life. News stories – or the appeal of the events which give birth to them – are perishable goods. More than that, where you can freeze fresh meat and vegetables to extend their useful life, you can't do that with a news story. Either it's happened today or it hasn't. Your new product launch is today or it isn't. The news 'peg' is today or it isn't. It really is difficult to 'fudge' this point, and journalists have very finely tuned instincts for detecting old stories dressed up as new. They deal in 'news' not 'olds'.

I come across this problem most frequently where a client has been unlucky and a big story has broken on the day of their major launch, so they haven't achieved much publicity. Inexperienced clients often ask if they can relaunch it at some date in the future. This is understandable for several reasons – they've put a lot of time, effort and sometimes money into it, and have often received encouragement from journalists they hope will cover the story on the day. Unfortunately, generally speaking, a launch is a once-only opportunity. Creative thinking, hard work and other events may produce other news 'pegs' and angles for feature articles, but if you've taken the plunge once and nobody noticed, your chances of making a bigger splash with the same trick the second time round are fairly remote. Journalists themselves tend to maintain the analogy with fresh food – they talk of 're-heating old vegetables' – wouldn't you prefer a plate of freshly cooked ones?

If you have a good story but bad luck keeps it out of the paper, the journalists who wrote the story will be sympathetic – after all, they want to get in the paper too. In reality, however, there is very little they can do. So please don't expect them to show much enthusiasm if you try and re-sell them the same line a few days or weeks later. Journalists tend to behave in a Casanovian manner – they're all over you when they want your story, but if you call them when the moment has passed, they're on to the next one and may not even take your call. Don't take it personally, they're just doing a job!

The importance of topicality then is not generally understood. Neither is the time when journalists use it most often – when you first contact them to try and persuade them of the merits of your story. During my entire career, from the bi-weekly *South London Press* to ITN and the *Daily Mail*, I have never known a shortage of potential stories. (You may find this difficult to accept when you look at what does get into some papers, but I promise it's true.) This means that I'm not generally sitting around waiting for your call. I have too much material, not too little. So when you call offering me more, I'm instinctively looking for reasons, in the words of Samuel Goldwyn, to 'include you out'.

Topicality (along with relevance) is one of the ways I do this. I'm listening for time-sensitive words which will allow me to reject your story because it doesn't fit our timeframe. This can mean it's either too late or too early (journalists are great at having their cake and eating it!). As a way of rejecting a story entirely, I'm listening for any clue which suggests it is too old for my newspaper/programme. Such words include, 'last week', 'today', 'this afternoon' and so on. If I can't kill it entirely another option is to move it off my own desk and on to someone else's, for example forward planning. In this case I'm looking for anything which suggests it is a story for the future. Then I can say, 'I'm sorry, I'm working on tomorrow's paper right now. Let me transfer you to forward planning.' Bear in mind that long-term planning in a news room means next week's paper.

An anecdote from my own career illustrates the relevance/topicality paradigm in which most journalists operate. When I was the editor of LWT News, one of the news desk journalists had a particular line of attack when PR people rang offering stories which were not relevant. His response went like this, 'Look...' he would say aggressively. 'The clue to what we're looking for is in the name of our programme. It's called *London Weekend Television News*. So to interest us it must be happening in London at the weekend, have good pictures, because that's what television needs, and be new. Your story, happening in Southampton on Tuesday, fails all four tests.' His routine certainly raised smiles in the newsroom. I hope it struck a chord with the callers too, and made them think about relevance and topicality before they rang us – or any news organization – again.

This total reliance on time-sensitivity has another consequence, which is less often understood: if the ideal news stories are ultimately time-sensitive, this leads to a devaluing of stories which are less so, and can be run on one of several days. This situation comes about in two ways.

If your story can be run say, anytime between Monday and Friday of a given week, on Monday it will be pushed into Tuesday because there will be other stories which can't wait. When Tuesday comes, the same thing happens, so it moves to Wednesday. By then it's becoming a bit of a wallflower – it's been hanging around the edges of the action but nobody's been sufficiently tempted to ask it to dance. And anyway, there are some dancers who are appearing for one night only. By Thursday it's been raised at so many forward planning meetings that people start to make jokes about it, and Friday ... well, Friday's programme has the sports preview, the paper has the weekend TV, the radio programme has the look at events coming up over the weekend ... so I'm sorry, it didn't quite make it. Much better to plump for one day, and work hard at selling it to us. The lesson here is to always make sure your stories are pegged to a specific day.

Additionally, there is the fact that news is different from features. Topicality is one of the defining credentials of a news story. If it hasn't got that, it may become a feature, but that's often someone else's job. (We will look at features in Chapter 4.)

Relativity

Napoleon was known to pray, 'Dear God, give me lucky generals.' The sensible client's prayer is, 'Dear God, give me the right news day.' You can follow all the advice above, work hard at making your story relevant and topical with good pictures and great interviewees, lay it on a plate for journalists, and still fail to get a line of coverage. This is because news value is not an absolute measure, but is relative to the other stories around. Earlier I used the analogy of a beauty contest. By this stage the selection process has become more like the start of a big horse race, with all the entrants jockeying for position. In fact, in some news rooms the story list for the day is conversationally referred to as 'the runners and riders' (though this may say as much about journalists' leisure pursuits as the nature of news!).

This can be good or bad news for you. A really big story can knock everything else out of the running, as we experienced when we were promoting a new arthritis treatment on the day John Major resigned as Prime Minister. Our arthritis story ran on the breakfast news bulletins, thanks to good case studies and interviewees, and just as I was talking to Sky News about its chances for later in the day there was a scream from the other side of the news desk. 'The Prime Minister's resigned!' someone shouted. That shout was the death knell for our story. Our client, sensible soul, heard the newsflash a few minutes later and rang me. 'I suppose that's the end of arthritis, then?' she said. Would that clients were always so understanding – and this means you! An essential element of successful media handling is to set realistic expectations and accept when, despite all your efforts, you've been beaten by a better story on the day.

Yet on a different occasion another big political story was responsible for getting one of our stories on to the national TV news. The occasion was Michael Heseltine suffering a heart attack in Venice. It so happened that on the very day we were helping to publicize a new study into heart disease. The story was not really strong enough to make it on its own merits, but as soon as I heard the Heseltine story I rang ITN to remind them there was another heart story that day. Helped by the sudden increase in topicality of heart disease, our story received national publicity.

On a normal news day where the news list doesn't benefit from prime ministerial resignations or other major breaking news, relativity still plays a large role in deciding what's in the news. Here, the editors and producers will try to produce a 'mix' of stories reflecting the wide interests of their readers, viewers or listeners. The process involves selecting items to cover a wide spread of subjects, such as politics, health, technology, finance and sport, but also trying to put together a mixture of heavy and light topics. We refer to this as 'light and shade', and the process is quite sophisticated. I've been running programmes myself on some days when we've had a preponderance of one type, hoping for something new to freshen up the news list. On most days something else happens, but sometimes it's just the wrong type of story – for example another 'heavy' one on a day where the news list is already looking a little heavyweight. In these circumstances we will say, 'It's a good story, but it doesn't help the mix' – it will only replace a current candidate, not add to the choice.

This has implications for you when you're trying to publicize your own stories. PR executives sometimes say they want a slow news day. This is only partly true – you also need the right type of news day. For example, if you're in IT, you don't mind that there are several strong health, political and financial stories around, as long as you don't come up against another strong technology development.

A common question on courses is, 'How can I avoid such a clash?' The straight answer is that it's very difficult, because the news list comes together so close to the day in question and arranging a launch takes so much time and planning. You can't wait to see what's around, then whistle up your spokespeople and opinion leaders, book a room and invite the media. This is really a plea for understanding when your PR advisers explain that they didn't meet your publicity targets because of competing news on the day. You can help your chances slightly by being aware of important diary events, for

example Budget day or the Queen's Speech which traditionally opens Parliament and sets out the government's agenda for the new session. The total eclipse of the sun which occurred on 11 August 1999 and dominated the media had been in the diary since 1927, so I really have no sympathy for organizations which staged launches on the same day! You can also avoid other difficult periods such as the political conference season (usually late September to early October) because many news organizations dedicate so many resources to them, leaving themselves thinly stretched for other matters.

If your story is still in contention here, it has cleared all the hurdles, and you can sit back and watch, read or listen to your story informing, educating or entertaining the public. Unless things change...

LEVEL 4

If your story has cleared all the hurdles, you've made it – you've reached the finishing post of coverage. There is usually a great feeling of triumph – congratulations. But a word of advice here. The feeling of triumph often turns very quickly to a close inspection of 'what did they get wrong'. Executives often go through cuttings and transcripts with a fine tooth comb and find something that's inaccurate or some aspect of the story that's not portrayed as they would wish. They then get on to their communications team and often start demanding that they write to the reporter or editor to complain. My advice here is simple: don't. Unless the error is serious, let it pass. Concentrate on basking in the glory of the winner's enclosure, and ring your communications team to thank them for training the horse well, rather than complaining.

HITTING A MOVING TARGET

The process explained above happens very quickly, and is constantly reviewed throughout the production period, which might be as short as a few hours on a 24-hour news programme or more than a month on a glossy magazine. So your story might be accepted then rejected, or vice versa. An attempt to court media publicity isn't over until the paper's on the streets. The speed at which journalists work can occasionally lead to mistakes (though the higher up the media ladder you go, the less likely this is – and you try getting a national news editor to admit to a failure of news judgement!). Anecdotally I reckon that your press release has about 15 seconds from 'in' to 'bin', that is from the moment the journalist picks it up to the time he or she casts it into the bin and picks up the next hopeful. If they know you or your company, or you're in the news for some reason, your initial call will be afforded more time. For example, when we were working on the broadcast publicity for the launch of the impotence treatment Viagra, I always had the journalist's attention and never felt under time pressure!

News editors and correspondents have their own system for deciding what's news. In the mornings, my own method involved a quick scan of the incoming mail to sort the 'possibles' from the 'no-hopers'. This would invariably produce a very full rubbish bin, and a small pile of releases which were worth another look. Another (slightly longer) sift would reduce the pile further, and I would then be ready to ask someone to make a few inquiries to find out more about what was left.

This process would produce a list of 'probables' to be discussed at the news meeting. Without fail, some of the 'probables' wouldn't make the grade, even though they were strong contenders, because they were edged out by other events. For you, this makes life unpredictable because you can never be sure the story will feature until you've seen it published. We do occasionally have clients who make the mistake of assuming they're definitely on air, or in the paper, and tell their colleagues. This can end in disappointment and embarrassment, particularly in the point-scoring world of many large corporations. My advice to clients is this: there are no 'definites' in the world of media publicity, only 'probables'. Start here to avoid embarrassment.

WHERE DOES NEWS COME FROM?

The processes described in the early part of this chapter describe the environment into which your story is pitched. Essentially, snap decisions are made against a constantly changing backdrop. Earlier I used two analogies to describe this competitive environment – a beauty parade and a horse race. You must accept, to continue the equestrian analogy, that a stronger runner may get its nose in front right from the gun, or another candidate may come up on the rails in the final furlong. But where do they come from? An understanding of the provenance of rival stories will help you to understand the environment, and as we have already agreed, information is power.

News is generally divided into 'diary stories' and 'breaking news'. They are then further subdivided into a number of other sources. You may be occasionally involved in breaking news stories if you are connected to something which is Stock Market sensitive and so cannot be revealed in advance, such as a merger or takeover, or the announcement of a large contract. Generally though, your involvement in the media will be with diary stories, so that is where we will start.

DIARY STORIES

All news organizations, from the smallest local weekly to the *Daily Mail* and BBC News, are run on a regimented planning system. At the heart of it is the news diary. It contains brief descriptions and contact details of every planned news event for a particular day – openings, closings, ceremonies, court cases, press conferences, speeches, demonstrations, celebrity appearances, photo-opportunities, 'first nights' and many variations of the above. In a big organization like a national newspaper each section will also have its own diary, so the business or City section will keep a record of AGMs, annual results, interims, new appointments and other company announcements. Today, the diary (or diaries) is generally held on a computer, but not so long ago it was a physical diary, with lots of annotations and comments scribbled at speed, unreadable to anyone other than the author. Thank goodness for technology!

The diary drives the news operation and is the first point of call for anyone wanting to know what's in the pipeline. It's the pre-delivery room for news-to-be. If you understand how it works your chances of success will be greatly enhanced.

The stories in the diary are distilled into a number of news lists. Some potentials fall at this early stage. The most important early list – and the one which you must aim to get into to give your story a fighting chance of inclusion – is the one for the weekly forward planning meeting. In most news organizations this happens on a Thursday, and its role is to consider the stories for the following week beginning Monday (or sometimes Sunday). This itself highlights a crucial difference between most businesses and the media – their operational timescale. As a senior executive you may be involved in planning for the next three or five years. The late Harold Wilson, when he was Prime Minister, once famously remarked 'A week is a long time in politics.' In journalism, a week is an age. To journalists, taking a long-term view means thinking about next week's paper. They work at such speed, and things change so quickly, that any longer view is irrelevant unless you're planning a big event such as the General Election. Speed is another trap that can catch people unawares, as we shall see in the next chapter on the role of journalists.

In many organizations the weekly forward planning meeting is chaired by the editor and attended by all the senior editorial executives, section heads and programme producers. You would normally expect to find the news editor, foreign editor, picture editor, features editor, women's editor, sports editor and so on there. This is their opportunity to flag their interest in a particular story, or make a case for its exclusion. In many organizations it's also a fiercely competitive forum as the participants vie to score points and make their mark with the editor. From your point of view, these are the people you should be approaching with your publicity. As they listen to you they're thinking ahead to the planning meeting, and asking themselves, 'How will this play in there?'

The format of the meeting is that the forward planning editor pulls together a list of the most promising stories from the diary for each day,

and presents them to this high-powered group. He or she is usually the lowest-ranked person in the room and in some organizations the other executives use the meeting for point-scoring over each other, hoping to impress the editor. The process can be quite painful, though the real cut and thrust happens under the surface – tempers and jealousies can sometimes break through, but are generally kept under control.

The main advantage of getting your story considered at this meeting is that the senior people there make their views known, so if they like it, it will gather a momentum which is likely to carry it right through to the day before publication or transmission. Conversely, if your story misses this meeting because you don't understand the process, it will have to take its chances on the day in question without the imprimatur of the senior executives. There are of course some mavericks left in the profession, but in general, up and coming journalist executives prefer to be sure about what the chiefs think before running a story off their own bat!

The downside, of course, is that if someone in the higher echelons of the organization takes against your story, it would have to undergo some Lazarus-like recovery to fight its way into contention. However, if you follow the advice in this book, your chances of being rejected out of hand will be reduced.

In today's multi-media environment, there is another big advantage to getting into the forward planning list – it is usually shared with other newsrooms in the same organization. We regularly get our stories into the BBC TV News list, for example, and as a result receive calls from BBC radio stations around the country.

If your story survives the weekly meeting, you may receive a call about coverage or asking for clarification of some aspect of either the story or the logistics. The journalist may ask you for a case study to ring, as part of the next stage of checking the story out. If this happens, it is clearly an encouraging sign. However, as we have seen above, it's no more than a sign – it's nothing like a commitment.

The next stage in the birth of a news story is the daily forward planning meeting, which on a daily paper usually takes place on the morning before the day for which the story is pegged. Between the two meetings there have been constant informal chats between executives, so your story may have been dropped or seized enthusiastically by the time the daily meeting takes place. This meeting is attended by some but not all of the senior executives, and by then the forward planning editor will be armed with a quite detailed knowledge of your story, enough to answer all the likely questions from colleagues.

By the end of this meeting a draft list of stories for the following day's paper or programme will emerge. The lack of balance, or 'mix' will often become apparent here, which is why your previously rejected story may be resurrected because it helps the 'mix'. Having done the forward planning job myself, I know the value of having stories up your sleeve for when the editor refuses everything else!

Assuming your story is still alive, all that's stopping it getting into the paper or on air are the vagaries of fate, changes of mind or any breaking news story.

INFLUENCING THE PROCESS – STORY PITCHING

Having explained the process, the next question is whether you can influence it. The answer is yes, to a degree. You can't prop up a weak story by knowing the system, or persuade journalists not to cover a big story because it's negative for you (but see the chapter on crisis management for what you can do). However, there are many stories every day which are far short of being 'must-haves' in the sense that it's obvious they're going to be covered. To maximize their opportunities of making the cut, you need to give them a nudge. This section explains how to do it. We call the process 'story pitching'.

For a moment, put yourself in the position of a news or forward planning editor, or a specialist correspondent on a reasonably sized organization, say your regional evening paper. He or she is sitting in the midst of what to anyone else's mind would be total chaos. People are constantly badgering them for attention and there is no time to think things through fully before making a decision. There is always someone holding

on the line to speak ... and faxes are ringi... 'ping' signalling an ... attention. They're tryi... for the next planning ... stories for today are alr... job is really chaos mana... name. Tempers are sho... even shorter. I organized ... pportunity for one client to spend a day in just such a newsroom, in a national TV news organization. At the end I asked how it had gone. 'It was so useful to see it from the inside,' she said. 'I realize now that instead of "please" and "thank you" people say "gimme" and "f*** off".' The lesson stayed with her for years, and she now behaves differently when trying to pitch stories into such an environment.

Back on the newsdesk, the phone rings and it's a PR person asking, 'Did you get my fax?' This is not the way to get your story into the paper. The reaction is likely to contain some old-fashioned Anglo-Saxon phrases, and is similar to lighting the blue touchpaper. In the list of 'heartsink' phrases in the journalistic lexicon, 'Did you get my fax?' is right there up front.

I have one colleague who's spent many years on news desks who has a standard answer to the fax question, 'I don't know. I haven't had time to check the fax machine because people keep ringing up with daft questions!' There are cleverer ways to influence the newsmaking process – and they all start further back. The first step is to build relationships with journalists. If you know the person you're calling, the relationship is entirely different from a 'cold call'. Imagine your reaction to a kitchen salesperson who calls you at home in the evening, compared to an acquaintance ringing up.

Let's assume the most difficult position, that you don't know them. The story pitch can be lost within a few seconds, so you need to be very well prepared. Before you pick up the phone you have three preparatory tasks. First, read the paper, watch or listen to the programme you're trying to interest in your story. You need to understand their audience or readership and exactly how your story will affect, influence or interest them. Second, you need to have 100 per

...nce in the story. This confidence ...shine through to the person at the other ...f the line. This is exactly the same as when ...ou're announcing a new process or procedure to staff. Whether it's good news or bad, you need to convey your total confidence in it, otherwise they won't be sold on it. Look at it this way – if you don't have 100 per cent faith in the importance or interest of your story, why should I? I've got thousands of things I can do today, and most of them involve people who're totally committed to whatever it is they're trying to achieve.

So let's assume you're OK on both these points. The third task is to know the time to call when you're most likely to get a reasoned response. Generally, you want to call as far from deadline as possible, but close enough to it to ensure that the journalist is engaged with your story. The various chapters on different types of media will give you an accurate fix on this, but for now let's assume you are calling at the right time.

There are several ways to approach the process of story pitching, but it generally involves a combination of phone calls and faxes (or increasingly e-mails). My own preference is to start with an initial call to the newsdesk or relevant correspondent, before I send anything in writing. There are three objectives for this call: to test the reaction to the story, to get someone to 'buy in' to it and promise to put it in the diary, and to get the name of someone who can take it on to the next stage. Getting names is a crucial element, as we shall see shortly.

In this initial call you're playing for high stakes. It can kill your story stone dead, or give it an uplift which will carry it through to a position of prominence, potentially to the dizzy heights at the top of the news list. So why do PR consultancies entrust initial calls to the most junior account executives? It is a source of wonderment to me – and frustration to many journalist colleagues. Journalists are very intuitive, with highly developed interpersonal skills. They respond well to a well-informed grown-up person who is, as we would put it, 'across the story'. The caller needs to be able to pitch the story and answer supplementary questions. Journalists can tell when they've been been landed with a hesitant junior who's been in the job 10 minutes, or worse, an over-confident Hooray Henry who may think he's God's gift to communications but in reality has much to be modest about. That realization speaks volumes – it means that either you don't think the story is important, or you don't think they are. Either way, it's bad news for you and your story.

In my many years as a practising journalist my impression of public relations consultants was formed entirely by how they performed on the phone either when trying to sell me something, or when I wanted something from them. I can still tell you now which PR firms were regarded as pretty useless, based on these observations. I won't, of course, because we have laws of defamation, but the point is still a strong one: get an experienced person to do the pitching when it matters. Yes, juniors have to cut their teeth some time, birds must fly the nest and all that, but don't take too much of a gamble. This is an important question to ask your PR consultancy, 'Who will actually be phoning journalists with our story?' Better still, ask it when they're pitching for the account.

HANDLING THE PITCHING CALLS

We run story-pitching exercises on some of our training courses, and it can be a difficult role to play. But struggle is good for the soul, practice makes perfect and the potential rewards are great, so it is worth investing time in it. There are three elements to handling the initial call successfully: be brief, be positive and be pointed. The need for brevity should be clear, given the typical newsdesk situation I have sketched out. Being positive covers a multitude of story-pitching sins. Athletes talk about the benefits of a positive mental attitude, or PMA. It's equally important here. Be positive about both yourself and your story. With media relations in general, you need to be convinced that your glass is half-full, rather than half-empty. In story pitching this simple truth is magnified. If Winnie the Pooh's friend Eeyore had been human, he would never have made a career pitching stories. You need to be able to withstand disappointments and still come back smiling.

Unfortunately this is not always the case. I've lost count of the times when PR practitioners (possibly still smarting from a previous conversation with a less helpful journalist than the author) start with, 'I'm sorry to bother you, but I thought you might be interested...'. The fact is, they shouldn't be sorry to bother me if they're offering a good story. It's like selling a new work pattern or remuneration package to your staff – even if you're not totally convinced, you need to sound as though you are. 'Hi, I've got a really good story for next Tuesday that I think is right up your street...' is a far better way to start. Journalists expect hype from PR people, believing that's what they're paid for, so it won't do any harm.

Some inexperienced pitchers behave like novice chess players – they rehearse their opening sequence, but are out of their depth when they're thrown on to their wits in open play. You need to start positive and stay positive. Here's an example of someone who starts well but then flounders.

Pitcher   Hi, I've got a really good story for next Tuesday that's right up your street. It's about a new way of stopping car thieves – it's a tracker device which will mean that if your car is stolen, you've got a 95 per cent chance of it being traced. It's called 'Car-track' and it's being launched at the Motor Show in Birmingham. And ... it's been developed by a local firm.

Journalist   Hmmm ... 95 per cent chance of getting it back? I assume that's only when it's been taken by joyriders rather than people who actually want to keep it or sell it illegally?

Pitcher   Well, yes. I suppose if someone steals your car because it's a nice car, or they want to sell it, then that's different ... but 60 per cent of stolen cars are taken by joyriders and most of them are dumped. Many of them are damaged.

Journalist   So most people who have their cars stolen get them back anyway. To clarify – this device doesn't stop them being stolen, it just makes it more likely you'll get them back? It would be better if it stopped the theft in the first place, really.

Pitcher   Yes I suppose it would. But getting your car back is a great advantage by itself, isn't it?

Journalist   Well, maybe. But if it's damaged and had the inside ruined you might prefer never to see it again. Might be better to treat it as a write-off and get the insurance company to pay.

Pitcher   Well, I suppose that's true. I had mine stolen last year and it was terrible when it came back. But then, I'd have had to wait for ages for the insurance company to pay up, so I just put up with it. But 'Car-track' is something to be going on with – until some kind of anti-theft device is invented. Don't you think?'

Journalist   It might make a piece. Depends on what statistics you've got – anyone famous going to be at the launch? Any celebrities had their cars stolen? David Beckham had one of his Ferraris nicked?

Pitcher   No. Sorry. We thought Jeremy Clarkson might do it, but he's driving in the Paris–Dakar rally.

Journalist   But maybe we could interview him about it?

Pitcher   I don't know. I mean, he's on the way to Dakar. And I don't know if anyone's actually asked him if he'll do it.

Journalist   Well, send us something over. Depends what else is on.

The pitcher here has started well, but the journalist has marginalized the story with his own Eeyore-type responses. He's doing this because these are just the types of points which will be made in the forward planning meeting. The caller needs to be more persistently positive. One way of doing this is to bring in more information at each stage. A better approach would be:

Pitcher   Hi, I've got a really good story for next Tuesday that's right up your street. It's about a new way of stopping car thieves – it's a tracker device which will mean that if your car is stolen, you've got a 95 per cent chance of it being traced. It's called 'Car-track' and it's being launched at the Motor Show in Birmingham. And ... it's made by a local firm.

Journalist   Hmmm ... 95 per cent chance of getting it back? I assume that's only when it's been taken by joyriders rather than people who actually want to keep it or sell it illegally?

Pitcher Yes, but that's the point. In some inner cities, up to 90 per cent of cars are stolen by joyriders anyway – the average is 60 per cent. The vast majority have been badly damaged by the time they're recovered. How Car-track helps is by tracking them down quickly by a remote device. So quick, that far fewer of them have been vandalized by then. In tests in seven major cities and three rural areas, the cars consistently came back in a better condition than those which were not fitted with Car-track. And of course, some cars never come back at all – Car-track can minimize the risk of that happening, too.

Journalist So most people who have their cars stolen get them back anyway. To clarify – this device doesn't stop them being stolen, it just makes it more likely you'll get them back? It would be better if it stopped the theft in the first place, really.

Pitcher Yes, as you say, most people get their cars back, but they're damaged by then, whereas with Car-track they're more likely to be unharmed. There are other devices such as immobilisers that are supposed to stop your car being stolen, but with 250 000 cars stolen every year, clearly that's not enough so we need something to help – that's where Car-track makes a difference.

Sold! If I'm that journalist, I'm doing that story. The person selling me the story is in control, has the information to hand and will give me all the ammunition I need to sell it to the grumpiest editor. They've remained positive throughout, and already I'm starting to imagine how we'll do the story.

As well as being a model of positivity, the short dialogue above illustrates the other two essentials of successful story pitching – it's brief and to the point. 'Be pointed' is the third element of a successful pitch, and should be the golden rule of talking to journalists in any situation – tell them the story up front. Too many people build the case in a rambling or chronological fashion. This is fine if you're having lunch with a journalist, but on the newsdesk we want

the story encapsulated in a few seconds. We don't have time for the scenic route – we're happy tearing down the motorway! Notice also the tone of the pitcher above – encouraging, but engaging the other person. It is very important not to be patronizing or pedantic. Journalists are human too – they react badly to inappropriate behaviour.

FOLLOWING UP

So you've got the journalist's attention, and their name. Now what? Send them some details. Chapter 6 on using PR goes into this in more detail. Here we'll concentrate on what happens next – the follow-up call.

The first point here is to know *when* to follow up. This is a delicate matter, and some of our clients try to badger us into chasing the news-desks so often it starts to sound like harassment. There is a balance to be struck between not sounding keen enough and leaving it totally to chance. Generally, if a journalist wants to cover your story, they will ring you. But a little nudge – and I do mean a little one – never did any harm. This, however, is a far cry from ringing up every hour saying, 'Are you covering it?' Another bad idea is to bother them as soon as they've come out of the forward planning meeting with an 'any news?' kind of question. Relax. If you've sold them a good story, it will happen. However, rather like a junior government minister waiting for the call from Number 10 on reshuffle day, be available.

During the first call you should have ascertained a level of interest and a likely timescale for coverage. When the time arrives, if they haven't been in contact, call them back. (This is where you have an advantage over junior ministers – they can't ring 10 Downing Street and say, 'Was the PM trying to get hold of me?') The same rules apply to the follow-up call as to the initial contact: be brief, positive and pointed. You are now on stronger ground than in the initial conversation, and should receive a more positive reaction. This is where having the name of the earlier contact proves very useful. 'Hi, can I speak to Suzie Smith?' sounds much more convincing than a hopeful story pitch. However, newsrooms being chaotic as they are, and working on shift systems, you are very likely to receive the response, 'She's not on today.'

This is where your PMA (positive mental attitude) comes into play once more. Many clients believe their story has been personally taken on board by a particular person, and if he or she is not there to take the follow-up call they feel let down. Don't be! Newsrooms are primarily process-driven, and many of the people in them are interchangeable (they won't generally admit this, so please don't go offering it as a view). Stay positive – even over-egg the positivity slightly. A good response would be, 'I spoke to Suzie on Monday about this great new anti-theft device for cars. It's called Car-track and helps you locate your car quickly if it's stolen. She was interested in coming along to a demo we're organizing at the Birmingham Motor Show.' Newsdesk journalists generally have instant recall of all the stories their organization is working on, but outlining the benefits of the story briefly in this way gives it another push. In case it hasn't been 'sold in' properly – unlikely if you've sent a suitably interesting news release (see the chapter on PR for more) – you've just had another go at plugging it.

AN OLD TRICK, BUT IT MIGHT JUST WORK

If you still meet any resistance, revert to the story pitch from the first call. If you're still meeting resistance which you didn't expect, there is one final tactic you can employ, though it is high risk: tell them their biggest rival is coming to do the story. Given the fiercely competitive environment in which journalists work, this can create a moment of indecision. They don't want to reject your story then see the opposition doing it well, as this may bring a rebuke from on-high. However, they don't want to sound indecisive to an outsider. They may say, 'That's up to them – that's why we beat them every night in the ratings', while making a mental note to pass this information on to the editor, just in case an error of judgement has been made. They might, alternatively, be confident in their own judgement and say, 'Good luck with them, then', or similar.

However, let's adopt our own PMA. Assuming your story passes the 'What is news?' tests outlined in this chapter of relevance, topicality and relativity, you should now be well on the way to publication or transmission. To revert to the earlier analogy of the birth cycle of news-to-be, your story is now in the delivery room. Good luck!

CHAPTER SUMMARY

- News doesn't happen. Events happen, and news is the reporting of some of them.
- News is produced by a well-defined process. If you understand that process you will improve your chances of achieving media publicity.
- News is divided into 'diary stories' and 'breaking news'.
- The media business is fiercely competitive – this is one of the main drivers of journalists.
- Newspapers, TV and radio stations have very clear ideas of what their customers want. You need to understand it too, to help your targeting.
- The news production process goes through a number of steps: Relevance and topicality are the key ones. Resources and budgets are also important.
- News is very time sensitive – many companies fail to obtain publicity because they don't realize this.
- News must be new – but this means 'new to the journalist'. It may not be new to specialists and experts.
- Journalists are attracted by absolutes – words such as best, worst, biggest, dearest, last and first. The more you have, the better your chances.
- News is change – but the change has to be big enough to be recognized.
- The easier you can make it for a journalist to cover your story, the greater your chance of success.
- Constantly ask yourself 'What does this mean to the readers?'
- 'News value' is not absolute – it depends on what other stories are around.
- Be aware of important diary events which may scupper your chances on the day.

- There are no 'definites' in terms of coverage – only 'possibles' and 'probables'.
- All news organizations have a rigid planning system – the more you understand it the greater your chances of taking advantage of it.
- Story pitching requires 100 per cent belief in the story and a PMA – positive mental attitude. Follow up the initial pitch call with the same positive attitude.
- Build relationships with journalists and your pitch calls will be better received.

CHAPTER TWO

The Journalist's Role

The previous chapter examined the end products of news journalism and began to explore how you can take advantage of it. Now I want to go back to the start of the editorial production process – the journalists who orchestrate it. Earlier I described a media interview as being like a game where only some of you know the rules. Having introduced you to the rudiments of the game, I now want to give you a briefing on the other players. Note that here I deliberately do not use the phrase 'the opposition' because in many cases you and the journalist are on the same side – you just need to be clear about what you both want.

I speak regularly at conferences explaining what journalists want and why we behave as we do. Depending on the audience I often begin like this: 'My name's John and I'm a journalist, but please don't tell my mother – she thinks I play the piano in a brothel!' It gets a laugh and sets the tone for a light-hearted, provocative presentation about the merits of the media. However, it also makes a serious point – journalists rank very low in public esteem. Journalism is said to be the world's second oldest profession – and its practitioners rank far below members of the oldest in terms of respect. In one poll, we came rock bottom with a 15 per cent approval rating. Lower than politicians, estate agents and cold-call telephone salespeople. I've spent my working life with journalists and I promise you we're not mad, bad or dangerous to know – we're just misunderstood.

At the start of our media training courses I ask the participants what they think of journalists. Many delegates have a fair, open-minded impression of 'people just doing a job' (or are too polite to say otherwise). But a significant minority believes we are unprincipled and biased with our own agenda, unlikely to accept any point of view that conflicts with our own. The most graphic picture was painted by a senior executive in a non-governmental organization. He said he visualized the media as a great, snarling beast, stalking the land with blood and saliva dripping from its jaws as it leapt from one herd of prey to another to satisfy its blood lust. His view was based not on normal business-related media interactions which you may have as an executive in a company, but on his previous role as a trade union leader which involved almost daily confrontations with right-wing newspapers. The scars were obviously very deep and had been caused by his occupation of a particularly difficult, high-profile post at a time of intense media interest in trade unions. This is far from typical, and the role was inevitably going to bring him into conflict with right-wing newspapers. However, when I asked about more recent experiences in his current 'normal' job he had hardly any complaints – a position I feel is more typical.

When I press participants on their comments, it often emerges that in essence their criticism is not based on a belief that we are forces for good or evil, but they're critical because they don't understand us. They have no comprehension of why we behave as we do, or what drives us. Having done an interview, they really have no idea how the end result may be presented. They have no understanding of what we do, our roles in the reporting or creation of news, or our motivations in doing so. If you understand those things, your chances of obtaining successful publicity are considerably enhanced. This chapter sets out to explain them. I invite you to put yourself in my place. Imagine you're a journalist, and try to see your potential story from my point of view. Think about what I want out of it, and what you can do to press my hot buttons.

CONFIDENCE IS THE KEY

Any successful sports person will tell you that confidence is an essential ingredient of success.

You need to believe you can do it. So it is with successful media handling. Let me begin building your confidence for forthcoming media interviews with this thought:

> The behaviour of journalists is almost entirely predictable. That's why public relations works.

Your PR advisers wouldn't go around suggesting surveys, photocalls, one-on-one briefings, opinion leader development programmes and casting other forms of media bait if they never got a bite. Once you understand what drives a journalist and why they react as they do, you too can predict their responses. That's what I want to help you to do in this chapter. My aim here is to introduce you to our motivations, show you our 'hot buttons' and illustrate how we see the world. If you understand these important basics, you'll know what makes us tick – and how to wind us up or stop us as the case may be!

IN LOVE WITH THE JOB

But before we put my journalistic colleagues on the metaphorical couch, a word in defence of my profession. It comes in the form of a quote from an American writer, the gloriously named H.R. Knickerbocker:

> Wherever you find hundreds of thousands of people trying to get out of a place, and a little bunch of madmen struggling to get in, you know the latter are newspapermen.

If he'd written that today, he would have included women, and of course TV and radio journalists, but the point is well made – we do many worthwhile things, sometimes putting our own lives at risk, in the pursuit of our chosen profession. The next time you see reports of conflict, whether in a faraway corner of the earth or on your own doorstep, think about Knickerbocker's madmen and the personal risks they've taken so that you can 'read all about it' at your breakfast table.

These are extreme examples, but they do illustrate the first character trait of journalists – we are dedicated to the job. Journalism involves long hours, years of dedication building a career and, for the majority of practitioners, the financial rewards are not great (most journalist's salary packages are generally well below similarly senior people in the PR industry, for example, and company cars and share options are just a dream for almost all journalists). If we didn't love it, we couldn't do it.

An old mentor of mine used to say that if the day ever came when I couldn't wait to tear the daily papers open to see what was inside, then I should give up. Ian Wooldrige, one of the greatest sports writers of the last 40 years, wrote that he regarded sports journalism as a great arrangement between him and the *Daily Mail*, where the newspaper paid him to be where he would have been by choice if he'd been wealthy enough not to have to earn a living. The feeling is not exclusive to sports journalists – most of us feel the same. John Prescott came under fire from hostile newspapers when he described his job as Deputy Prime Minister as 'better than working for a living'. Ironically, it is a phrase that journalists use about their own profession. That is the first lesson on a journalist's motivations – we love the job.

Hand in hand with loving the job goes the excitement we feel when we're on a big story. Sometimes executives on our courses believe the media, or sometimes individual journalists, are in some way 'out to get them'. We're not. We are, however, out to get a good story. That can be good or bad news for you, but that is of little consequence to us. We are generally motivated by our news instincts, not malice. In a sense, we take a fairly amoral view of how it affects you. A story from one of our clients illustrates how this works in practice – and how it may affect you.

Pharmaceutical companies are occasionally the target of attacks by animal rights activists, who believe it is wrong to use animals in medical research. There was a surge of such activity in the early 1990s, and as part of it some activists claimed to have poisoned a famous soft drink made by a large pharmaceutical company. The bottles were cleared from the shelves and nobody was hurt. Being a very famous drink, however, the story attracted national publicity. The media reaction was very informative in terms of how journalists view each story as separate, sorting the parties into villains and victims for that one time only, and possibly re-casting them for the next time, depending on the cast list.

Journalists had two potential places in which to lay the blame – the company for using animals in medical research (as required by law) or the activists who had potentially put many lives at risk by poisoning a drink favoured by millions of children. The decision was clear – the company was acting perfectly legally, but the activists had committed an illegal act and put innocent lives at risk. The mainstream media sided with the company.

The corporate affairs spokesman found himself in great demand for TV, radio and print interviews. As a superb professional he handled them all very well. His one uncomfortable moment came, he told me later, as he was waiting to appear live on the BBC TV National News. Standing outside the pharmaceutical company headquarters with the reporter, he was waiting for his 'cue' to go live. As the moment of truth approached, the reporter smiled at him and said, 'You know, it's a funny old world, isn't it?' 'What do you mean?' asked the spokesman, smiling nervously as the colour drained from his cheeks at the worry about what was coming next. 'Well, you know. Here we are today taking your side and helping you out of a spot. Then tomorrow if one of your drugs has killed or harmed someone we'll be back again – but going for the jugular.' To the reporter, the pharmaceutical company was an important part of the story – being on one side or the other for anything longer than this one incident didn't come into it.

WHAT IS A JOURNALIST?

Journalist is such a catch-all term that many people are confused by who it includes. The first point to make is that it could be you – in the UK anyone can call themselves a journalist. There is no mandatory formalized training, no minimum qualifications, no enforced apprenticeship. You can give up your job today and be a journalist tomorrow. Whether you make any money out of it is, of course, another matter, and increasingly journalists are graduates who have undertaken an approved, yet still voluntary, training course. There are, however, many thousands of students undertaking media studies courses believing it will equip them for a career in the media. Sadly, they're wrong – it may equip them to study the media, but not work in it. It's like the difference between being a film critic or a director – doing it requires different skills than writing about it.

Today all sorts of people call themselves journalists, but more of them later. The important thing is that a journalist is anyone concerned with the editorial side of a newspaper, TV or radio programme, magazine or any of the new media outlets such as web pages. They include everyone from the editor of a national newspaper to the youngest junior reporter on a small-circulation quarterly magazine. The news editor, sports editor, feature writers, sports reporters and photographers are all journalists, as are the layout artists, camera crews and videotape editors.

In TV and radio news, researchers, producers and reporters are journalists too. The trend these days is for TV and radio news presenters to be journalists – a far cry from the days of Jack de Manio, the first presenter of the BBC *Today* programme whose original contract described him as a 'compere'. Anyone who accused his tough modern day equivalents of being comperes would get very short shrift! Outside the hothouse of news programmes, though, presenters can come from any background – they may be actors and actresses, ex-weather girls or even married or related to someone famous. They could be the prime minister's brother, or his wife's sister – both stood in as TV and radio presenters in recent years.

Occasionally radio stations in particular use desperate measures to attract ratings, and hiring an untrained 'celeb' as a presenter is one example of a high risk, high profile strategy. That's how Mandy Allwood, the British woman who became pregnant with eight babies, became a stand-in presenter on Talk Radio, the UK's first commercial speech-based radio station. It was a publicity stunt which worked in so far as it got Talk Radio talked about. What it did for the morale of the real journalists who could have done a much better job is a different matter. In these ratings-conscious days, all kinds of people become celebrities and Andy Warhol's prediction that 'In the future everyone will be famous for 15 minutes' no longer seems outrageous.

With such a wide group of people lining up behind the banner 'journalist' a crucial part of your preparation for an interview is to establish what type of journalist you are facing. This is important for many reasons – not least that their levels of knowledge and understanding will vary greatly. So will their interviewing skills (a much-neglected element of the job – everyone thinks they can be an interviewer, but try it and see) and their objectives for the interview. As a rule, professional presenters want you to put your point then question you on it – amateurs getting their 15 minutes of fame just want to look good and work out a way to stay in the limelight.

However, you still need to be prepared, because it's sometimes the obvious question that can knock you out of your stride – and if it's that obvious, it can come from anywhere. I once heard an executive of a potato crisp manufacturer who'd launched hedgehog-flavoured crisps (presumably as a publicity stunt) thrown by the first exchange, which went like this:

Interviewer   So tell me – where do you get the hedgehogs?
Interviewee   Well, of course, they're not made from real hedgehog – they're just hedgehog flavour.
Interviewer   OK – so who tasted hedgehog to find out what it tastes like?
Interviewee   Well actually, nobody did.
Interviewer   So they're not really hedgehog flavour, then, are they?

Establishing your authority can be very difficult after an opening exchange like that.

But if you're well prepared, even the most banal questions are opportunities to put your points across. Take, for example, a consultant neurologist who went on a local radio station to be interviewed about a new migraine treatment. The show format was records and chat, a sort of poor man's Jimmy Young show, where the interview is broken up and sandwiched between records. Unfortunately many local radio stations operate on a shoestring, so the presenter didn't have the benefit of JY's extensive research team – he had to go on air almost totally unprepared and 'busk it'. His first question was so unexpected that it would have thrown many expert interviewees. However, the consultant, having been media trained, was ready for it. The opening question went as follows: 'Thank you for joining us doctor. Tell me, I've always wondered – is it *meegraine* or *mygraine*?' Even this not-very-promising opening offered an opportunity to communicate his key message. His reply? 'It doesn't matter how you say it. What matters is that it affects about five million people in the country, and now most of them can be treated.' Inspired! The interviewee had got his first key message into the first answer, and taken control. He had slipped into the driving seat and from that moment he was steering the interview where he wanted – down the road clearly marked 'my agenda'.

When I tell this story, executives sometimes say, 'I bet the journalist didn't like that, did he?' That's not true. As far as the presenter was concerned, he had in front of him a real expert, who was in command of his subject and actually *had something to say*. For many local radio presenters, their daily show involves conducting maybe six interviews on subjects about which they know very little. So when they're confronted by someone who does know it, and can mix some wit with the wisdom, they relax because that's one interview they don't need to worry about.

Having something to say is a vital element of preparation. Please do not confuse it with its close relative *knowing what you want to talk about*. The biggest problem faced by expert interviewees is they can talk about their chosen subject all night long. Unfortunately, they need to summarize their point in just a few seconds. In the words of a feminist campaigner interviewed by Alan Partridge, the spoof TV chat show host, 'Alan, are you asking me to summarise 60 years of feminist struggle into one media-friendly soundbite?' To which Alan replied, 'If you could, yes.'

JOURNALISTIC TYPES AND CHARACTERS

The hedgehog and migraine stories illustrate an important point about most journalists – they are generalists. Even specialist journalists rarely have your own level of knowledge. Journalists can be divided into many groups, but they generally all conform to H.L. Mencken's job spec. for a journalist:

> A pleasing manner, a little literary ability and a dash of rat-like cunning.

Each of the three elements illustrates an important point about journalists, and they can all trip you up if you don't fully understand them.

A PLEASING MANNER

The first element is an essential component of that part of the journalist's tool kit which is often under-recognized – getting stories. An important part of a journalist's job spec. is an ability to get on with people. 'A pleasing manner' has also been the downfall of many an executive who's told a reporter something they should have kept to themselves. It can confuse interviewees, who mistake the relationship they have with a journalist for a personal one, when in reality it is entirely professional. Building relationships with journalists is a good thing, but always regard them as you would your bank manager, accountant or lawyer – whatever you say may come back to haunt you!

One large client came to us for the first time after their organization had been rocked by revelations in the financial press about takeover targets and criticism of the performance of a joint venture partner. It came about because a senior manager had met a journalist at a conference and found himself sitting next to him on the return flight home. Having been seduced by the reporter's pleasing manner, the manager chatted as if they were old friends and confided his doubts about the results of a recent merger, and the difficulty of merging the two company cultures. He went on to identify new joint venture targets who would in his opinion, deliver more value. The manager only realized something was wrong when the reporter rang him two days later to check the spelling of the name of a key player!

The hapless manager was then doubly unfortunate because the story happened to appear in the country's leading financial paper on the day of the European directors meeting – the one day in the year when it was guaranteed maximum exposure among the senior executives. The mole hunt was short, retribution was swift, and the manager was soon an ex-executive.

The journalist was only doing his job and getting a story, and I'm sure had not sat down next to the manager with entrapment on his mind. Part of a journalist's job includes a responsibility to inform the public – who in this case included shareholders, investors and customers – and people tell journalists things. I have been the recipient of very good stories over the years because for some reason I can't quite identify, people tell me things. I have many colleagues who are the same. We just get on well with people.

The story illustrates another important point about journalists – we are never off duty. This leads to a simple rule for executives who are likely to run into us – if you want a journalist to report something, tell them about it; if you don't want it reported, keep it to yourself. Telling a journalist something and expecting it to go no further is like telling an off-duty police officer that you've committed a serious crime – they're bound to use the information. Apparently if you're lucky enough to win the National Lottery and don't want any publicity the organizers' standard reply is that in that case you should not tell a soul – if you do, it will get out. I urge you to deal with journalists in the same way – be discreet. If you start from that point you won't go far wrong.

There is another aspect to this – journalists are great gossips and even if they do agree to keep your story out of the paper they'll very likely talk about it when they're next in a bar with fellow hacks. Journalists are human too and like to tell their colleagues things they didn't know. It's also not uncommon that the reporter who's guarding your greatest secret can't remember which part of your conversation was 'off the record' anyway, so they may feel they're not breaking confidences by revealing it. Many such requests to go or stay off the record involve the interviewee saying something like, 'You won't use this, will you?' I may agree to this request, but a week later when I'm in a bar with my mates I'm not *using* it, I'm just telling a story among friends. What's wrong with that? The friends, of course, have made no promises to you. It's easy to see how things get out, isn't it? The moral of this story is simple – however pleasant they are, don't tell journalists anything you'd be embarrassed to see on the front page. Remember, a plausible manner is part of their job spec.

A LITTLE LITERARY ABILITY

This phrase damns us with faint praise. It suggests that you only need a little literary ability to be a journalist, as opposed to truly artistic professions such as novel and screenplay writing which demand it by the bucketload. Journalists won't generally agree with this assessment, but in many cases it's true – particularly in news reporting, where speed, clarity and accuracy are more important than style. In a newsroom, given the choice between an excellent writer who can't make the deadline, or a workmanlike scribe who can turn in copy to order, every editor will choose the latter. 'Not perfect' is better than 'not ready', though there are a handful of exceptions who can write very well and fast. In other branches of the profession, however, a good writing style is highly valued – in the features department for example.

Just because we don't need to be great writers, however, doesn't mean we can't write. It's an important element of our job, and most journalists enjoy it. It's just a different type of writing than you'll find at your local literary evening. We're more concerned with economy of words than flowery phrases. You need to understand the processes which happen behind the scenes, however, to fully understand the way a story is formed – in particular the way a story as it appears in the newspaper or on TV can be the end result of many people's efforts. This is one reason why we can't generally let you see the piece before it appears in the newspaper – once the reporter (your point of contact) has written

it, he or she sends it through to the next part of the production process, where it may change dramatically.

There is another element of the way journalists work which is very important to you – the way we put words together. We will form an impression of a story, company or issue and convey it to the readers, viewers or listeners. Words are our tools, and we use them like master craftsmen – with consummate skill. As a senior executive you play a major part in forming that impression. Very often, it is difficult for outsiders to understand just how we promote our own impression of people and organizations we meet without overstepping a legal line and landing in trouble. But we do.

A DASH OF RAT-LIKE CUNNING

This aspect of journalists can affect you in a number of ways. Journalists are no great respecters of authority and are very resourceful. They're always pleased when they can circumvent the system – whatever that system is. So if you have a company policy that all media interactions must go through the public affairs department (as many large organizations do) we will, when it suits us, try to get round that. One typical way is that we meet someone at a conference or on another story, use our pleasing manner to make friends with them, then when your company is in the news again, we ring them up, rather than callling the public affairs team. The importance of this to you is that you must ensure your company/media arrangements are watertight.

Figure 2.1 illustrates this point neatly. It represents an hourglass where the top chamber is labelled with the name of your company, and the lower chamber is marked 'media'. The narrow neck is your PR department. They are the gatekeepers to the media, whichever direction the traffic is travelling. They are responsible for handling all initial media inquiries and should be the first point of contact for all journalists. Often they will set up interviews with the relevant director or spokesperson but journalists must go through them to get to the interview. Impressing this on your staff can be challenging but is the only sensible way to have any chance

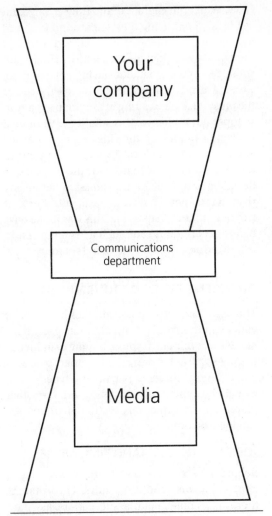

Figure 2.1 Using your communications department to filter media inquiries

are regularly media trained so [...] most of the opportunities.

If you build relationships wit[...] will also find less attempted c[...] your PR department, because it just won't be necessary. Whoever is handling media inquiries, though, the three watchwords should be honesty, openness and timeliness. This means, 'never lie, be open in all cases except where commercial confidence absolutely prevents it, and always get back to a journalist in their time frame.' From your point of view as a senior executive, you must also give your PR department the information they need. Don't send them naked into the debating chamber. If you and they can

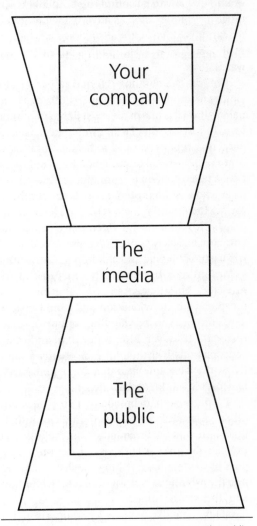

Figure 2.2 The media are the gatekeepers to the public

of communicating consistent messages and controlling your company image.

It must be acknowledged, however, that in recent years the hourglass model has changed slightly in some companies which have adopted a more open media policy, allowing more people to be quoted. Other factors here are that PR departments have become more attuned to journalists' needs and the number of media interview requests has mushroomed, necessitating an increase in the number of spokespeople. Even here, however, you need a clear policy on who is and is not authorized to speak to the media. It's also important that all potential spokespeople ccomplish these objectives, you are more likely to achieve a fair press than if you adopt a closed door policy.

The hourglass analogy gives us another opportunity to consider why you should talk to the media at all. Figure 2.2 illustrates this point. In this version the top chamber is marked with your company name, and the lower chamber has many possible different labels – customers, investors, regulators, workforce, unions, pressure groups and so on. The narrow neck in this instance represents the media. They are the gatekeepers to the general public, the group represented by the myriad of names on the lower chamber. Like the journalists in the previous example, you can go round the bottleneck with other techniques such as advertising and direct mail, but positive editorial coverage is what will really send your sales graph and career skywards.

The rat-like cunning referred to earlier also alludes to another ever-present feature of a journalist's life – it is one of the most fiercely competitive industries on earth. And journalists, in particular reporters, need a dash of cunning to overcome the opposition. When I was at ITN we gave a video camera to Tom McLean, an adventurer who was attempting to break the record for rowing the Atlantic single-handed. The plan was that he would record a video diary of his epic voyage exclusively for us. Towards the end of this trip we took his wife and children to Cornwall so we would also have exclusive pictures of the expected emotional reunion. Putting them together with the video footage would give us a major 'beat' over the BBC opposition, we reasoned. However, after a few days and many conversations with helpful radio hams around the world, it became clear that Tom, though safe, had lost his way in the Atlantic.

By then we had broadcast two pieces and other journalists had arrived in Falmouth to greet him with us, threatening our exclusive. To protect our investment, we did the only thing possible – we hired a fishing trawler and set off into the Atlantic to look for him. It took four days and the search made finding a needle in a haystack seem like a picnic by comparison, but we did find him – with a little help from the Royal Navy. When the captain of the trawler saw Tom in his tiny boat being buffeted around in the 30 foot waves, he memorably explained 'Christ, I thought we were looking for a man in a boat – not some **** in a canoe!' But having got our man, we were faced with another problem – the rest of the press pack was waiting in port for us, ready to scupper our exclusive. Our solution? We hired a helicopter to pick up the video tapes out at sea and fly them to the local TV station for onward transmission to ITN. In this way the piece could be edited and ready for transmission before any rival hacks got anywhere near our hero. It worked – though I stress that this was in the days before accountants took such a keen interest in where the news budget was being spent!

DIFFERENT TYPES OF JOURNALISTS

The term 'journalist' poses another problem for you if you're trying to learn about its practitioners, as I recommend if you're hoping to influence them. As well as covering a wide variety of jobs, it covers a great range of personality types. As an essential element of a briefing on the other players in the game, this section gives you the rundown on both.

JOB DIFFERENCES – AND SIMILARITIES

Behind the scenes in journalism are a variety of jobs, many with confusing titles. For example, there are so many editors: sub-editors, assistant editors, managing editors, section editors. In TV there are also the tape editors. There's also, of course, *the* editor. The various chapters on newspapers, TV and radio spell out the differences between them because it is important that you understand what happens to your story before it appears in the newspaper or on air. For now I want to concentrate on the journalists who will interview you, whether over the phone or in person. They are generally reporters though in reality some of them may be correspondents or even editors.

The differences between reporters and correspondents are very important to you because they imply different levels of knowledge, familiarity with the subject and sometimes seniority. They can also signify the amount of influence they wield back in the newsroom. Asking what their role is in the organization, therefore, is an important part of your interview preparation. Reporters are the people who get the story and write it in first draft form. If news is the first draft of history, as has been claimed, these are the people who write it.

Reporters tend to be generalists, and this is where many executives go wrong in their dealings with the media – they know so much about their subject that they forget how little non-experts know about it. This is easily the most common error made in talking to journalists. You are immersed in your world full-time, so it is easy to lose perspective and forget that others are not. The problem is neatly alluded to in my favourite definition of journalism:

> Journalism: A profession whose job it is to explain to others what it personally does not understand.
>
> (Lord Northcliffe)

Though there is clearly a hint of bitterness here, there is also more than a grain of truth. As a generalist, a journalist's knowledge has been described as being 'a mile wide and an inch deep' – they know a little bit about many subjects. As an expert on your subject, your knowledge is the opposite – a mile deep and an inch wide. Figure 2.3 sums up this crucial difference, and shows you what to do about it.

You can see from the diagram that if you and I are going to have a sensible conversation or meaningful interview, we have to start in the shaded area – our common ground. Having established where this is, we can move forward together as you take me deeper into your knowledge base. A word of warning, here, however. Journalists are not stupid, and like any of us, hate any suggestion that they may be. They just don't share your knowledge. In the words of an American wit: 'We're all ignorant, just on different subjects.' To avoid falling into the most common trap, my advice for dealing with reporters is this:

> Never underestimate their intelligence. Always underestimate their understanding.

If you stick to this advice you won't go far wrong.

A REPORTER'S LIFE

The life of a general news reporter is varied, interesting and hectic. For example, they may start the day with a press conference on a subject they've never covered before. By late morning they've written their story and filed it back to the office, either via laptop and modem or dictated by telephone to a copy-taker. Then they may be off to another event such as a photo-opportunity or demonstration timed to catch the lunchtime news programmes live. Then it's back to the office to write up that story, and possibly get involved in a number of others which need chasing, finishing or starting. As a news reporter in the office I might be handling three stories at a time, and be waiting for calls back on all of them. So if I've called you and you ring me back, forgive me if I don't immediately recognize you – you may be in cars or computers and I had my mind on genetically modified crops!

General news reporters tend to be quite smart, fast learners and quick on the uptake. We also have finely tuned antennae for when someone is being evasive, uncomfortable or making statements which cannot be substantiated. This can make us suspicious and we are then likely to

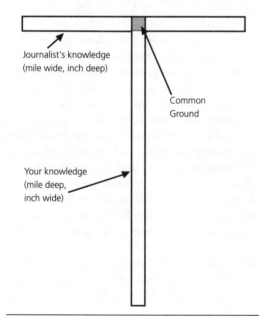

Figure 2.3 'Start with the common ground'

probe deeper into the uncomfortable aspects of the agenda for you. The clear implication is that you shouldn't try and bluff or be evasive. So if we ask you how much your new drug is, with the implication that it will be a severe drain on NHS drug budgets, tell us. Weasel words will not do. The next step is to put it into context, which we will discuss later. But not answering the question is not a good strategy. If you don't know, or the price has not been set yet, tell us.

There is no routine background of a general news reporter in the national media. They have generally climbed up the journalistic hierarchy from local radio or papers but there is no other common pattern. There are some elements, however, which do not vary, and if you understand them can give you a big advantage in realizing what makes news reporters tick.

We're only human, and all humans come with baggage. We all have our own opinions on important subjects, which influence our reactions to events and news. Journalists are the same. We also live in the country/community on which we report, so if your story has had previous publicity we are likely to have heard it. Another factor affecting our initial reaction is that if you're launching a new product or service, some of us will have personal experience of the subject. For example, if you are launching the car tracking device mentioned in the previous chapter, it is possible that inner-city journalists will have had a car stolen at some time in their lives. Even if they haven't experienced it personally it is very likely that they will at least know someone who has been a victim of autocrime. This experience colours the judgement of the journalist covering the story. If you're in computers, we've all now got PCs, use laptops for work and are familiar with e-mail and the World Wide Web. If you're in finance we all have mortgages, and many of us have personal pensions, ISAs and insurance.

It's said that 'a little knowledge can be a dangerous thing'. But not always – and in this case it's definitely not. With a well-researched product and well-prepared brief, the journalist's previous exposure to the idea or problem work in your favour because they will immediately see the benefits. If you've got a genuinely new product or idea, and you can explain how it is better than existing products, technology or services, we are likely to be receptive as consumers. However, if you're peddling a half-baked idea which has been heavily 'spun' so that it appears to fly in the face of what we judge to be accepted wisdom or common sense, then we will be sceptical – and critical.

We're great ones for putting ourselves in the position of the reader, and also, in business stories, of the potential user. For example, I ran a media training course for some executives who were launching an online department store. I shop online personally for some items such as books, IT equipment and occasionally groceries so have some experience of their world. In fact, I'm a potential customer. But at the start of the course I couldn't see what the new service was offering that couldn't be bettered by specialist online retailers such as Amazon or e-toys. So I began the role-play interview by asking, 'People use a real department store because it pulls together many different departments under one roof. But the Web does that anyway – through one computer screen we have access to specialist electrical, IT, clothing, books, toys and many other retailers. So why do we need a virtual department store? What do you think this Jack-of-all-trades approach will offer that isn't already being done by specialist retailers?'

The interviewees didn't have a convincing answer, so I wrote a negative, sceptical piece as a training exercise for them. By the end of the course we had worked out an answer to the question, along the lines of ease of use, one-stop shopping and the advantages of navigating around one site rather than the whole Web, particularly for novice web-users. By giving the communications programme a slight 'flick' in this way, the story sounded more believable, and journalists would receive it differently. It also became an important element of the business's sales pitch, so the benefits of the media training course, as so often, were far wider than just talking to the media. The web site was subsequently launched to favourable reviews and has turned into a big success – because they were able to sell its advantages.

Another important element in the reporter's

world is what academics call 'agenda-setting'. Given that journalists all come with their own baggage, it is important to think about how that baggage may be influenced. Stop for a moment and ask yourself what you think are the most powerful influences on a journalist's opinions. Is it the government, pressure groups or PR practitioners? In fact, it's none of these groups – the answer is 'other journalists'. From listening to the radio or watching TV news in the morning, to being briefed by the news editor on the day's assignments and attending events with other colleagues, a journalist's day is punctuated by colleagues telling him or her what, in their view, is important.

This has important consequences for you: it shows how important the media audience is, given its persuasive power, and illustrates how crucial it is for your organization and its products or services to be portrayed positively in the media.

CORRESPONDENTS

The people who come to interview you may also be correspondents. A correspondent's role differs from a reporter's in several crucial ways, all of which can affect your story. The main differences are the correspondent's specialist knowledge, their internal influence and advisory role, and differences in background. Let's look at these in turn.

Specialist knowledge

A correspondent is a specialist in his or her subject area, so you can expect a higher level of knowledge. Be careful, though, because here the term 'specialist' is used widely. Journalistic specialists will not be aware of the minutiae of every aspect of your subject. Consider, for example, the role of a health correspondent, either on TV, radio or in newspapers. Their 'beat' includes all the diseases and treatment areas known to humankind, as well as all the new ones which crop up. This means they are the first call for information on any of the rare health threats which appear from time to time.

During the late 1990s these included the Ebola virus, necrotizing fasciitis, a new variant of bubonic plague allegedly on the way to the west

from India and the new variants of CJD and links to BSE which were initially denied by government scientists. They are also called upon to keep up with developments in new technology, for example cloning and xeontransplantation, and write about them quickly on demand. In addition they are expected to have a wide knowledge of health politics, including arguments over funding the NHS, the drugs bill and doctors' pay. Given this wide brief, it is not surprising that they may not be immediately aware of the highly specific way in which your new treatment differs from the commonly used competitor.

Internal influence

A correspondent's views generally carry more weight in the organization than those of a reporter. The best way of gaining publicity for your story is to find someone inside to champion it and argue its case against other, similar stories. The correspondent is best placed to do this – if you get them on your side, you're almost home and dry. Because they spend all their time working in one area, they are also more likely to be keen to establish relationships with sources within it. For you, this means it is well worth the effort to cultivate specialist correspondents, whereas this is not so often the case with general news reporters.

Advisory role

When a news story breaks, the News Desk directs the reporters in terms of outlining the angles they want covered and by whom. This produces a one-way relationship with generally the News Desk in charge of the reporters. But the relationship with correspondents is more one of equals – when a story breaks in a specialist area, the News Desk asks the correspondent for advice, which may vary from the basic, 'Was this expected?' or even 'Is this important and why?' to very detailed, specific questions. In this way, the specialists play a leading role in shaping the day's news agenda – another reason to get them on your side.

Different backgrounds

Correspondents' backgrounds also vary, but not

as much as general news reporters. The main routes to being a correspondent are:

- having qualifications in a subject, in particular scientific areas where specialist knowledge is very important
- a background in trade magazines in the relevant area which allows the reporter to build up specialist expertise
- as a general news reporter, showing an interest or aptitude for a particular subject

This last condition can be drawn quite widely – the health editor of a national TV news station explained to me how she obtained her own position. 'I was made the health correspondent after I had time off to have a baby. They said, "You obviously know about health and hospitals – you can be the health correspondent." Then when I had a second baby they made me health editor.' There's an element of cynicism here but the point is well made – the term 'specialist' can be used quite loosely.

TRADE JOURNALISTS

A word here about journalists who work on trade magazines, and what this means to you. In the trade press you will normally find a deeper understanding of the subject and a greater level of knowledge than with the general press. This is generally true, but I would still urge caution with reporters whom you have not met previously. This is because even trade journalists have to start somewhere, and tend to have journalism skills first, then add the subject knowledge by on-the-job learning. So the reporter from *Rubber and Plastics Weekly* who's interviewing you about your new guttering which is guaranteed never to clog up with autumn leaves might be new on the magazine, and only the previous week have been very comfortable interviewing a derivatives dealer for an investment publication.

This situation has come about for a number of reasons. One is that most trade magazines are owned by huge media groups such as EMAP, Haymarket or IPC. The career path for a journalist within such a group will usually involve taking on increasingly senior roles on several titles. Depending on the titles in a group's portfolio, a journalist may move from cars to chemicals then the day before your press release lands on their desk take a senior post on a computer magazine. If you don't realize it and it all comes out wrong, your learning curve may be as steep as theirs at this point.

The way to avoid problems here is to establish the reporter's level of knowledge before you start the interview – not enough people do this. In fact as a general rule, interviewees don't ask enough questions of the reporter before the interview starts. You can do it and we won't mind! It will even help us to get the story right – and that suits both of us. There is no harm in asking a journalist whether they've covered this subject or type of newspaper in the past, and trying to discover how much they know about it. Then you can tailor your answers to their level of understanding. Importantly for you, most journalists feel exposed when they move into a new subject area, and will be delighted if you start with a non-patronizing ABC of the subject. They will also be very much in your debt, and owe you a big favour – a good position to be in!

EXPERTS

You will occasionally encounter real experts among journalists. They tend to be on the trade magazines, often as the editor, though if they are really knowledgeable they will have quite a wide number of outlets. For example, David Learmount of *Flight International* and Richard Hope of the *Railway Gazette* are highly respected in their fields. If they interview you, expect them to be very knowledgeable indeed – this will be no easy ride. However, if you convince them of the merits of your story they do have huge influence in the wider media. All these people – and there are many of them – write regularly for the national press, and are called upon to comment on industry-specific issues when big stories break. With their credibility, influencing them is very tough, but worth investing a lot of effort in.

COLUMNISTS

Columnists are an essential tool as a newspaper seeks to define its own character, and they often express the views of the readers in a very clear fashion. To read Lynda Lee-Potter in the *Daily*

Mail is to listen to the voice of female Middle England, the paper's heartland. Not being hampered by facts or restricted by considerations of balance, columnists are employed to have opinions and express them trenchantly. They are also very powerful. 'My own column' is a dream of many journalists, particularly feature writers who have more latitude in their subjects than news reporters. Once they get there, the choice of what they include is theirs and theirs alone. That does not mean, however, that a little lobbying won't occasionally pay off. If you're launching something which you think may interest them, send them details. The key here, as ever, is making it relevant.

Columnists on trade magazines are a different matter from their colleagues on the nationals. They tend to have a good understanding of the industry and can play a significant role in shaping the success of your launches. Where there is a strong trade magazine in your subject area, make a point of getting to know the columnists. Try and find out what they like and what irritates them. Because of their standing in the industry, they have a strong opinion-forming role among their journalist colleagues as well as the readers – and influencing journalists and readers, after all, is your objective.

CHAPTER SUMMARY

- Don't think of journalists as 'the enemy' – you and they are often on the same side.
- Many executives are critical of the media because they don't understand what journalists want. They commonly regard journalists with a mixture of fear, suspicion and misunderstanding.
- Confidence is the key to successful media handling.
- Journalists take an amoral view of how their stories affect you – they're just after a story.
- You need to establish what type of journalist you're dealing with, their level of knowledge and their understanding about your subject.
- Ask the journalist how familiar they are with the subject before you agree to be interviewed.
- Journalists want you to be a good interviewee.
- Before you agree to an interview it is vital that you have *something to say*. This is much more specific than *something you want to talk about*.
- Journalists are never off duty. So there's no such thing as 'off the record'.
- Journalists like getting round systems – so make sure your company procedures for dealing with them are watertight.
- Make sure your spokespeople are media trained regularly.
- A journalist's knowledge is 'a mile wide and an inch deep' – your knowledge is the opposite, so you must start in the common ground.
- 'Never underestimate their intelligence, always underestimate their understanding.'
- Journalists see you from the point of view of their readers or editors.
- Trade press journalists are often very knowledgeable about their area – but not necessarily so.

CHAPTER THREE
Television

Television is the world's most powerful communications medium. Television commercials are the most expensive form of advertising, and hard-hearted media buyers will focus on the bottom line and hand over millions of pounds a year because they know how influential television is. Increasingly, surveys show that TV is the primary source of news for many people. Other surveys also show it is much more trusted than newspapers. The effects of TV are said to be so powerful that they changed military strategy in the Gulf and Kosovo conflicts, and regularly influence western politicians debating whether to send aid to distressed regions of the world.

In the same way that TV pictures and reports can move armies and galvanize nations, they can be a major influence on the way you and your company are perceived. But though politicians and generals have been quick to understand the power of TV, large parts of the business community choose to ignore it. This may be because they don't watch it, as senior executives often tell me. How you spend your time is of course your business, but your customers, staff, shareholders and competitors spend some of theirs watching TV. If you ignore it, that gives them a competitive advantage. In the slogan of the *Sun*'s million pound bingo game, 'You got to be in it to win it.'

A story about one managing director of a global business illustrates how many senior executives regard television as trivial. At a time when his company was attracting lots of media publicity he agreed to a recorded interview in his office with a CNN business reporter. They did the interview twice, but the reporter felt the executive seemed distracted and could offer a more succinct answer to an important question. 'Do you mind if we just do that question one more time?' he asked. 'That's OK. But can you make it quick, because I've got to get back to work,' said the MD. His media adviser sitting in the corner of the room buried his head in his

hands. His boss had a golden opportunity to talk to large numbers of the business community in his key markets across the world, and he didn't regard it as work! Yet only the previous week he'd taken a half-day out of his schedule to rehearse his presentation to the AGM. He just didn't realize that the TV interview was at least as important – arguably more so.

Apart from not being TV viewers, there is another obstacle to big businesses courting TV publicity. They – and their advisers – don't understand it. PR consultancies (with a few exceptions) are famously weak on their knowledge of TV, and human nature being what it is, their reaction is to either just pay lip service to it, or ignore it completely. This attitude, of course, rubs off on their clients or employers, who ignore it too. To test your own organization's TV-savviness, compare the reports you receive about press coverage with those about TV. Most large companies receive a regular press cutting service – you probably see the cuttings yourself. But when did you last receive a videotape of a TV programme which featured your company? And when did you last watch one?

Given the power of television, I am constantly struck by how many large corporations don't have a TV set in their executive offices, or even in their communications department. My company spent some time helping a large multinational corporation prepare to announce a round of job cuts in the UK. Early on the morning of the announcement we moved into the managing director's office, which was to be our operations room and press office for the duration. My first action was to go out and buy an aerial for the TV set which had sat in the corner for almost two years but had never been switched on. I came back with videotapes so we could record the coverage. I also bought a radio. Without these basic broadcast tools, we would have been working in a vacuum, unaware of what the other interested parties were saying about the story.

This chapter starts to fill in those gaps of knowledge about television and its reporting of business stories. By the end of it you should be able to discuss the merits and problems of appearing on TV, know the difference between the various programme types, and understand what TV producers want from you.

TV – A WINDOW ON THE WORLD

The first common misunderstanding about television is its huge variety. It really is a window on the world – and what you see depends on where you're looking. Saying 'I want to be on TV', or indeed 'I don't want to be on TV', is like saying you're catching a plane but not telling me where or when. You need to be far more specific. And just as you need an airline timetable and a map for that, you need to look at the TV schedules before you launch yourself. So we'll start with that basic kit – a map of the TV landscape.

When executives do consider trying to court television coverage, they generally mean one of two types of programmes – news or documentaries. There are several problems with this approach. A news item and a documentary programme are very different animals. They demand hugely varied resources and timescales to produce, and the demands they will make on you, your company and your time are dramatically different. They also have very distinct focuses. TV news tends to tell a story as it appears on the day of transmission, which may be favourable or critical of the subject. Documentaries, however, have an element of investigation or revelation about them. As a consequence, they tend to favour the underdog, and are less likely to promote your corporate viewpoint – positive documentaries about big businesses are unusual, unless there's an even bigger villain in the frame, often the government. (In reality because of the financial pressures on production budgets, the investigation is often superficial and tells us little that wasn't known, but the impression can still be damaging to you.)

However, the idea that TV means just news or documentaries is a mistake for other reasons. It ignores huge areas of the TV landscape. In particular, it's ignoring the great growth in specialist business and financial programmes. TV producers are very inventive, and are constantly coming up with new formats. As an example, in autumn 1999 a new business TV show achieved prominence on Channel 4. Called *Show Me The Money* it was based on a panel game where the contestants bet on shares – a sort of Fantasy Footsie. Anecdotal evidence suggests that just about every share which was tipped by the panellists immediately rose as private investors, aided by the boom in online dealing, backed it. This sort of behaviour can produce a volatile share price particularly with smaller plcs, or AIM-listed companies. If you're a senior executive in one such business, you need to know about anything that can move your share price (particularly if you're about to exercise some options!).

But *Show Me The Money* was more than a panel game. It also featured a slot called 'Sixty Second Pitch' where senior executives of (generally) small to medium-sized plcs had one minute to pitch their businesses to the panel. As the programme built a following, particularly among the investment community, this became quite an opportunity to raise the profile of the companies featured. The programme was quickly commissioned for a second run starting early in 2000.

The point here is that *Show Me The Money* would not appear on any list of news or documentary programmes. In comparison with ITN or the BBC *Ten O'Clock News**, it's not even on the radar screen, so you'd have to look very hard to find it. It's just the type of programme that is ignored by media advisers who are less than comfortable with TV. It also illustrates how widely you have to cast your net to catch all the available publicity opportunities.

The inventive nature of producers means that no list can be exhaustive and risks becoming out of date as soon as it is compiled. The best way to keep up is to look through the TV listings – or ask your advisers to do it. You must also, however much this may go against the grain, watch some of the programmes. Here are the main types of TV programmes which offer opportunities – and threats – to your business:

---

* As this book went to press . . .

- national, terrestrial news programmes
- 24-hour news channels, usually with an international audience
- business news bulletins
- feature programmes, usually broadcast weekly, e.g. *The Money Programme*
- interview-format programmes, e.g. *Sky Business Report, Bloomberg Business*
- investigative and consumer programmes
- documentaries
- sofa shows, e.g. *Richard and Judy, After Nine* on GMTV
- chat shows, e.g. *Clive Anderson, Michael Parkinson, Larry King Live* on CNN
- specialist slots and programmes, e.g. personal finance, lifestyle, health
- quizzes and panel games.

Whatever their focus and attitude, whether they're a general news or special interest programme, investigative documentary or a cosy chat on the sofa, most television programmes likely to feature business fit into one of three types:

- programmes based entirely on location shooting, pre-shot and edited, usually joined together by introductions from a presenter
- studio-based programmes composed of interviews
- combinations of both, such as news programmes, *Newsnight* or sometimes *The Money Programme*.

Businesses feature prominently in all three types of programmes. The requirements of journalists on location or in the studio are fairly universal, whatever their eventual programme output, so I will examine them in detail, and show you how to take advantage of them to maximize your chances of gaining publicity for your company or organization.

NATIONAL TERRESTRIAL NEWS PROGRAMMES

A word first about the great beasts of the TV jungle – the 'national news'. In the UK, although we have five terrestrial television channels, their news programmes are all produced by just two organizations – ITN and the BBC. ITN produces the news for ITV, Channel 4 and Channel 5, giving the organization a massive influence over what comes across the airwaves or, increasingly, down the cable. The BBC produces its own news programmes for BBC 1 and 2 and its various and expanding cable and satellite shows. It is also the oldest and most credible broadcast news organization in the world.

Sky News is the other big beast. In the ten years it's been broadcasting it has established a first-rate reputation for proper TV journalism. Its standing in the journalistic community can be measured by the number of reporters, presenters and producers who have moved there from ITN and the BBC. It now stands shoulder to shoulder with ITN and the BBC – you should regard any requests to appear on it with equal seriousness.

The furore over the ITV companies' decision to move *News at Ten* from its prime time slot and the intermittent rows that break out over accusations of anti-Conservative bias on the BBC show how seriously these programmes are treated by many parties from the government to the rest of the media. This is also where the glamour boys – and girls – of TV journalism ply their trade. When clients talk of 'getting on the news' this is usually what they mean. And it is guaranteed to make your media adviser's heart sink. The reason is that journalistically, these programmes are at the top of the tree – and reaching that height is very difficult. The need for a reality check is not exclusive to senior executives, however. Some of the worst culprits are product or brand managers, whose belief in their product is unshakeable. From a corporate standpoint this is very important – if the product manager doesn't think the benefits of his or her product should be trumpeted to the world, no one else will. However, this can lead to a warped sense of what's important. It's not unusual for such people to think that a change of packaging colour from one shade of blue to another merits national publicity. If so, that's what advertising is for. A challenge for media advisers – including your in-house PR department – is to keep at least one eye on the real world. And in the real world, packaging changes very rarely make it on to the news.

So 'getting onto the news' is the most difficult thing in media handling. You can, however, increase your chances by understanding what TV journalists want. Many items on the wish-list of TV news producers and journalists are the same as those who inhabit other parts of the TV landscape, so I will go into them in some detail.

THE ESSENTIALS OF TV NEWS

Although it is essential to keep an eye on other parts of the TV world, it is on TV news where you are most likely to appear. And TV news – whether it is a tiny regional station or the BBC – is at once fiendishly complicated and deceptively simple.

Not all the elements of the job of a TV news reporter appear on screen – in fact TV reporters and producers tend to develop a rather peculiar set of skills. The basic elements of news also hold good for any programme which includes location reports in its mix, such as feature specialist programmes. It is therefore worth exploring those basic requirements in detail and how they affect you. The essentials of TV news can be divided into two categories: what's required from a story as a whole, and what's required from interviewees. Let's look at category one first.

WHAT'S REQUIRED OF A NEWS ITEM

Here are the essentials of a TV news item, particularly as they relate to business stories:

- pictures
- time
- logistics
- people.

Let's look at them in more detail, how they affect you and what you can do about them.

TV NEWS IS ABOUT PICTURES

Whenever a TV journalist is told of a potential story, assuming they like the sound of it their first question (or thought) is '...and what will we see?' Let me state a point which may sound obvious, but in my experience is not considered early enough in the story-producing process: the biggest problem for many business stories is how to illustrate them. Put it another way: if you can illustrate your story with relevant, interesting up-to-date footage, your story leaps right to the front of the queue. I like to imagine potential TV news stories as show horses in a gymkhana. If your story has good pictures it's like getting a bye through to the final, where it is paraded around the ring with the other finalists. It still won't necessarily win, but at least it's in there. Its chances are then dependent on other factors, some of them appropriate to journalists in any medium (for example relevance, timeliness, newsworthiness), others specific to television.

To illustrate the pictorial problem, consider the fastest growing sector of all the world's major stock exchanges, the Internet-based companies, or the 'dotcoms' as they've become known. Dotcoms play an increasingly influential role in the performance of the markets, and stories about them get huge amounts of airtime. You may even be running one yourself. So let's say you've got a story which will attract a fair amount of publicity in the print media, and you're expecting to make a similar splash on television. Ask yourself – or your advisers – the journalist's question: 'What will we see on screen?'

The problem with many dotcoms is the dearth and lack of variety of good pictures. Shots of computer screens, web pages, rooms full of people clicking away and a few close-ups of mouse and keyboard work and your animated logo will only go so far. (This is not to say, however, that you shouldn't supply such pictures to broadcasters – if you watch business stories on TV, you will see that the majority of those concerning dotcoms are composed entirely of the above, plus an interview with a senior executive. A TV producer's wish-list is like a child's letter to Santa – you don't always get what you want. But if you can give it to them, you'll find yourself very popular.)

Assuming your story passes the tests discussed earlier – newsiness, relevance and so on – the more pictures you can lay on, offer or supply, the higher value it takes on. 'Great pictures' is a phrase in common usage in TV newsrooms. For example, if your company specializes in late-booking holidays, or last-minute sales, or discounts which are only available because you wait until you reach a critical mass of orders and can then bulk buy, you have the opportunity for pictures outside the normal dotcom world. So if you are planning a TV story, arrange access in advance to the other locations which will supply the pictures. Or better still, get them professionally shot and supply them to the journalist as a tape of core footage. This will ensure that you approve of (and approve) the pictures used, and leaves the journalist free to concentrate on other, less predictable pictures.

As an example, in autumn 1999 a large IT company wanted to reassure customers about the range of support available to enable them to avoid the effects of the so-called millennium bug. We shot all the pictures listed above, but also included pictures from one of their customers, in this case a traditional, low tech engineering company in Wales. Going to the customer's premises offered us the opportunity to include pictures of heavy engineering, which contrasted neatly with the high-tech images from the IT firm. The combination of the two worked well, and resulted in much TV coverage.

In contrast, we were asked to advise the same client on the TV potential, if any, of a survey they had conducted about how people relate to their PCs. This entailed not only questions about the extent of PC usage across Europe, but also more wacky issues such as whether different nationalities are more likely to kiss or hit their PC, where they rated it compared with other household equipment such as dishwashers and washing machines, and to what extent they felt they could live without it rather than their partner. Our advice was that the lack of pictures made it a difficult story to do for television, and they should concentrate on the press. We did, however, suggest that if they had the right type of spokesperson who could be both serious and light-hearted as required then they would have a chance of making it on to some interview-based TV programmes – and they did.

TV journalists put a lot of effort into planning the shots they want for a TV piece. You should do the same – and it needn't be difficult.

One criticism of TV news today is that it has become formulaic and the pictures are all predictable. I'm not convinced how recent this phenomenon is, when I remember that on my first day as a TV researcher more than 20 years ago I was sent to cover a gas blast in a block of flats. My news editor's brief was very clear. 'Don't bother with anything flashy, just get the usual – wide shot of the scene, the white tape saying "Police, do not cross", close-up of the street sign, pull back to the blasted windows, police searching through the debris and a couple of cutaway shots of people watching. Then knock off a couple of voxpop interviews with the residents.' I was very impressed with his prescience when I arrived at the scene and found the whole story could be illustrated exactly as he predicted. The cameraman and I did just as requested and the piece made the evening news. If you watch the news today, you will see a great similarity in the pictures used to illustrate the pictures in your own industry. With the right forethought and advice, you can plan the pictorial elements of your own stories with great accuracy and a similar amount of success.

TV NEWS IS ABOUT TIME

Some years ago I attended a course for TV news executives in the USA. During one exercise we were each given a lump of modelling clay and asked to make something which symbolized our work. Three people in the group made timepieces of various designs. (I made a camel, once memorably described as 'a horse designed by a committee', because I feel TV news bulletins are the camels of journalism – generally put together by committee, rather than one person's vision of what the news is that day.)

This obsession with time is more acute with TV news than any other form of journalism. It's also the aspect of our job which causes most problems for would-be subjects. If you have aspirations to TV news publicity then you need to understand its restrictions and how to cope with them. That's what I want to explore now.

Time for a TV reporter poses three problems:

1 the speed with which we need to set up the story
2 the lack of time we have to put the piece together, and
3 the small amount of airtime we have to tell the

story in the bulletin (typically between 45 seconds and two minutes).

Each of these poses particular challenges for you. Let's examine them and see how you can overcome them.

Setting up the story

The typical day of a TV newsroom is roughly divided into three segments, each one ending with one of the day's three main programmes:

- early morning until the lunchtime news
- lunchtime until the evening news
- early evening until the late night news (the BBC's *Ten O'Clock News*, or *Sky News at Ten*, for example).

Each segment ends with a programme because each bulletin editor wants his or her programme to include as much new material as possible, either new stories, or new angles on 'running stories'. This puts enormous pressure on the production team, as in many cases they only have the length of time between bulletins to set up the story. This entails arranging all the interviews, foootage and library material within a very short timeframe. This is the first challenge for you – you need to be prepared to react quickly to requests for an interview or permission to film. Yet the culture of big business is generally not consistent with fast decision making, where important ones are generally agreed after much discussion at several levels. Another problem is that given the packed nature of senior executive's diaries, making time for an interview often means some other important meeting or person loses out.

The fact is that it's rarely convenient to do an interview at an hour's notice, but if you want to use TV to raise your profile or communicate your messages, you have to be flexible enough to agree. If you don't, you're likely to turn on the TV and find your competitors getting the airtime instead. There are always many logistical reasons to say 'no'. What's challenging is to find a way of saying 'yes'. I hope that the importance of using the media is such a clear message of this book that you will regard TV news opportunities as at least as important as other meetings on the day. Most other meetings will wait for a few

hours – in that time, the opportunity to reach millions of people will be lost.

A word of advice here – 'reacting' means reaching a decision quickly whether the answer is going to be 'yes' or 'no'. It's important for your relationship with the journalist that you don't dither, or worse, lead them to believe you will help, when you won't.

Reporters working for the 24-hour news channels such as Sky, CNN and BBC News 24 are under even greater pressure than their colleagues on 'traditional' news programmes who are aiming for specific bulletins at fixed points in the newsday. Their time challenge is simple – how soon can I get this on air? CNN reporters talk of 'feeding the beast' – the beast in question being a 24-hour news programme with a voracious appetite. Underlying all this time pressure is the constant worry about what the opposition are doing, and the knowledge that back in the newsroom my own editor is watching the opposition's output, watching for any hint of an angle I may be missing out on the road.

To outsiders, this relentless time pressure appears to produce a frantic way of working which is difficult to understand and in the views of some mitigates against doing a thorough job. In truth, there are many occasions in a TV newsroom where getting it fast can easily become more important than doing the best job possible. This is very different, however, from not working hard to portray a story accurately. 'Getting it right' has always been the first maxim of journalism, and the fact that TV journalists generally work faster than others does not mean that accuracy is sacrificed – on the contrary, it's just accepted as another hurdle to be cleared as we hurtle our way to the next bulletin.

Putting the piece together

It is one of the paradoxes of journalism that although reporters are fully aware of how important time is to their own schedule, they rarely understand the time pressures on the interviewee. This is an important point and can lead to other problems for you. During my years as a TV journalist my starting point, as with all journalists, was an unshakeable expectation that interviewees would regard being interviewed as a privilege or a duty. Journalists feel they can take liberties with your time, being blissfully unaware of how they've devastated your diary for the day. When I'm putting the story together, this can affect you in two ways. The first is that I may be in and out so quickly that when I've gone you feel I didn't give you enough time to explain your point of view accurately. I know how frustrating this feels for senior people, but the good news is that it doesn't need to happen. You can avoid it by being fully prepared with what you want to say. See the final chapter on 'putting it all together' for techniques to ensure that you get your messages across, but essentially the starting point is to work out in advance what they are. This enables you to turn the lack of time to your advantage – if I'm in a hurry I want you to be very clear, and will regard your clarity and brevity as a help, not a hindrance.

By contrast, my lack of appreciation of the value of your time can have a very different effect – even though I'm under great time pressure, I still need to go back to the office with a *good* interview clip and/or the best possible pictures. I will keep trying until I get what I need – and if this takes longer than expected this will eat further into your diary. You may have agreed to the interview believing it will take 15 minutes, but after half an hour I'm still there, still trying to get what I want. The way to avoid this is by setting a time limit in advance, and sticking to it. If you're adamant that I only have 15 minutes, I can cope with that – even though I will try and persuade you to give me more time when we're together. One way of enforcing your limit is to do the interview in another room, away from where you are working. Then the crew can set up and get it just as they want it without disturbing you – you just turn up and do the interview.

Lack of airtime

How long do you think a typical TV news story lasts? The answer varies depending on the programme, but on *Sky News* it will usually be about a minute and a half. On the BBC's *Ten O'Clock News* it may stretch towards two minutes. When I worked on ITN's *News at 5.45*, one minute and fifteen seconds was the target. In that time we would endeavour to explain some fairly compli-

cated issues about the economy, foreign affairs or politics – and usually make a good job of it. This is important to you because it illustrates two things:

- how brief your contributions have to be, in terms of interview clips, and
- how simple and clear your arguments need to be to work in this tight timeframe.

This last point in particular seems to evade many executives. There may be many good, detailed reasons for reaching the decisions you have made, but TV news is not the place to explain them in detail. TV news – indeed most of TV with the possible exception of interview programmes – is about being clear, brief and simple. In advance, you have to realize how much explaining you can do in a 20-second interview clip. Start with that idea and you won't go far wrong.

Soundbites

The need for brevity leads me to a thorny subject which often crops up in discussion of TV (and radio) journalism – our love of soundbites. A 'soundbite' is a very short interview clip which summarizes your position as a whole. Soundbites get a bad press in the UK. In 1999 the Conservative opposition started to claim that the Labour government was 'all soundbites and no substance' – ironically, this was such a good soundbite that it was used repeatedly on TV and radio news. It met all the requirements of a good soundbite – it was short, memorable and summed up a more complicated position, that is that the government was more interested in presentation than policies (another good soundbite). Research conducted in the USA found that the average interview clip during the Presidential election in 1966 was 43 seconds, but in 1992 it was eight seconds. Can you make your point in eight seconds? You probably can with preparation. British TV news tends to include longer 'soundbites' than its American counterpart, so you do have slightly more time available – aim for 15 seconds.

Much of the criticism of the 'soundbite culture' has come from politicians who feel that politics is too important and complicated to be reduced to bite-size pieces in this way. Rather than going into that here, I hope it will be more useful if I give you some illustrations of good soundbites. Politicians, for whom getting on the TV is an important element of their job, have given us many great ones. Neil Kinnock, the former Labour leader and a man not usually known for his brevity, scored highly when he was in opposition with 'The government knows the cost of everything and the value of nothing.' Archbishop Desmond Tutu criticized the Mandela government in South Africa with the words, 'This government stopped the gravy train – just long enough to get on it.' Tony Blair produced what's thought to be the first soundbite without a verb or object, 'Education, education, education.'

But 'giving good soundbite' as TV reporters describe it is not a skill exclusive to politicians – I quote them because their utterances tend to be recorded and they have more opportunity than most to practise their art. A spokesman for Richard Branson, during one of the Virgin v. British Airways rows, memorably said, 'Calling yourself the world's favourite airline because you carry more passengers than anyone else is like calling the M25 the world's favourite motorway.' This is a good example of another thing which makes a good soundbite – a word picture. Where possible, think of something visual to illustrate your point.

The key point about these and all good soundbites is that they're planned in advance. If you don't do this, you can end up with a rather unfortunate construction, as with the spokeswoman for a pressure group who was criticizing a new government initiative. Live on national radio she started very well, but her soundbite came out as follows: 'It's just no good. The situation's out of control. They've created a Frankenstein's monster, and now they'll never get it back into the bottle.' She then realized what she'd said and become flustered, with consequent collapse of authority. With planning and careful thought, you can avoid this kind of trap and produce good soundbites of your own.

TV NEWS IS ABOUT LOGISTICS

Logistics – the practical aspects of compiling the story and getting it back to the studio in time for transmission – pose a greater challenge to TV news journalists than those working in either radio or print. If you understand the problems and help journalists to overcome them then your company will be in a small minority. Most companies gear their media relations to print journalists so if you follow the advice in this section TV reporters will be grateful and other things being equal are likely to come back to you rather than your rivals. It will also give you – or your communications department – a head start in building relationships with broadcasters, which itself will increase your chance of take-up.

Most of the logistical challenges concern the nature of TV news and the people and equipment required to do the job. A crew usually has two people plus the reporter. They carry a lot of equipment so they must travel by car and be able to park near the location, with all the problems that entails for driving and parking in congested cities. When they arrive they need a power supply (though the cameras can run off batteries they do need power for the lights). They also need more space to operate than their print or radio counterparts so tend to make small offices look very crowded. They also like an interesting background for interviews – this is an opportunity for you to get your company logo on screen.

Having got the material 'in the can' the reporter or crew then have to get it back to base where it can be edited in time for transmission. This usually means they have to leave the scene as soon as possible, or at least give the tape to a despatch rider – you will often see the DR standing by waiting for the interview and filming to finish.

News conferences provide extra challenges for TV news. A row of people making statements and answering questions is not visually exciting, so TV reporters usually want to conduct their own interviews with the main players from the conference. Print and radio reporters may also want to carry out interviews too. Given the time pressure you can collect more brownie points by allowing TV reporters to go first. You should also set aside a space or a room – with your logo in the background – where they can conduct the interviews uninterrupted and undisturbed by extraneous sounds.

Here then are some rules to make yourself popular with TV crews:

- take advice on the timing of news conferences and TV-focused photo-opportunities – TV journalists need time to get the material back to base and edited
- arrange car parking in advance and make sure the gatekeeper has their names and car registration(s) if necessary
- make sure reception know where to direct the crew on arrival
- make sure the interview set-up has an interesting background which reflects the subject matter, for example laboratories, computer rooms, factory floors. Then let them get shots of it in operation as voiceover material
- if the interview is to be in an office, set up a company logo in the background
- if you're holding a news conference, set aside a separate space or room for TV interviews
- ensure there are adequate power supplies near the interview point
- be aware of the sound requirements – a low-level hum of general office noise in the background is OK, but don't start that huge photocopying job just as the camera starts running
- send a memo (or e-mail) telling people what's happening and what you expect them to do
- put signs on the doors saying 'Quiet please. Filming in progress'
- make sure the telephones in the office can be turned off or diverted for the duration of the interview.

Interview locations

My first point about the essentials of news was that television is about pictures. This is equally true whether the pictures are of your exciting new product in operation, or most of the screen is filled with an interview and the pictures are 'only' the background. If the interview is to be done on your premises, you have a great opportunity to provide pictures which reinforce your image. Research done in the early 1960s suggested that 55 per cent of a message is conveyed by how people look, 38 per cent by how they sound and only 7 per cent by what they say. The

exact percentages have been queried since, but the fact remains that on television the images are an important element of the message.

Chapter 8 gives advice on how to dress, look and behave during a TV interview. For now I want to address the other part of the picture – the background. In corporations, the potential power of the interview background is often ignored. An example from my own experience serves to reinforce the point. In the early years of my career on the local TV news in London a colleague went to interview a hospital manager about a strike in the laundry. The manager met the film crew on arrival and suggested they did the interview in the laundry with the mountain of unwashed sheets, pillowcases and pyjamas in the background. As they walked into the laundry he took off his jacket, rolled up his sleeves and put a chair in front of the mountain of washing. My colleague was delighted because this was just the type of background we wanted – so different from a man in a grey suit at a desk.

It was only when we watched the interview being transmitted that evening that we realized what he'd done. The combination of the rolled up sleeves and his concerned manner against the backdrop of dirty laundry created the impression that as soon as the interview was over he was going to turn around and make a start on the sheets! An inspired piece of strategic thinking which reinforced the idea that the management were leaving no stone unturned in the effort to sort out the problem.

By contrast, consider the story of the man from the transport ministry who was contacted by a local news programme about a fast road that had become an accident blackspot. He agreed to do an interview standing by the busy road. No sooner had the words 'The accident rate on this road is no worse than average' left his lips than there was a pile-up behind him (no doubt caused by fast-moving drivers struggling to see what the TV crew was doing!). The moral of this story – and a golden rule for all executives – is never to do an interview where you cannot control the environment. This includes outside locations, where there may be drunks, demonstrators, pneumatic drills or barking dogs just ready to spoil your day – it is impossible to sound authoritative shouting against the noise or struggling to concentrate against other distractions. So keep locations on your own premises where you can stay in control. But that should still give you plenty of scope.

TV NEWS IS ABOUT PEOPLE

Television, more than print or radio, is a medium which operates best at a surface level. It is not generally good at debate or in-depth exploration of issues (there are some notable exceptions in the current affairs world, though these are few and far between). Very often the way of presenting an issue is by telling it as a personality story. An early beneficiary of this trend was Sir John Harvey-Jones, when he was Chairman of ICI (he was such a hit as an interviewee that he became a presenter himself). Today, stories about News Corporation are presented as items about Rupert Murdoch, Microsoft means Bill Gates, Amstrad means Alan Sugar – and of course Virgin anything means Richard Branson.

This cult of the personality can have pluses and minuses, but you need to be aware of it to be able to deal with it. You need to decide whether you want to build someone (maybe yourself) up to a level where they are recognized as 'personalities' by TV reporters. The more recognizable your senior spokesperson becomes, the more often he or she will be approached for comment on stories, and the higher your company profile will be. Of course, the real problems may be more to do with internal rivalries and jealousies, but it is something you should consider – forewarned is forearmed.

Case studies

This leads to the most important tip of all for getting onto TV programmes, though it also applies to all other types of news. Supply good case studies. Television in particular needs this because of the nature of the medium. If you think half a million people in an area are going to benefit from your new water filtration system, that's great. Unfortunately we can't show pictures of half a million people. So to illustrate it we need one or two examples. In this case they might be people who've been taken ill because

the previous filtration system was inadequate, backed up by a public health specialist saying 'clean water made the biggest contribution to public health in the twentieth century'. The TV station would also need pictures of the public health specialist at work in a lab to illustrate that aspect of the story. Another important element is that case studies build empathy with the viewer. They make them think, 'That could be me' – the ultimate hot button for journalists.

This section has covered the first essential of TV news – what's required from a story. Let's now turn to the second – your role in an interview.

YOUR ROLE IN AN INTERVIEW

In reality your role in an interview starts before the phone rings – when you (or your communications department) realize there may be a media opportunity on the horizon. This is when you need to start the serious discussions about whether you want to get involved in the likely media attention. It is also when you need to prepare for such an opportunity. Even if you do decide in advance, I know of many occasions when managers' publicity hopes have fallen at the first hurdle of the initial inquiry from a journalist. Here are some of the main reasons they fail:

- There are too many people in the way of the interviewee, making the journalist jump through an unreasonable number of hoops to get to them.
- They can't be contacted quickly enough on the day the journalist needs them.
- They won't, or can't, make themselves available at the right time.
- They need approval – for their appearance and their statements – which takes time.
- They're not clear what they want to say.

They also fall because of their secretaries, who in large corporations are often experts in preventing callers getting through to the boss, behave as if they're handling a routine call, and don't give priority to the journalist's request. By the time the request has been passed on, it's too late.

Every one of these events is a missed opportunity. And every one of them can be avoided. I offer you two rules to help you ensure that you get the chance to put your case on TV:

Rule 1: Prepare, prepare, prepare
Rule 2: Question, question, question

RULE 1: PREPARE, PREPARE, PREPARE

The Duke of Wellington famously claimed, 'The battle of Waterloo was won on the playing fields of Eton.' What he meant was that the preparation of his officers gave his men the edge over the French. Preparation is just as important to you in your plans for TV publicity (and any other form of media handling). Reconnaissance is the first stage of preparation – you need to be aware when opportunities or threats may be about to present themselves. We call this 'horizon-scanning' and the people on the bridge in this instance are your communications director and team, assisted by your external PR consultancies. You may be the company's voice, but they are its eyes and ears. If you work together you'll reap maximum benefits of teamwork – if not, you're more likely to resemble the three wise monkeys. So keep open lines of communication with them. However senior and/or busy you are, you need to make time to listen to their advice.

Once you know what the opportunities are, you can begin to prepare thoroughly. The first step here is to get yourself up to speed on the company messages. Media training or message development is an excellent way to achieve this – an outside consultant can facilitate a message development session far better than an insider, because they are not so worried about internal politics and upsetting their superiors. Becoming comfortable with the messages has several advantages: naturally it arms you for the forthcoming interviews, but it also gives you a clarity of thought and expression in other areas including internal meetings. This clarity can be career-enhancing if you display it in the right corridors of power.

When you are clear about the messages your next step is to prepare and approve written material which can be sent or given to journalists. This may be in the form of backgrounders,

press releases or a variety of other documents (see Chapter 6 on using PR for a detailed breakdown). The important point is to prepare them in advance – and get them approved. I can't stress this point sufficiently. If the BBC calls you at 10 a.m. and wants a piece for the lunchtime news, that is no time to start drafting materials. Preparation and advance approval can cut right through the process and give you a head start on your competitors.

Having done this you are then in a position to make an informed decision, with your PR advisers, about whether you want to be interviewed and in what circumstances. This leads to another important point: if you have been selected (or have volunteered) as the company spokesperson, make sure others are aware of it, and in what circumstances you want to be contacted personally for comments. Commonly, senior managers will talk to the high profile media themselves, leaving the communications department to talk to other media organizations, such as the trade or local press. To avoid confusion you need to be specific about which calls you want to take personally, and which should be referred where. For example, you may not want to talk to the local paper, but it is likely that you definitely do want to talk to the BBC *Ten O'Clock News*. All other media requests fall between the two, so you need to issue clear guidelines about your likely response. In my experience the last thing you want in such circumstances is people using their initiative.

The first steps to getting on air, then, are all taken some way in advance of the call coming from a journalist. Some calls do indeed come out of the blue, but many more can be prepared for – and remember the old maxim: 'Failure to prepare is preparation for failure.'

RULE 2: QUESTION, QUESTION, QUESTION

My second rule is this: the conversation is a dialogue, not a monologue. Most potential interviewees do not ask enough questions of the journalist before they decide whether to take part. Once you have asked them, you then need to ask yourself some crucial questions too. Only when you have answered both sets can you make an informed decision. Here are the key questions from both points of view.

Ask the journalist

Who are you, what programme do you represent and what are you asking about?

Journalists will identify themselves and their organization to your secretary or whoever answers the phone, but it is useful to clarify this. In particular, be specific about the programme. In broadcasting more than in print it is easy to get the wrong end of the stick. For example *Newsround* and *Newsnight* are both BBC programmes and may sound similar (particularly to busy executives who never watch either) but the first is a news programme aimed at children, while the second is fronted by the most feared interviewer in television, Jeremy Paxman. You would not want to confuse the two! There are so many TV programmes today you can't be expected to watch them all. So if you're not sure what the programme is, what it's like and who it's aimed at, ask the journalist. Ask in a spirit of cooperation, though – better to say something like, 'Excuse my ignorance, but I don't think I know that one. What type of programme is it?' Avoid dismissive phrases such as one I encountered when I was the editor of a satellite programme and rang a famous agony aunt, 'I don't do satellite or sofa shows anymore – I'm too busy. Is your programme one of those?' If you're looking for a way to put a journalist's back up, this attitude is about as good as it gets.

It may seem strange to ask about the subject of the call, but any large organization is likely to have several newsy issues at the same time and mistakes in communications do occur – you need to make sure they are calling about your subject.

Sometimes, interviewees ask for the questions in advance. This is virtually never possible, for several reasons. The first is that I don't know what my second question is going to be until I've heard your answer to the first one, and so on for the rest of the interview. On a wider level, however, I don't want to feel that I'm giving you control over the interview – my job, remember, is to ask the questions anyone would ask if they had the opportunity, and with respect I probably

have a better idea what they would be. However, you are perfectly entitled to be given an outline of the issues I want you to address – otherwise how can I decide whether you're the best interviewee or not?

There is no need for you to worry on this count – with preparation you can anticipate virtually all the questions anyway. There are two ways forward here: employ the services of an external media consultancy to help you prepare (they don't suffer from being so close to the subject that they miss the obvious) and get your own colleagues and staff to come up with the most difficult questions – that is where the really tough questions will surface! No journalist can put you on the spot the way your colleagues or superiors can. If you analyse why people are occasionally caught on the hop by TV reporters, it's more often the unfamiliar environment of the studio or the paraphernalia of the equipment than the incisiveness of the question. Remember you are the expert – that's why they've come to you.

Who else are you talking to (and, if possible, what are they saying)?

This is a crucial question which is rarely asked – yet the answer is one of the most important of all. Knowing who else they are talking to will give you a pretty accurate 'steer' as to the thrust of the piece. The other interviewees may include third parties sympathetic to your case, or an opponent. Most pieces involve an element of opposition or 'putting the other side of the story'. As we saw in Chapter 2, journalists see this as a normal part of the job. The identity of others taking part in the piece is a valuable pointer to your own decision as to whether to do the same. If the journalists are talking to your opponents and/or competitors, for example, you may regard it as vital that your company's viewpoint features in the story.

Alternatively, it may be that the story is based on a claim or a survey (journalists love surveys) from an organization whose credibility you regard as suspect. Here you may decide to use the opportunity to flatly contradict their claims while explaining why your own position is so reasonable and far-seeing. Or you may decide privately not to touch it with a bargepole. In this last instance publicly, of course, you would politely decline the invitation to become involved. (Any suggestion that you are pouring scorn on their claims may result in a 'row' story, which is fine if that's your objective, and takes you back to the previous position.)

Will it be recorded or live?
The great majority of TV news interviews are recorded in advance of the programme's transmission, then edited into a news report. If you watch the news you will see that most live interviews don't involve real interviewees at all, but are discussions between the presenter and another journalist. Then when real live interviewees do appear, they're often chosen from a select group of people we've all seen before. One reason is that the format of many news programmes only allows for one or two live interviews at most. Another is that there is a risk in going live with an inexperienced interviewee in such a pressurized environment. So if we don't know them we often prefer to record the interview and reduce the risks all round. TV journalists are very aware of the kind of presence required to give a good live interview, so if they do ask you to go live they have made the decision that you can do it – take that as a vote of confidence.

An important difference between the two forms of interview is that if you go live you will probably be given more airtime, but of course you only get one shot at it. If you make a mistake in a recorded interview you can always stop and ask to start again. Another consideration is that 'going live' entails a lot more equipment, cables and people, so it can be much more intimidating than a recorded piece. Even your own office will feel like a different, possibly intimidating place in a live situation.

Earlier I mentioned a word which comes up more often than any other in discussions with executives about what it is they fear about television interviews – editing. They sometimes claim that their comments are 'taken out of context' in some way, and occasionally say that the editing process mixes up the questions and answers, as though we are trying to twist what they said. Let me make it clear that in my experience this never happens, at least not deliberately, though the speed at which we work means that mistakes are made. What does happen is that a journalist will often ask the same question two or three different ways, in attempting to get the shortest, most succinct answer possible. We might then put question version one with, say, answer version three, but the effect is to make the interviewee sound better. This is a far cry from twisting the interview. If you do feel your words have been twisted or taken out of context, ask your communications director or PR adviser for their view. If you both agree that you have been unjustly treated, my advice to you is to complain to the journalist concerned, or the editor of the organization.

Serious complaints against TV news programmes are rare, but if you are going to make one, here is my tip: be very clear about what you want to achieve. Are you asking for an apology? A retraction? A promise not to repeat the offending words? A promise to be more careful in future? As in life, the clearer you are about what you want, the more likely you are to achieve it.

Where do you want to do the interview?
This logistical question has already been covered in detail. Here, suffice to say that you have as much say over the location as they do. Be reasonable and keep in mind that the interview might well be more beneficial to you than to them, so be prepared to put yourself out in the right circumstances. Remember that if they want you to go to the studio this will take up more of your valuable time.

How long do you want?
There are two elements to this question – how long will the interview take (including setting-up time) and the length of clip they are looking for in the final report. With today's lightweight, portable technology and light-sensitive cameras which require little extra lighting, most TV news interviews can be done fairly quickly. As a guide, assume they can be in and out of your office in about half an hour to 45 minutes for most 'talking head' type interviews. Although cameramen (nearly all of them are still men) are under the same time pressure as the reporter, some of

them will spend ages getting a shot just right if you let them. There's a simple answer to this – don't. Stress how keen you are to help but be clear about how long you can give them. They will then work to your deadline as long as it's reasonable. What camera teams hate is starting to rearrange your office furniture so the daylight comes in the best direction then just as they're at the transitional stage where everything is in the worst possible place the interviewee says, 'I've got an important meeting in 10 minutes – that should give us enough time, shouldn't it?'

The length of the interview clip in the final piece is a difficult question to address. To a degree it depends on what you say and the way you say it, but as a rule the answer is 'as short as possible'. The real answer in a TV news piece may be '10 seconds maximum'. However, we rarely give you such a straight answer because non-journalists often freak out – they don't think you can say anything meaningful in 10 seconds! In reality you can, particularly with preparation. In general, however short you think your answer should be is still too long. As a guide, national news, where the time pressures are greatest, wants everything as short as possible, while further down the scale the local magazine programme might let you have a bit more time – say 20 seconds. Many pieces will also include more than one interview clip, so you do have longer than you may think.

This focus on the actual length of the clip, however, misses an important point. Your interview – and your off-camera discussion with the reporter – is a great opportunity for you to influence their commentary, or the voiceover which links the interviewees in the report. This is where you start to put across your key messages – if they're short, succinct and relevant, you'll be surprised how often they appear in the final piece. So remember, the right interview clips are very important, but only part of the story.

Who will be doing the interview?

In TV news it is quite common for researchers, producers or news editors to set up interviews for reporters. This doesn't necessarily imply different levels of seniority, though it can. It may simply be that the reporter is out doing other interviews while you are being asked whether you will take part in the same piece. This way of operating means that you need to first make your mark with the person on the phone, then start again with the reporter who turns up to do the interview. Some people find this disconcerting, believing they have to go through the whole questioning process again when the reporter arrives. You don't, but you should go through the points which are still relevant, particularly the issue about who else is featuring in the piece. You should also take them through the points you want to make before the interview starts – and remember this is a chance to influence their commentary and the general tone of the piece. You also need to check with the reporter that the general area of discussion you agreed on the phone still stands – by the time they get to you the reporter may have spoken to two other experts and may be forming a different impression.

This list is a guide to the kinds of questions you should ask in general. There will always be others, depending on the specific circumstances, and they will flow naturally from the above. The point is that you need to engage the journalist in a discussion about the piece.

Ask yourself

Having been satisfied on the first front, you then need to ask yourself some questions. The answers may well have become apparent during the discussion, but here are some points to consider.

Why should I do this interview and what will I/we get out of it?

There are many reasons for doing an interview, including the need to put your company viewpoint forward in a current issue or public debate, raising your company's profile (and your own, with subsequent benefits) gaining publicity, explaining a position or, occasionally, correcting a misinterpretation or mistake.

What will the journalist get out of it?

Think about the basic elements of a news story discussed in Chapter 2 – newness, relevance, etc. Then reassure yourself that all these elements are in fact there, and that this 'newsmaking' process will not distort your story. Also make sure that the journalist understands the story as you see it, and is not labouring under some misapprehension.

Is this a key audience?

The way television works today interviews are seen as a great resource and as such are syndicated around the broadcasting world on a complicated exchange arrangement. For example, an interview on ITN's *Lunchtime News* may well crop up on local radio just as your chief executive is driving home tuned to the local station to catch the traffic news (this, of course, can be a two-edged sword!). Your BBC TV *Breakfast News* interview may appear in the news bulletin on the *Today* programme, listened to by many influential people. The fact remains, however, that none of this happens automatically, so you should assume that your interview will only be seen and heard by the primary audience. Based on this, you can then decide whether to go to the trouble and put up with the disruption involved.

What are my key messages?

You will, of course, have worked these out in advance.

Am I the right person?

Being approached by a journalist – especially a senior or famous one – is very flattering and can lead to people agreeing to interviews which would be best left to someone else or even to another company. Too many have an eye on telling the story down at the golf club when they should be concentrating on the questions outlined in this chapter. The process which leads a journalist to an interviewee is a haphazard one at best, so don't assume you are necessarily the best person for the job. That may be someone else in your own organization, in which case tell the journalist you will get someone else to call them back. Then contact the person concerned immediately. If the journalist's call comes via the PR or communications department and you've gone through the preparatory steps I've outlined, this is another matter entirely and you should have no worries on this score.

The big question: can I make things better?

Whatever questions you ask, they are all supporting bouts to the main event, which is this question: can I make things better by doing the interview than by not doing it? The answer clearly must be 'yes', otherwise you should decline. It is important to realize that 'making things better' may not necessarily mean you and your company come out smelling of roses or clinch the chairman's knighthood. It may in practice mean 'making things less bad'. This is particularly the case when your company has been criticized and your role is to explain corporate actions or behaviour. See Chapter 7 on crisis management for more on this point.

Putting the pieces together

This is the last part of the TV journalist's job, and if you have followed the advice here you will have already influenced it as far as you can by the clarity of your points, the reiteration of your key messages and your performance in the interview. In these circumstances there is every reason why you should be happy with the result – always remembering that this is a piece of editorial, not a commercial! One further hint here – the majority of inexperienced spokespeople find one tiny mistake and focus on it to the point of obsession, some of them using it as evidence that the media can't be trusted or can't get things right, depending on their own prejudice. This is a huge mistake – focus on the big picture. Chances are that nobody outside the company noticed the error, because nobody else was paying anything like as much attention as you. I promise!

OTHER FORMS OF TV PROGRAMMES

Earlier I presented a list of different types of TV programmes. The arguments and issues I have presented here are relevant to all of them, though each type of programme will alter the mix of ingredients to suit its own recipe for success (or perceived success). In particular the time constraints are slightly looser in programmes which don't go out every day, and even worse in rolling news programmes. As we have already seen, the key to media success is relevance. In television this, of course, means answering the key question, 'What does this mean to the audience?' But in an ideal world it also means supplying interviewees with whom the audience can identify. Ideally, the interviewees should appear to be the same 'type'. So if you're a stereotypical golf-playing, rugby-supporting ex-public schoolboy in a dark suit, cufflinks and breast pocket handkerchief (I know I exaggerate, but you get the point) you might be great on *Business Breakfast* but if you're invited on to Richard and Judy's sofa show, you may be better off finding another interviewee – or loosening up a little.

The most important thing you can do as part of your preparation is the one thing which executives rarely do – watch the programme. See if you can imagine yourself on it. Would you feel comfortable? If so, great. If not, ask yourself why not. Then get yourself some media training.

This last piece of advice is particularly important for any programme with a consumer or investigative edge. *Watchdog* is a particular *bête noire* of many businesses, to the extent that many executives now refuse to appear. This is not always the right response, but I will discuss this more in the chapter on crisis management.

CHAPTER SUMMARY

- TV is the primary source of news for increasing numbers of people – it has a major effect on perception of your business.
- Many business executives and their advisers steer clear of trying to obtain TV coverage because they don't understand it.
- Make sure you have the basic equipment to join the TV world – buy a TV set for your office so you can see what's on it.
- Watch the programmes you're aiming to get onto.
- There are great variations in TV programmes – be clear about your targets.
- All national terrestrial TV news in the UK is produced by either ITN or the BBC – and Sky is now just as highly regarded.
- Getting your story onto the national news is very difficult – set realistic expectations.
- TV news is about pictures – think of how you can illustrate your story.
- Get a tape of core footage shot by professionals and distribute it to the main TV programmes – then they'll use the right pictures when they run your stories.
- TV news is about time – the journalists don't have any, so you need to react quickly to avoid missing opportunities...
- ...but when they come to your office they don't appreciate how busy you are too. Set a time limit on the interview to avoid this problem.
- TV news is about logistics – the more you can smooth the crew's way, the more they'll like you.
- TV news is about people. This may mean business personalities.
- Good case studies are the key to TV success.
- The first rule of getting good TV coverage is prepare, prepare, prepare.
- The second rule of getting good TV coverage is question, question, question.
- Don't expect to be given the interview questions in advance, but you have a right to know what areas will be covered.
- News conferences don't make good television – TV reporters will want another room set aside to do their own interviews.
- Think carefully about interview locations.

CHAPTER FOUR

The Newspaper World

Whatever the attractions of the glamour of television, the accessibility of radio and the immediacy of the Internet, newspapers are likely to be the main focus of your attempts to raise your media profile. The sheer size of newspapers offers you more publicity opportunities than any other branch of the media. They have adapted to the threats from TV, radio and the Internet – and to the changes in the way people live – in ways which are great news for executives with good products, interesting stories and creative minds. One manifestation of this is the huge rise in interest in the business world. As millions of Britons have become share owners and more have started investing in pensions, ISAs and other investment schemes, so their interest in the world of business has grown. And newspapers, who excel at recognizing the changing times, have responded by dramatically increasing the amount of news about business throughout the paper.

Just a few years ago most business stories were buried away towards the back of the paper between the TV listing and sport, aimed at a specialist audience and presented in a dry, dull fashion seemingly determined to deter outsiders from reading. Now, leading business people are household names and their business dealings reach the highest audiences possible through high profile treatment. As I write, the papers are devouring the news of the world's biggest merger, between America Online and Time Warner. Their respective executives are smiling out of the front page of every national newspaper from the *Independent* to the *Sun*. The business story has come of age in the newspapers. Business editors, who used to supply the little 'filler' paragraphs for the news pages, now stride into news planning meetings with a confident air, knowing their stories have as much chance of making a big splash as anyone else's. It's not just the national press either – take a look at your local paper, or regional evening, and you will see the same trend. Business news is big business. If you have a good story or interesting new line and know what you're doing, the opportunities for using the media to raise your profile have never been better.

Newspapers have also adapted in another way to the changes in society, and this too offers great opportunities for you. Much of what appears in today's newspapers is not 'news' at all in the sense of the event-driven and time-focused happenings discussed in Chapter 1. Increasingly, newspapers cover a wider spread of subjects including trends, developments, sectionalized interests and so forth. These 'non-news' items represent the biggest growth area in the media after the Internet. They also offer huge opportunities for publicity – providing you understand how they work. This chapter will introduce you to both the news and the non-news elements of today's newspapers and show you how to take advantage of them.

But why talk to the press at all? Because newspapers are woven into the fabric of British society and have a massive effect on how you are perceived. The UK is one of the newspaper capitals of the world. There are 11 national daily newspapers, 14 national Sunday papers, 19 regional morning papers, 70 regional evenings and about 500 local weekly newspapers – a choice unrivalled anywhere in the world.

Together they offer you the biggest audience imaginable – every day 30 million people read a national newspaper, and many more read regional and local papers. That's why what appears in them about you or your company is so important. However, even though they're so familiar to us, the workings of a newspaper remain a mystery to outsiders. To you as an executive this means you're at a disadvantage when it comes to trying to use them for publicity. To journalists it means they're constantly irritated and frustrated by incompetent, irrelevant approaches by public relations practitioners acting on behalf of companies. This chapter aims to bridge the gap between the newsroom and the boardroom. By the end of the chapter you will, I hope, have a firm understanding of how to maximize your chances of getting your stories into the press, whether local or national. You will also understand the opportunities available to you from the 'non-news' parts of the newspaper landscape.

LAND OF OPPORTUNITY

The UK press, from the national dailies to local weeklies, is the most varied in the world. This variety produces opportunities and challenges for you in trying to make the best of it. With planning and understanding you can select and target the audience most important to you – and as we've seen, if your story is important to them, journalists will like it. Your challenge is to target the right newspaper(s) and work up your story in such a way that it stands proud of all the other offerings of the day and makes itself visible to the editor. The actress Lesley Joseph was once asked for her philosophy of life: 'Trust to fate – but lean forward, so that fate can see you' she said. I'm often reminded of this quote when I talk to executives who have had good stories which might have run if the people behind them had only helped the stories 'lean forward'. The fact that they never saw the light of day is a missed opportunity for everyone. On any day on any news desk you will find hundreds of stories being offered. One national news editor likens it to playing space invaders: 'The stories stream at me down the computer screen – I just pick off the ones I fancy.' As in space invaders, most of the characters look the same until you look closely. Your first task is to get yours noticed.

In story terms this means making it relevant, interesting, available and timely. It also means putting yourself out so you can talk to the journalists when they want you. Reporters on national papers in particular have an arrogant view of the rest of the world – they assume an executive will drop everything to get their story into the paper. If you don't, then they'll find someone who will. The first lesson of dealing with the national press is that you have to accept

that they will be in charge of the timescale. I once saw national newspapers described like this:

> Daily newspapers – a daily miracle of
> just-in-time creation.

This is a great phrase which sums up your first challenge in trying to get into the national press – speed. With the right planning and internal procedures this shouldn't pose any problem for you, but I am still surprised by how many supposedly well-prepared executives it does catch out. The phrase also goes some way to explain why national newspaper journalists are in so much of a hurry – they have so much to do and so little time. This is why the story-pitching process is so important to them. The national press is at the summit of journalism in the UK. Getting your story there requires a lot of hard work. It demands time, effort, creativity, contacts, an understanding of what they want – and a slice of luck so that nothing else will appear to knock it off just as the summit comes into view. But the effort is worth it for the view when you get there – when did you last have the chance to speak to 25 million people?

To understand what national newspaper journalists want, consider the picture of journalists I painted in Chapter 1 – time-pressured, fiercely competitive, irritable, with finely tuned instincts as to what their readers want – and think of the most extreme cases. The life of a national newspaper journalist can be summed up in four lines:

> Deadline
> Headline
> Good line
> Bottom line

If you can deliver these, you're on the right track. Let's look at them in some detail.

DEADLINES

The deadline is in many ways the most important, because in the national press, deadlines are absolute. We hear so many stories of deadlines being extended in other walks of life – for new roads and rail routes to open, for discussions and talks, for public service targets to be met – that a deadline can appear to be a moveable feast. In the national press, it's not. The distribution network which guarantees that every national newspaper will be available for virtually every breakfast table in the UK is highly sophisticated. If the paper is to catch the delivery run or train, it must be there on time. To you, this means that if the reporter can't get to you when he or she wants you, they'll move on to somebody else. 'I'd really love to include your point of view but I must have it in 15 minutes' is a common statement from national reporters. Elsewhere in the book we will discuss what you need to do in terms of preparation for this call. For now, the important point is that deadlines are sacrosanct, and to make the most of the media you must respond to them.

HEADLINES

The headline is the shop window for the story. Headlines are what induce readers to read on, and much effort goes into writing them, but the result may not be to your taste. Headlines seem to touch a raw nerve with executives more than the stories themselves. This is because summing up a complicated story in just a few words can give the wrong impression, but also because the reporter who writes the story doesn't write the headline. The headline is an important concept for you, however, in your story pitching. In training exercises I often ask, 'What's the headline?' You may find a news editor asking you the same question – so be ready. They won't expect you to come up with a fully formed, perfectly polished gem – that's their job – but a very brief summary will be a great help.

GOOD LINE

A 'good line' in journalistic jargon means a good quote or a soundbite. People who 'give good quotes' are much loved by journalists. That's why Richard Branson is so popular. For best effect, your quote needs to be short and memorable. Ideally it should also be a word picture. The crucial thing is to work it out in advance. See the section on 'soundbites' in Chapter 3 for more on this (p. 39).

BOTTOM LINE

There are two meanings to the bottom line. First,

when the chips are down, what are you saying? Company spokespeople have a tendency to use jargon more suited to an MBA course. If you speak like a management consultant, the journalist will translate it for you – and many mistakes and misunderstandings are made in translation. Don't speak in code. Use plain English so your position is in no doubt whatsoever. Clarity, along with brevity, is a highly prized asset in the land of journalism. Your approaches will be greeted more positively if you exhibit it. This is a particular issue with press releases where the story seems to be frequently obscured by a smokescreen of gobbledegook.

Second, my own bottom line is that I can't hang around. If I can't get what I need from you, I'll go somewhere else – either to someone else to talk about your story, or to another story entirely. So react quickly.

REGIONAL, LOCAL AND TRADE PRESS

The UK press is about far more than just the nationals. Quite apart from the vast range of newspapers quoted earlier, there are also thousands of trade magazines with others opening and closing every week. The Audit Bureau of Circulation, the body that verifies newspaper and magazine circulation, has more than 3500 titles under its remit. The regional and local press vary hugely in terms of circulation, coverage areas and the way they work. The leading regional morning and evening papers such as the *Yorkshire Post*, *Western Morning News* and *Manchester Evening News* are well resourced and respected. They guard their patch jealously and pride themselves on being in touch with what's going on in their area in a way the nationals cannot be because of their nationwide remit. These big regional papers tend to work in the same way as the nationals, with a number of specialist correspondents, a general reporters pool and their own business and parliamentary staff. You should treat them accordingly.

All the regional, local and trade press can play a role in establishing or enhancing your corporate image. Any of them can also play a significant role in publicizing your story. This leads to an important point about the media in general, and the press in particular. Once your story is out, it flows all around the media world, often at great speed. The media world has its own ecosystem, where different sectors of the press feed off each other. As in life, the bigger beasts feed off the smaller creatures – so stories which begin in local papers are often devoured by the regional evenings and sometimes the nationals. Many stories are first reported in the trade press, scientific or academic journals and are sold or syndicated to bigger organizations where they then receive national publicity. As I write, the newspapers are giving prominence to new safety problems with the Millennium Eye, the giant ferris wheel erected on the Embankment in London to mark the turn of the century. The story was first reported in *New Civil Engineer*, a trade magazine, but now British Airways is having to respond to national criticism about it. This is one reason why you can't afford to ignore the local and trade press. Maintaining contacts with trade and local press will often provide an early warning of trouble on the way.

The way in which stories flow like this confuses many companies. Because they don't realize how it works they often ignore the local press in particular, or treat them with contempt. This can cause serious problems as the local press often have great influence on the community in which they are based. I remember driving through one large town where it seemed almost every other window featured a poster from the local paper saying 'Megastores mean mayhem. Keep them out.' If you were the executive who'd planned a new megastore in the town you'd feel you were losing the battle with such a wave of resentment from local people just ready to be unleashed on the public inquiry which would no doubt be the consequence of the paper's campaign.

Campaigns of this type are part of the lifeblood of local and regional newspapers. Graham Glen, editor of the multi-award-winning *Nottingham Evening Post* summed it up succinctly: 'A part of the community, not apart from the community'. If your business is affecting the community – and all businesses do, for better or worse – then it is crucial that you put your case to the local paper. You want them to understand what you're doing, and when appropriate give you the credit for the local employment you provide. It may not be worth your personal while spending much time on it, but someone should make it their business to build a relationship with the local press. Many companies now have community action programmes and often appoint community liaison officers – they can be good candidates. Then your role as a senior executive is to turn up for the occasional function and give the odd interview on locally important matters.

Another reason for courting the local press is that more than any other type of reporter, their staff have the time and inclination to build relationships with you as a prominent employer. Many locals operate on a 'district' system where each reporter has a responsibility for a geographical area. Over the years they know you are likely to be a good source of stories, so are keen to get to know you. On locals you are also likely to find the same person doing several jobs, for example the senior reporter may become the chief layout person the day before press day. If you are hoping to court them for publicity, the first task is to identify which reporter(s) is most likely to cover your stories. Most local paper journalists are not as precious as their national colleagues and will give you the time of day if you call at an appropriate time. This generally means the morning after the paper has come out, before the mad rush to the next edition is in full swing. So ring them up, introduce yourself and ask who you should contact. They are unlikely to send you away with a flea in your ear, but will be even more receptive if you have a story to tell them at that moment – always bear in mind that the way to a reporter's heart is through the paper.

FREESHEETS

For the sake of completeness, a word here about freesheets, or local free newspapers. They're generally regarded as being at the bottom of the food chain and are often part of the same media groups that publish the local paid-for newspapers. Their influence varies hugely. If they are part of a big media group the stories they carry often come from the paid-for papers anyway, so your efforts with the paid-for press will also see results in the freesheet. Most independent freesheets have little local clout. However, because of the nature of journalism it is impossible to predict where the next story is coming from, or where the next good story will end up. Don't invest inordinate amounts of time in cultivating them, but don't go out of your way to alienate them either. Remember, too, that the big stars of tomorrow's journalism have to start somewhere – and that may be on your local freesheet. It's never too early to start making friends.

DO'S AND DON'TS

As with any activity, there is much merit in practising for the hardest case. With media handling this means handling the national press – if you are confident about that you will feel correspondingly comfortable with other sections of the media. I now want to turn, therefore, to typical mistakes which companies make in their dealings with the national press, and how to avoid them. The lessons are equally applicable to the rest of the media. Here are some of the comments journalists made in a survey of how they regard contacts from businesses:

'The sheer weight of material is ridiculous. Most of it is of little interest to the national media.'
'I get the occasional thing that's completely unintelligible – it's geared for a specialist audience, either the City or a technical journal.'
'Most of what I get is highly promotional and short of news content.'
'The material is often too technical or too corporate. It's aimed at the wrong audience.'

The most common mistake was summed up by a specialist correspondent on a national broadsheet newspaper:

The problem is they are apparently writing one press release for an enormous range of media, and obviously it's not going to satisfy everybody. If

they can target what they send out better, although it involves a lot more work they might see a better result. It doesn't take a genius to work it out.

In the previous chapters I talked about the importance of relevance and targeting. I would now like to build on that with a 'wish list' of what journalists want. Use it before you or your PR team approach them to assess your story's chances of success:

- read the paper before you approach them – you may be surprised what's in it and how it's changed since you last looked
- remember that journalists work on the editorial pages and have no brief to promote your products – expect to be challenged on what you say
- keep press releases short – two pages maximum including a very brief 'note to editors'
- don't overburden them with information. The key points are enough. If they want more detail they'll ask for it
- write several versions of the press release aimed at different audiences – and alter your story pitch in the same way
- be honest about the claims you make for your product
- be sensitive to their reaction – don't badger them and risk turning them off
- be aware of deadlines – ring daily papers in the morning before the time pressure starts to build up and they've made their plans for the day
- focus on the human element wherever possible – remember journalists want to know how your story will affect their readers
- offer third party opinion leaders who can back up your claims.

JOURNALISTS' SOURCES

So you've pitched your story and the journalist seems interested. Now what? Journalists on national newspapers rarely take what you tell them at face value. Checking the facts is part of their job, as is obtaining another view on your story. Executives are often surprised at how widely reporters spread their nets in following these and other lines of inquiry. National newspapers have vast resources to do this. If you understand what the main sources are you will have a better picture of how your own story may be reported, and in some cases you may be able to influence it in a small but significant way.

CUTTINGS LIBRARY

This is the first port of call for a journalist given a story to work on. The library on a national newspaper is a huge resource. As all the nationals are part of established media groups the cuttings library usually goes back to the days when their oldest newspaper was founded, or at least to the period just after the First World War. That's right – if you're a large corporation there are cuttings on your business going back to the 1920s in a cuttings library near you!

Many executives fail to understand two crucial elements about the library. First, the library does not just contain that newspaper's cuttings. It includes pieces from all the major (and some of the minor) publications in the UK, as well as big international magazines such as *Time* and *Newsweek*. On major stories the librarians will file a cross-section of cuttings reflecting all the angles from serious to silly. The effect of this is that if you have had publicity anywhere in the national press – good or bad – the journalist will find it. This is a very important reason for you to put a lot of effort into making sure that any stories about your business are reported accurately because there is always a danger that any mistakes and misconceptions in an original story will be perpetuated by subsequent publications. So the idea that 'today's news is tomorrow's fish and chips wrapper' is only true if you're a reader. To a journalist, today's news is tomorrow's source material.

Second, what the journalist finds about you in the library has an important bearing on how he or she regards you (positive, negative, caring, driven, sympathetic, cynical) and how they approach your story. Just as you or I form an impression of someone by what we hear, see and read, so a journalist's impression is formed by the contents of the library. If such a conceptual thing as a corporate image can be said to exist anywhere, your cuttings file is its manifestation.

THE INTERNET

The Internet is changing many aspects of media relations, though most of the changes are still in process. See the Appendix for more information.

THIRD PARTY OPINION LEADERS

A journalist's next port of call, and one that you can directly affect, are the opinion leaders. Opinion leader development should be a major plank of your public relations programme. See Chapter 6 on using PR for more on this.

NEWS AGENCIES

Checking the incoming wire stories is another obvious source for journalists and another one which you can affect to some degree. The Press Association has a strong influence on how journalists report stories and should be on your list of media targets. It is also famed for its balanced reporting, so can be a big help in ensuring that your point gets across – not just in newspapers but across the media spectrum. Take advantage of this by talking to the PA whenever you get the opportunity.

PHOTOGRAPHS AND ILLUSTRATIONS

The first rule for successful press handling is to read the paper or magazine you're targeting. If you follow this advice you'll realize that not only are the papers much thicker than previously, but they're also very visual. They're also mostly in colour. This leads to another publicity tool which many companies ignore – photographs and illustrations. Some business stories get into the papers purely because they're very visual. Others are very complicated and need an illustration to explain them. The business pages are particularly bereft of good visuals – you should take advantage of that. Wherever possible avoid the 'grey men in grey suits' type of shot and go for something more creative.

You can provide this in two ways. First by commissioning a press photographer to take the pictures for you, and distributing them with your press material. In this case be sure to keep the photographer's creative instincts on a tight leash – leave creativity to the photographers whose job it is to know what the particular newspaper wants. This is the second tactic – the photocall. Here, be sure to give the photographers enough variety of possibilities, allow them enough time to get what they want, and ensure that you can control the background. For example, if you're launching a new bus service, you don't want to hold a photocall where your rival's buses are likely to be trundling past as there's a danger they will get the publicity.

NON-NEWS – THE GREAT GROWTH AREA

Look at your morning newspaper. Ask yourself this question: how much of it is 'news' in the event-driven, instantly perishable sense as I have outlined it so far? And how much is 'non-news' – articles that are still relevant and topical but don't have the words 'today' or 'this week' in them? Items that may be longer and more considered than the news stories? Much of it is the latter. They may appear either in sections or in supplements, or in the body of the paper. They may cover specialist subjects or sectionalized interests such as finance, health, sport or IT, or take another view of an item in the news pages. These 'non-news' items are grouped together under the heading 'features', and they offer great publicity opportunities for your company. With the right forethought, these are the parts of the paper where you can hope to achieve most of your coverage. That's what I want to look at now.

THE DOMINANCE OF NON-NEWS

As an example of non-news at its most dominant, look at the *Daily Mail*, the UK's most successful newspaper in terms of constantly rising circulation. On a day when there is a big story it is untouchable in terms of breadth and quality of coverage. But on 'normal' days, its feature content dominates. It has led the way in branding each day with a different feature topic, and publishing an entire high profile section devoted to it. Typically, that breaks down as Monday sport, Tuesday health, Wednesday 'Money Mail', Thursday 'Femail' and Friday entertainment. Within these topics are many other sub-topics. For example, 'E-Mail' is the technology section and 'Enterprise' is the small business section inside 'Money Mail'.

Over time the days and subjects may change, but the feature mentality will be with us for many years. The Saturday paper is even more feature-dominated. It has pulled off an impressive trick, and transformed itself into a lifestyle magazine while still retaining the attributes of a newspaper – and crucially, not only retaining readers but picking up more on the way. Every one of these subject areas has potential for business stories.

Every other national newspaper is the same, as are the big regional dailies and evening papers. Newspapers are digging deeper into the stories, issues and subjects to combat the appeal of television news, which covers stories very quickly and memorably but only thinly. Consider how thick the papers are now compared with just ten years ago. The difference is in the amount of feature material. (Specific feature supplements or sections are also popular with advertisers who target a more informed, specialized but smaller audience than in the news pages.)

So to journalists and newspaper executives in pursuit of defining their product, setting it apart from the pack, non-news is an increasingly important element of the character of a newspaper. The following sections outline the various types of non-news and explain how to take advantage of them. I also quote many examples where creative thinking has produced positive media publicity from an unlikely source. This in turn should help you to think laterally and develop similar opportunities for your own company or organization.

IDENTIFYING NON-NEWS NEWS

As with any aspect of communication, to succeed you must first identify the audience you want to convince. In contrast to news, which always falls within strict parameters, almost anything can be a feature. Indeed it can be said that while the nature of news *excludes* most things, features, being more widely drawn, *include* things. This looseness makes defining a feature more difficult, but I hope the examples in this chapter will assist and illustrate how you can begin to take advantage.

It is helpful to start by considering the difference between the two types of editorial coverage. In particular, one criticism of news is that it is just like a journalist's knowledge – a mile wide and an inch deep. The features pages of newspapers attempt to address this drawback. In particular, the specialist features pages with their total focus on one area (health, finance, IT, lifestyle and so on) can be said to be just the opposite – an inch wide and a mile deep.

You may remember this schoolchild rhyme from Rudyard Kipling:

I have six true and honest friends
They taught me all I knew
Their names are what and where and when
And why and how and who.

It still summarizes the main questions journalists will ask. Generally, news focuses on what, where, when and who, where features concentrate on how and why. These days, there is always another important question you have to answer: how much?

Here are some essential differences between news and features:

News	Features
Event-driven	Subject-driven
Needs a 'news peg'	May reflect news, doesn't report it
Time-sensitive	Topicality not the prime driver
'Just the facts'	Adds background or colour
Broad brush strokes	Fine detail
Fast turnaround	Time to prepare (sometimes)
Highly perishable	Longer shelf life
Short	Less restricted by space
'Initial reaction'	Generally more considered
Changing picture	Stable situation, or snapshot

The number of conditional words in the right-hand column emphasizes the facts of features life – while a news story is squeezed into a corset or straitjacket soon after birth, a feature lives a much more liberated, even relaxed life and is shown a greater degree of tolerance. It also lives longer – a feature generally has several chances to appear, whereas as we have already seen, a news story generally gets one shot at fame. Indeed, every newspaper, TV and radio news programme has a shelf of fairly timeless, ready-to-run features to compensate for the days when the 'mix' of stories is wrong, the amount of breaking news doesn't fill what's left of the schedule or there's some last-minute hitch with a news story, threatening white space on the page or silent airtime. Non-news is the reason you never see white space or hear silence on air.

This lack of obsession with topicality is the first advantage you have if you're aiming for feature coverage – you are less at the mercy of fate and stronger stories edging you out. Features are more likely to be 'held over' until the next issue, or indeed often hang around waiting for a topical 'peg' to freshen up the intro. Yet this is a two-edged sword – because the parameters of features are less distinct than news, they are much more open to personal interpretation. So one journalist will think an idea is a 'must have' while their colleague, doing the same job the next day, will think it's dull and boring. As journalists are only human, they also bring their own strengths, weaknesses and tastes to every decision.

Take as an example a company whose business is what's known as spread betting – betting on whether the financial markets will rise or fall, and by how much. The first time they tried to gain publicity and get a journalist interested, they failed miserably. Spread betting is quite complicated, and it became apparent that the journalist didn't really understand how it worked. Undaunted, they tried again a few weeks later. This time the man on the features desk understood it perfectly, and once they'd agreed on the kinds of case studies they needed to bring it to life the story was topping the features list.

This also illustrates an important element of story pitching – never give up. I'm not advocating the flogging of dead horses here, rather that a change of tack or target often reaps dividends.

TYPES OF FEATURES

Because the nature of a feature is more creative, less rigid than a news story, virtually anything can be turned into one. However, there are a few traditional types which appear almost daily.

Recognizing them will increase your chances of obtaining publicity and I hope provide food for thought. Here are the main types.

Backgrounders

As the name suggests, these features provide a detailed background to an event in the news. In newspapers they often appear on the page facing the news story on a leading topic. So when AOL announced it was merging with Time Warner most national newspapers ran backgrounders. The angles ranged from the histories of the two companies to what we as users could expect from the new alliance. Consider another example – the Bank of Scotland takeover bid for Natwest in autumn 1999. As you would expect the public relations machines of both companies went into overdrive (as did all the other activities of the communications departments). On day one, the features pages concentrated on the rationale behind the bid, and profiled BoS as an aggressive Celtic terrier not afraid to pick a fight with its bigger Sassenach rival. Two days later Natwest launched an aggressive fightback which achieved prominent publicity in the news pages. On the features pages, the background features looked at the reasoning behind the fightback with head-lines such as 'Natwest – the bank that likes to attack'.

The key to successful backgrounders is to use your media contacts. You want to be confident that the reporter will have a good grasp of what may be a complex issue, and won't betray your trust. The best way to make this likely is to invite in journalists you know or at least those whose work you are familiar with, so you and your fellow executives know roughly what type of piece to expect. Playing the backgrounder game well can achieve millions of pounds of publicity and play a crucial role in the battle for hearts and minds of investors, analysts and customers.

Explanations

How will the new generation of mobile phones work? How does the so-called 'whispering jet' engine work and what makes it significantly quieter than current engines? What about the super chemical which makes crops invulnerable to frost? These 'how it works' types of features

are very common when you have a breakthrough product, particularly one which has potential to affect the lives of millions. Be ready to offer explanations in layperson's language. If you haven't got anyone who can do this, get them media trained. More than any other type of feature, success here often relies on being able to provide understandable graphics, illustrations and photographs – in colour.

Reporter involvement

An excellent way to get publicity is to involve reporters. In advance of launching a new pro-duct or service, offer a journalist the opportunity to try it out under embargo, so his or her report will appear on launch day. Offering journalists exclusives is often a good way to increase the likelihood of favourable publicity – if you choose the right one. The word 'exclusive' after a byline increases the kudos of the writer and the news-paper (in a small way) and as long as you can back up the claims you're making for whatever it is you're launching and have a good relationship with the writer, they're unlikely to bite the hand that feeds them. Travel features, of course, are founded on exactly this. Increasingly, though, the practice is spreading to other parts of the newspaper.

Ford's design centre in Essex received a huge amount of favourable publicity in the *Daily Express* when their researchers developed a suit which can replicate the problems older drivers have in new cars. It was an interesting story any-way, but when they allowed a young Express reporter to 'test drive' the suit and become an old man for a day the piece really came to life. Internet-related stories are naturals for this treatment. Offer a journalist the chance to take part in an online auction, buy or sell a house or get cheap travel, and you've got a great chance of good publicity … as long as it works!

This leads to another general point about courting publicity – even if you don't invite them to, you must always be aware that journalists will legitimately test your claims. Occasionally exec-utives have horror stories of appalling reviews they've received for new products or services, and ask me how they could have avoided it. Usu-ally the answer is simple – don't launch it until its ready. Be sure your sins will find you out. Notice that I do not make any reference to 'free publicity' in this section, or anywhere else in the book. If you do receive good publicity via the media, you've normally had to work very hard for it indeed.

People profiles

The increased amount of 'celebrity journalism' in the UK media attracts some criticism when it's applied to TV, film and sports stars. Profiles of business leaders, however, are a different matter. They can be critical but as long as you're aware of any skeletons in your chairman's cupboard (or your own) they can generate very positive publicity. The first challenge is to identify a newspaper (or journalist) which you are confident will be generally favourable; the second is to persuade them why your senior executive (or you personally) are worth a profile piece. Like most features, this type of piece needs an element of a hook. This might be an exciting new development or product launch, better than expected interims or annual results, a change for the better in company fortunes or a bold move which surprises the City.

If your company is involved in a takeover bid of any newsworthy size, you have an excellent chance of getting your chairman or CEO featured in a profile piece. This is particularly true if there is an element of surprise or audacity about the move – journalists love characters and a common complaint from older practitioners is that boardrooms are increasingly full of dull, faceless clones. A few words of advice here: make sure the subject knows he or she is being interviewed for a profile piece, and that will mean letting some of their personality and interests through. And a word of warning: don't overdo the personal publicity – it can lead to false (or even accurate!) impressions that your enterprise depends on one person, and the City may not like that. Being naturally conservative they're worried about what would happen if the chosen one fell under a bus – a common question asked of large corporations led by a charismatic figure of stature and vision, for example Rupert Murdoch or Sir Richard Branson.

A second word of warning: only put your CEO up for it if they enjoy this type of thing. Journalists hate to try and write personality profiles when the interview is like pulling teeth.

A third word of warning: pride sometimes comes before a fall. A criticism of the media is that they like to build people up then destroy them. Ask Gerald Ratner. His personal stock was at an all-time high when he made his deprecatory remarks about some of his jewellery. Previous personality profiles carried headlines including 'Me and my cats, by Gerald Ratner' and 'What the well-dressed millionaire is wearing'. He was a media darling, but it didn't save him when it mattered. Think carefully before you volunteer executives for these kinds of pieces. Ask yourself 'Is this the image we want?' Of course, if you have a publicity-seeking chief executive it may be just what they want.

Anniversaries

The chapter on crisis management examines how milestone anniversaries of a crisis often provide a peg for negative publicity to return. With some careful preparation of the ground, the same technique can work in your favour and lead to pieces marking positive anniversaries. We all love looking back to how things were, or how such a product, service or company has changed our lives – journalists are no different. With careful thought and planning, some of these anniversary pieces can be blatant product plugs. For example, to mark 25 years of McDonalds in the UK the *Express* produced a list of 'fascinating facts' which the marketing team behind the golden arches could have only foreseen in their dreams!

Soft news

'Soft' news is a term used in journalism to describe stories that fit the criteria of timeliness and event-driven nature described elsewhere, but don't really involve life and death decisions or heavyweight topics. Many of them are based on surveys, studies, reports and other common tools of the public relations industry. To be honest, the majority are spotted as 'PR plugs' but with the right planning and targeting, you can gain massive publicity for your service, product or organization.

Comparisons

Sometimes a story crops up where the UK experience is directly comparable with another country's, either for better or worse. This can be another opportunity for coverage, providing, of course, that the portrayal of your company in the UK is positive. We're so used to seeing British industry criticized in comparison with other countries that this kind of story will catch the eye of journalists ... providing you tell them! I'm constantly surprised at how many executives I meet who tell me great stories of productivity, ground breaking deals, unheard of targets, and complain that 'The media aren't interested in good news.' I hope the examples quoted in this chapter have started to persuade you otherwise, but my reply is always the same, 'Have you tried telling them?' The executives concerned usually shrug as if to say, 'What's the point?' The point, quite simply, in the words of a wise colleague is, 'If you don't tell me, I won't know about it. I'm not a mind-reader, and I haven't got a crystal ball!'

There are many other types of comparative features such as big v. small, regional v. national, old v. young. Most of them need a news peg to give them the edge over other equally interesting but timeless ideas. Here's one stunning example, brought about by creative thinking. In autumn 1999 Wal-Mart's takeover of ASDA caught the imagination of both the business pages and the general news sections. It spawned seemingly acres of print, much of it focused on the Wal-Mart 'Pile 'em high and sell 'em cheap' philosophy, or on the likely effect on the face of the high street (a classic case of answering the question, 'What does it mean to me?'). The deal sparked rumours of the other supermarket giants looking for merger partners and a close interest in their performances.

Outside the famous four of Tesco, Sainsbury, Safeway and ASDA, there is a northern supermarket chain, Morrisons. The executive chairman Ken Morrison is son of the founder and at the time of the ASDA/Wal-Mart deal they were turning in record profits by sticking to what they unashamedly called 'good old-fashioned practices' and ignoring current marketing thinking.

For example, they have no loyalty cards and no gimmicks but reported profits that the 'big four' could only dream about. During 1999, the year of the ASDA-Walmart deal, they were also celebrating their 100th anniversary, so the story had two pegs – a supermarket success story and an anniversary. A good news story if ever there was one – and recognized as such by the *Independent*. The newspaper most likely to turn away PR gimmicks was so impressed by Morrison's story it became the cover story of the 'Business Review' section – a huge piece in a prominent part of the newspaper with photographs of a store and Ken Morrison and columns of positive coverage. What a gift for the company's profile. You can't buy that type of publicity. It was spawned by creative people having an eye for an opportunity.

News to use

This is a concept first invented in the USA – and good news it is for businesses. The concept is simple – our readers want information that they can use, whether it's a new way of getting more miles to the gallon from their car, a new treatment that might help them preserve their skin or a faster connection to the Internet. It flies directly in the face of the old-fashioned journalistic idea that if people want to plug products they should call the advertising department. Journalists and editors now realize that part of the secret of a successful newspaper or magazine is to provide a service to the readers. The acid test, as ever, is *relevance*. Ask yourself how relevant your new product is to the readers/viewers/listeners of your target media. If you can make a strong case, make that call.

SUPPLEMENTS AND SECTIONS

It's clear then that features play an important role in a newspaper, and can provide great opportunities for publicity with a little creative thinking and judicious lobbying of the right journalists. Most of the features I've mentioned so far have appeared in the main body of the paper – on the features pages. But there are vast tracts of newspaper land as yet untouched by this book, which provide rich seams of publicity opportunities. If there were a signpost pointing towards this part of the newspaper world it would read 'supplements and sections'. This is very important to any attempt to raise your media profile, as your cuttings files will probably confirm – most corporate publicity can be found in the supplements and sections. To gain an idea of the importance of this part of medialand, take a look at any daily or Sunday newspaper. Mentally compare it with the same publication ten or even five years ago. If you recall the older version your first impression will be of the enormous difference in size. When I was a newspaper delivery boy I used to ride my bicycle with my bag full of papers slung nonchalantaly over one shoulder. Now, the boys often need carts or barrows to carry the huge weight of newsprint. Almost the entire difference in size is down to the huge increase in supplements and sections published as part of today's newspapers – and the advertising which they attract.

The good news for you is that all these new pages (as opposed to news pages) offer golden opportunities for effective publicity among your target audiences. They offer a focused audience who have turned to that part of the newspaper and stayed with it because they're specifically interested in the subject matter. They're a fast track to the people who matter to your company. It is also often easier to get stories into the features supplements or sections because you can build relationships with the journalists who run them based on your common interest. General news reporters rarely talk to the same sources more than a handful of times. Editors and writers on supplements, however, regularly talk to the same sources.

This section looks at what's required to obtain coverage in the supplements and sections and includes examples of the type of coverage other companies have obtained. I've assumed that if you're in a relevant sector then you, or your communications team, are already in touch with writer and editors on the evergreen sections such as gardening, motoring and food sections. Even they have taken on a new lease of life and begun to launch their own superstars such as Jeremy Clarkson, Charlie Dimmock and goodness knows how many celebrity food writers.

Also included is a list of the supplement subjects as of the later part of 1999. As you read it, however, bear in mind that a newspaper is in a state of constant change. In the words of Lord Rothermere, the late proprietor of Associated Newspapers who died in 1999, 'A newspaper should be like the sea – always the same, yet always changing.' New sections spring up and old ones are dropped as part of that process of change, so the picture will be different next year and again the year after. This list, therefore, is a snapshot of the world of supplements and sections at the time of writing. You can update it by glancing through the newspapers. It will, I hope, give you food for thought.

THINK LATERALLY

The supplements and sections parts of newspapers offer great opportunities in ways which may not be obvious. Dream up ideas for the supplements which focus on your own sector by all means – but don't stop there. The editors of sections are often more excited by the opportunity to include something outside their normal remit than by churning out 'more of the same'. For example, in the run up to the London Motor Show, while most motor manufacturers were targeting the motoring pages, Honda provided the *Guardian*'s careers section with the opportunity to run a piece on its training scheme for the engineers of tomorrow. 'We don't call them mechanics anymore – you're more likely to find them with a pen in their top pocket than a spanner in their back pocket. Today's new cars have more computing power than the Apollo space rocket that took men to the moon,' said the Honda spokesperson, guaranteeing the company bucketloads of free publicity. He was also reiterating some of the company's key messages.

It's important to realize that the two approaches are not mutually exclusive. Honda didn't ignore the important motoring sections in favour of the careers pages – it courted both. You should do the same wherever possible. Generally speaking, however, newspapers don't want to be turned into a propaganda sheet for a company, so if you've worked up several ideas, spread your approaches around several titles, and maybe several weeks.

THE DIFFERENCES

The words 'supplement' and 'section' refer to different ways of presenting a part of a newspaper dedicated to a subject or a concept. A 'supplement' is supplementary to the main newspaper, and comes as a free extra part on certain days, such as a 'colour supplement' with the Sunday papers, or 'ES' magazine with the London *Evening Standard*. A 'section' may contain the same sort of information as a 'supplement' but it is an integral part of the newspaper. So 'Femail' is a section of the *Daily Mail* devoted to feminine topics, and 'Night and Day' is the paper's Sunday supplement. For our purposes I shall use the words interchangeably because it is the ideas behind them which you need to understand to enable you to start taking advantage of them.

Both supplements and sections are based on either subjects or concepts. One very popular subject is 'entertainment', where the supplement contains TV, radio and cinema listings and includes entertainment-based features. Other supplements are based on looser concepts such as 'the weekend' which may include listings but also features on sport, leisure and 'things to do'. Increasingly, there is a third type of supplement – the review. Particularly in the broadsheet papers, this is an eclectic mix of features and articles by columnists (who're employed to have a point of view and aren't restricted by concerns of balanced reporting). As we shall see, however, another common feature is that they provide many opportunities for business publicity.

TYPICAL TOPICS

There are some topics which every newspaper covers in some kind of section. They include health, money or finance, IT, fashion and entertainment. Others are currently limited to just a few newspapers, but if imitation really is the sincerest form of flattery then many newspaper section heads must be feeling good – successful sections are soon copied. The best way to keep up with what's happening is to read widely and try to spot the trends. Then suggest ideas to your PR consultancy or department. If you have a good PR consultancy they will be doing this already – check that they are. Here are some of the most popular subjects featured in supplements at the time of writing, together with example features. With each example I've tried to identify what it is that makes it worthy of inclusion, though so often it's just 'news to use'.

Health

Doctors and health professionals are only outnumbered on TV news programmes by politicians and policemen, and surveys regularly put health at or near the top of what people want to read and hear about in the media. For some years now health has been the dominant growth area in the features world. More than any other subject, it meets the prime objective of relevance to readers – we all get sick, and we all have an interest in staying healthy. Our families and friends get sick too, so even if it's not directly relevant to us personally, most subjects covered in the health sections can impact our lives. Because health and treatment provokes so much debate, newspapers increasingly feature an 'alternative' health column. Both traditional and alternative sections offer many opportunities for profile-raising.

As there is a current tendency to regard health in a holistic fashion, the subject often comes with a partner. So we have sections and magazines dedicated to health and fitness, health and well-being, and health and beauty.

Computers/information technology

If health has been king of the supplement road for some years, the new kid on the block with the cocky swagger is information technology. This is the current 'must have' supplement for everyone – and the phrase IT is defined very widely. It covers just about any aspect of technology, computers or gadgets, and with a little creative thinking and a good pitch to the editor you've got a great chance of being featured. Subjects featured in my own sample include numerous guides to the Internet and World Wide Web, many pieces about online commerce, including shopping, share dealing and banking, and a host of columns identifying and rating new web sites. In the business sense, there is a great interest in how traditional companies are adapting to, or making use of, what's been called 'the second industrial revolution'. So if you're a leading estate agent and are putting property details on the Web for the first time, you might invite a journalist to try it out. Offer other case studies of satisfied customers, and include outline costings and you're on the road to very favourable publicity. The key here is versatility and creative thinking – if any part of your business has an IT element, it may give you enough of an edge over the competition to make a feature.

Here's a surprising example of coverage which illustrates an important point: the first online landlord has opened his doors to Web users – so we may never again hear the cry 'Last orders, please!' Real ale is now available on the net. It can be ordered without leaving home and delivered to your door the next day in time for your party. Here the rather surprising combination of 'real ale bores' and 'computer nerds' – previously all they had in common was beards – was enough to spark the attention of the *Daily Telegraph*'s 'Connected' supplement, where it received prominent publicity. The point it illustrates about the national press in particular is that perception and reality are often not even on nodding terms. Newspapers evolve, and section editors in particular are very receptive to fresh ideas. In an effort to widen their constituency of readers they will risk a little bit of alienation or boredom at the edges of their sphere of influence. I wouldn't have been surprised to find this story in the *Guardian*, where we expect to find a large number of real ale fans – but the *Telegraph*? It shows how outdated the image of crusty old colonels and 'Disgusted of Tunbridge Wells' is – or at least how incomplete it is. The lesson here is that you need to keep up to date – you may be surprised at what you find.

Another story which appeared in 'Connected' concerned travel firm Stagecoach, who are trialling smart cards instead of tickets on trains, trams and buses in Manchester. Yet another featured the opening of Fabric, a huge new dance club in central London. It had five floors and more dance space than any other club in the UK, but what got it into the *Telegraph*'s technology section was the state of the art sound system which was linked to the various parts of the building by computer. Two more good examples where lateral thinking achieved very favourable publicity in less than obvious places. The latter would have been less surprising in the entertainment section, while we might have expected to find the former in the travel section, or maybe as a news story. The lesson is the same – be creative, and think laterally!

Personal finance

The great rise in share dealing and interest in personal finance in all its forms has spawned a great number of supplements and sections. Every newspaper now has a personal finance section, from the *Mirror* to *The Times*. Crucially, the pieces they carry are finely targeted at their readers. So the *Mirror* carries regular updates on privatized utility shares, which it believes its readers have bought, and cheaper shares, while the *Independent* runs pieces about what to do with your spare cash when you've taken up your quota of ISAs – aimed at readers with higher income and a more sophisticated grasp of finance.

Primarily these sections offer opportunities for companies in the finance business. If this includes you, you need to have them constantly in your sights.

Property

Hand in hand with the increased interest in personal finance there has been a rise in interest in property. Again, these pages are more likely to offer opportunities to companies in the property business, but this can be quite a wide definition. Anything to do with house furnishings and decorating, for example, sits naturally here. So if your company is in the electrical appliance business, makes or sells furniture or has anything to do with DIY, this is a prime target for you. You can also come up with a radical new view – one house building firm achieved publicity in the *Express* because they were building houses without car parking spaces, believing that car ownership would go out of fashion. Stories like that stimulate debate, which is partly what newspapers aim to do – the secret as ever is in the targeting.

Appointments

Another section which appears in different guises depending on its placing is 'Appointments'. In the *Daily Telegraph* it's a straight, nononsense 'Business File', in the normally egalitarian *Guardian* it's 'Careers' and within it the unashamedly elitist 'Crème de la Crème', and in the *Mirror* it's called 'The Mirror Works'. This last one includes 'Workline', a section within the section, dedicated to features about living, travelling and working in London. Whatever the name, this section can reveal surprisingly rich pickings. The *Daily Telegraph* version in particular is worth spending time on. It includes a 'Movers and Shakers' column which chronicles senior moves in the business world – a sure way to raise your profile and make colleagues a teeny bit jealous, or in some cases green with envy.

The same newspaper offers another opportunity for profile-raising – 'My Week' where a senior business figure outlines his or her upcoming working week. The column has an excellent reputation and so does manage to attract the great and the good – Niall Fitzgerald, Chairman of Unilever, was one occupant of this column. If someone in his position thinks it's a good place to be seen, your own chairman is likely to agree.

Shell and BT also received favourable publicity in a piece about the benefit of work experience aimed at A level students looking for a way to spend their summer holidays. They talked about how open they are to youngsters looking for a short placement, and how such schemes were valuable in job searches in later years. The piece enabled managers from the two companies to publicize one way in which they're 'putting something back' into the community. Not exactly putting their name in lights, but in these days when corporate community programmes are increasingly expected, every little helps.

Education

Education is another widely drawn definition where a little creative thinking can pay great dividends. The broadsheets, the *Daily Mail* and the *Express* all have weekly education sections,

and all the daily papers publish special supplements at crucial times in the academic year, for example on GCSE and A level results days. Take a look and you may be surprised. In the words of the *Radio Times* TV advertisement, 'I never knew there was so much in it.' For example, BT received positive publicity in the *Independent* for a new phone system it has devised to help stroke victims keep in touch. This type of publicity is never going to make or break you, but it can only help in the development of your public image. It will also look good in your annual report and will provide you with ammunition for aggressive interviewers.

Another benefit of getting to know what these supplements feature is that it will help you with your targeting. As we've all been to school, education is one of perhaps two or three subjects of which we all have direct experience. This applies to journalists, too, and affects the way they view the subject – you need to understand their viewpoint if you're to target them successfully.

Business

Not to be confused with the highbrow business sections of the broadsheets or the *Financial Times*, which I assume are already occupying the time of your investor relations and corporate communications people, the business sections of the mid-markets and 'red-top' tabloids generally look at small and medium-sized businesses. They like personality-based stories, or features where the success of a business is based on a clever or original idea. They also like stories about growing businesses reaching milestones, which may mean in terms of turnover, or coming to the unlisted markets.

Lifestyle

'Lifestyle' is one of the great buzzwords of our times. Lifestyle sections are one of the great growth areas of newspapers and magazines, as they strive to provide something which TV and radio cannot – depth as well as breadth. It's a subject relevant to virtually anyone who sells to the public. Almost anything can count as lifestyle – health, entertainment, gadgets, clothes, holidays … you can fill in your own here. Lifestyle sections come under various names, often including some version of 'Life' (*Daily Express*, Fridays) or 'Style' (*Daily Telegraph*, Fridays). Whatever their name, they all start from the same point – 'How can our readers improve their lifestyle?' All decently sized newspapers have a lifestyle section, and once again they offer excellent opportunities for publicity.

Special supplements

In addition to the weekly supplements and sections, the broadsheets publish occasional special sections dedicated to a particular geographic region or industry. These can be surprisingly narrow, but still offer effective publicity opportunities because of the very accurate targeting of their audience. Again, this is a fast track to the people you want to reach. The *Daily Telegraph* published a two-page 'Special Report' on the Scottish electronics industry, for example, which offered good publicity opportunities for the main players including Hewlett Packard, Racal and Motorola. The advertisement departments of the newspapers will tell you when they're coming up because they want to sell advertising around the features. Your objective is to find out who's writing it and contact them to try and sell them an idea.

The examples quoted here are just a small percentage of the wide variety of positive business stories featured in supplements and sections. I hope they have inspired you and your communications team to read widely, think laterally and target carefully.

PITCHING TO MAGAZINES

Magazines are one of the great success stories of the age and your efforts at raising your media profile would be incomplete without including them in your media plans. With good targeting they are another place where you are likely to find your company cropping up regularly – and good targeting is also the key to their success. Even more than newspapers, they offer you an entire readership focused on the subject matter. Magazines can be divided into two types: general and specialist. I assume you are already familiar with the latter, for example if you're in electron-

ics, cars or cameras you know the magazines in your own sector. General magazines, however, also offer great publicity opportunities, particularly for some sectors such as health, gadgets, personal finance and travel. Articles are usually longer than newspaper items so you do need to be ready to go into your story in some depth. Another big difference is that magazines tend to stay around longer – often ending up in the doctor's waiting room – so you can expect feedback from customers over a longer period of time than with a newspaper article.

A key point here is to recognize that magazines are started and closed almost every week, so you, or somebody on your behalf, really need to keep an eye on what's around. The magazine sector is very varied and there are many long-standing publications with huge circulations and excellent writers. They have a very clear idea of what they want, and are in no way an easy touch or the poor relations of the dailies. So plan your approach to a magazine as carefully as you would when calling a known-to-be-difficult specialist correspondent or section editor on a national newspaper.

The strategy for getting into magazines is very similar to getting into the supplements and sections – the first step is to identify one in your target area and develop story ideas relevant to the readers. As with newspapers, this means reading widely to discover what's around. Your pitching and contact-building can then continue in the same way as with newspapers. There is one big difference, however – magazines work on a much longer timescale than newspapers. It is not unusual for a monthly magazine to be working three or four months ahead, so rather like the fashion shows which feature woolly garments while we're basking in a summer heatwave, if your new product will revolutionize Christmas you need to be selling the story by August.

The longer deadlines and more collegiate decision-making in magazines also has another effect – generally speaking you're less likely to get a quick decision. My advice here is to be patient and don't be surprised if you need to follow up your initial call several times. But as ever, be polite. It costs nothing and might gain you a lot.

WORKING UP FEATURE IDEAS

I hope this chapter has given you a good start in understanding the world of 'non-news' and how to take advantage of it to achieve favourable publicity for your business. The key words are relevance, flexibility and lateral thinking. The rest is up to you, but as a start try this story-spotting technique.

I said earlier that journalists' favourite words end in 'st' such as first, last, cheapest, fastest, biggest, smallest and so on – they like absolutes. Some of your own products or services may be a 'first', 'cheapest' or whatever. If so, you should now be able to pitch the story to the news desk. Even if the whole idea isn't a 'first', however, it is always likely that part of it will be. In the example of Fabric, a new London club that was featured prominently in the *Daily Telegraph*'s technology section, it was the 'first' time a major club's sound system had been based on a computer. This was enough to provide the features 'peg'.

What I urge you to do is to gather the people who've been involved in a particular project, and get them to complete these sentences:

This is the first time that ...
This is the fastest ...
This is the biggest ...
... and so on.

You won't be able to complete them all, but in my experience you will identify a significant number of potential stories. It will also encourage your colleagues to start thinking in a publicity-conscious way. One more tip – if you do identify stories in this way which finally achieve publicity, send your colleagues a copy of the cuttings – it's a great morale booster.

CHAPTER SUMMARY

- There is huge media interest in stories from the business world and this works clearly in your favour.
- Much of what appears in newspapers is 'non-news' rather than the time-sensitive, event-driven news discussed previously. This is where you can expect to achieve most of your publicity.
- Journalists have a very clear idea of who their readers are – you need to understand this too so that you can target your stories effectively.
- Produce different versions of press releases to increase the 'What does this mean to our readers?' factor.
- In the press, deadlines are absolute – you must understand this and meet them.
- Don't ignore the local press – they have a huge agenda-setting role and are highly trusted in their own area.
- Expect journalists to check your story and get the 'other side'.
- Cuttings files are the first port of call for a reporter – it is vital that the contents accurately reflect your corporate image and actions.
- Supply good quality photographs and illustrations (in colour) to enhance your story's chances of success. The business pages in particular are in great need of good visuals.
- Understand the difference between news and features – and take advantage of it.
- Be creative and think laterally when you're trying to produce ideas for supplements and sections – don't just aim for the ones in your specialist area.

CHAPTER FIVE

Radio

Radio is the world's oldest form of genuine mass communication – and the way some executives regard it you'd think it had already been pensioned off. Many people regard radio as simply television without the pictures – a second-rate medium that belongs in a bygone age. This is a mistake, and if you ever suggest such a thing to a radio journalist they'll give you very short shrift. Britons listen to the radio for an average of 23 hours a week. Of all the traditional media outlets, radio is the one experiencing a growth spurt – consider how many new radio stations were launched in the UK in the final years of the twentieth century. Relaxed regulation and cheaper technology have combined to make radio, the most accessible medium, even more available. In many big cities in the UK there are several stations, each targeting a different audience. Many of these stations are speech-based and have an insatiable appetite for news, features, current affairs and topical discussion. With the right knowledge, approach and planning, any of this can include you or your company. This chapter gives you the keys to the door. It shows you how the needs of radio producers and journalists differ from those of their TV and print colleagues, how to approach them to best effect, and what to expect in dealing with radio.

British radio is some of the finest, most respected in the world and favourable publicity on it can do wonders for your public image. For millions of us, radio is part of the national psyche – we've grown up with it and trust it in a way not necessarily the case with other media. The British Social Attitudes Survey of 1998 found that radio had the highest trust rating of all the media – 70 per cent of respondents said they trusted radio journalists, compared to 15 per cent who trusted the national press. This unrivalled credibility rubs off on the interviewees and companies featured on the programmes. Because of the way and the places we receive it (in the bedroom, the bathroom, sitting around in our dressing gowns, driving the car) radio is seen as the most intimate medium. More than any other journalists, local radio reporters in particular are seen as being 'on the side of the listener' – so conveying a favourable impression is an absolutely critical factor in building or maintaining a positive image.

However, many executives I meet have a totally distorted impression of speech-based radio. Their views are formed by listening to *Today* in the mornings on Radio 4. If this is the extent of your own radio listening, it's understandable if you've come to believe that all radio news is confrontational and all interviewers are like John Humphrys. Understandable but wrong. *Today* is possibly the most confrontational arena in British journalism. It's an excellent programme and is rightly the flagship of BBC radio. It is not, however, typical, so please don't take it as such. Much radio is exploratory and information-seeking, rather than confrontational. Radio offers a wide range of programme types with publicity opportunities – from the highly professional *Jimmy Young Show*, where you may find yourself sandwiched between pop records, to late night local radio phone-ins where you wonder if the spotty-faced youth in the presenter's chair is old enough to vote! Both these extremes and everything in between have their place in raising awareness of you, your company or products. Your first task is to decide where to invest the time and effort based on the potential reward.

Outside the news bulletins, radio offers many more types of programmes where you can get your message across. Where TV has a preponderance of news programmes and bulletins, much speech-based radio is composed of more loosely defined 'talk' – whether between presenters, pundits, experts, interviewees, the public or any combination of these. These outlets also offer you the opportunity to talk in more depth than on the news about your company and products, often in a non-threatening way. With so many programmes and styles to choose from, therefore, it is important that you don't become fixated by the thought of the *Today* team bearing down on you. It doesn't have to be like that. This is not to say that the rest of radio is a soft touch – quite the contrary, the presenters will still ask tough questions and you need to be fully prepared. The less confrontational style, however, should make you feel far less uncomfortable – even welcome – compared with *Today*.

RADIO REACH

As an illustration of the ever-present nature of radio, think about your own routine. What did you do this morning? However much you were hurrying to get ready, see the children off to school, catch a flight or arrive early at the office and get some work done before the phone started interrupting, you almost certainly listened to the radio. Whether in the shower, at the breakfast table or in the car – or even all three – the radio was probably on. It's most likely that it was tuned to the news. That illustrates the size of the opportunity available when you understand radio. More than any other medium it gives you the chance to have a word in the ear of millions of people. Approximately nine out of ten adults in the UK listen to radio at some time during the week – that's the size of the stakes for which you're playing.

Think again about your routine and you'll realize another crucial point about successful radio handling. Though you may do much of your radio listening alone, you virtually always do it while you're doing something else. Whether you're waking up, showering, shaving, driving or talking, radio is usually 'on in the background', particularly during peak-time news programmes in the morning and early evening. Remember those pictures from years ago of a family sitting round the radiogram listening to the World Service or Light Programme? That really is a bygone age. Never again will we sit round a radio and listen with rapt attention. The transistor, which made radios portable, changed all that. We move from room to room vaguely aware of what's on in the background, rather than sitting

in rapt attention. This leads to a point about radio journalism which you need to understand to be a successful interviewee:

> Good radio interviews contain an element of showbiz.

To have an impact on the audience with nothing more than a voice, the presenters need to have big personalities, and the interviewees have to perform. The BBC charter sets out one of the objectives of the corporation as 'inform, educate and entertain'. Radio news, uniquely, does this all at once, while TV generally spreads these responsibilities around the schedule. Good radio interviewees are 'good performers'. They make the programme more interesting by the way they say it as much as by what they say. You need to aim for that too.

I'd like to make one other point about the power of radio to reach different sections of the public, that is your customers, investors, staff and other stakeholders. Consider your morning routine once more and think about how many radios you have in your own home. Quite a few, I suspect. They are probably all used by different family members, each tuned to a different station aimed at their needs and tastes. This is a notable advantage of radio over TV – there are so many more radio stations that whatever audience you are trying to influence, you can reach them.

THE RADIO NATION

So far from being a cinderella industry, radio is a lively, pioneering, important sector of the media with its own traditions and requirements. With so much local radio in particular, it also offers the best opportunity for publicity for you and your business, and a very high chance of reaching your target audiences. Radio, therefore, should be an important element of your communications plan. To make the most of it you need to understand about radio – the vast range of its programmes and stations, what makes a good radio story, and what you need to do to take advantage of that. That's where I am going to turn now. The pace of change in the media means that very detailed information about particular stations and programmes risks becoming out of date very quickly, so with a few honourable exceptions you or your team need to identify specific targets yourselves – by listening to the programmes. This section, therefore, concentrates on an overview.

As of January 2000 there are nine national radio stations in the UK and 270 local or regional ones, split between the commercial and BBC local radio networks. Together, they attract an astonishing 42 million listeners per week. This single statistic illustrates the size of the prize on offer. How else could you get to talk to 42 million people about your company or product for a fraction of the cost of advertising? The radio stations can be loosely divided into music, speech, or music and speech stations. Our focus here is on the last two categories.

STATION v. PROGRAMME

As with any section of the media your first step to success is to know the audience. With radio stations this is more difficult than with newspapers because a radio station's audience changes during the day as large tranches of the population tune in and out based on their routine. If you're asked to take part in an interview, therefore, it is important that you are very clear about the audience for that specific programme, rather than for the station as a whole. The changing audience – and the time they have available – also has a bearing on the style and tone of the programme. At breakfast time, for example, when listeners are in a hurry, most stations offer a fast-moving news programme, often fronted by two presenters. The aim is to cover as wide a range of the important or interesting stories of the day in as short as time as possible. Any interview you give here will need to be short, punchy and to the point.

By mid and late morning, though, the audience contains more women at home with families, and the programme style and content changes. On BBC Radio 4, for example, the flagship news programme *Today* ends at 9.00 a.m., and after an hour of studio chat is followed later by *Woman's Hour* and *You and Yours*. Both of these programmes run longer, feature-based items in recognition of an audience that has more time and different interests than people rushing off to work. They can cover items in more depth, be more reflective and take on a wider agenda. What this means to you is that if you are invited on to one of these programmes you will be quizzed in more depth about your subject than you will on the news. Your preparation, therefore, needs to reflect this.

Radio stations have a general style, within which the individual programmes fit. Programmes too have their own style, and to be a successful interviewee you need to be aware of both. As an illustration of differences in tone, consider BBC Radios 4 and 5. Both are national radio stations with all the credibility and resources of the BBC, but they are very different in tone and style. Radio 4's news programmes have a heavy (some would say too heavy) agenda biased towards political stories and a general 'heavyweight' feel as reflected on *Today*, *PM* and *The World Tonight*. Radio 5 Live, on the other hand, still covers most of the important items of the day but does so in a more conversational manner. Though the *Today* interviewers are among the most feared in the land, those on Radio 5 are more likely to catch you out with an unconventional question (as opposed to one for which you have prepared). Again, your media training must reflect that – make sure you roleplay a fast-moving, slightly irreverent interview as well as preparing yourself to face John Humphrys and the heavy-hitters.

LOCAL RADIO AUDIENCES

To group all the non-national stations together as 'local' is a little unfair because the group includes such a huge variety in terms of size, audience and resources. They vary from Capital Radio plc, a Footsie 350 company which owns 11 local stations around the country, and the big London speech-based programmes LBC and LBC Talk, both part-owned by ITN, to tiny stations in rural areas where the sheep outnumber the audience. The rules are the same, however, wherever you're aiming to appear. Local radio tries very much to be a part of the community. Its presenters speak with the regional accent (generally – if not, they usually make a feature of the difference) and understand the big issues in the area. Because local radio transmission areas are generally more limited than their TV counterparts – they really are local rather than regional – local radio sets out to reflect the feelings of the community. The stations and progammes, and as a consequence the reporters and interviewers, are clearly on the side of the listeners. This can affect you if, for example, you're announcing new jobs or cutting employment in the area.

The tone of local radio is often very different from the big national stations. It's usually more chatty, and aims to provide a feeling of eaves-dropping on a conversation. It's important that you pick up these cues because you can sound domineering if you use the wrong tone. Before you attempt to target any one station get one of your team to do a little research to produce basic facts about the main programmes, such as who they see as their target audience, including their age and sex profile. Try searching the Internet as a starting point, including the Radio Authority web site. The sites will also tell you what types of special interest programmes stations run, which may find stories from your business sector very attractive. Most stations today have slots which cover all those favourite subjects that hold such sway in the rest of the media – finance, sport, health, travel, cars, IT and so on. Your communications team can help you to target these.

Another important step is to understand who produces the editorial content for your target station. This information will tell you who to approach to increase your chance of success. The bigger, speech-based stations tend to produce much of their own UK-based material and rely on either ITN radio (for independent stations) or BBC News for major foreign stories. Assuming you're a UK-based executive, though, you can ignore the international elements. One similarity with television is that you will find that the same two organizations – ITN and BBC News – take up the lion's share of news and feature production. All BBC radio news and most features are supplied by the BBC, and ITN supplies more than 200 stations with news, features and other topical programming. It follows, then, that ITN and BBC Radio will be your first ports of call for important stories which you hope will achieve national publicity. There are also inde-

pendent radio production companies which produce features and documentaries for the bigger stations, but they will normally contact you if you're operating in an area of their interest for a particular programme or series.

On top of their arrangements with ITN or the BBC, many stations have their own reporters who will cover local stories. Your approach, then, needs to be tailored to which part of the operation you think is most likely to be interested. As a general rule, if your company is a national or international concern then announcements you make may attract national radio. This will certainly apply to financial results and announcements of investment, launches and cutbacks. Local stories, on the other hand, will be of interest to the local stations.

NATIONAL v. LOCAL RADIO

One of the biggest differences between radio stations is that between a national and a local broadcast. Trends set at national level are often copied by local stations, so in a way this distinction is an artificial one – a good interviewee needs broadly the same qualities whatever the target programme. There are, however, important differences and similarities between national and local radio – the more you understand them, the better your chances of success. Here are the main differences and similarities:

National	Local/regional
National and international story focus	National and local focus
National and international arena	Limited geographic area
Specialist and generalist reporters	Mainly generalists
Experienced interviewers	Wide variety of skills
Generally well resourced	Resources can be limited
Smooth operation and infrastructure	Organization can be chaotic

Let's look at some of these elements individually and examine how they affect your chances of obtaining publicity.

Story focus

In terms of editorial coverage, when we talk about national radio we mean BBC Radios 4 and 5, some inserts into Radio 2 programmes and the short, snappy but highly regarded Radio 1 *Newsbeat*, aimed at a young audience. There are also BBC radio news bulletins which are transmitted at various times on other BBC outlets including BBC Radio 3. National music stations such as Classic FM tend to include short hourly news bulletins, then there is the UK's first commercial speech-based radio station, launched as Talk Radio then relaunched early in 2000 as Talk Sport. (The content and character – indeed even the future – of Talk has been the subject of much change and speculation, and it will take some time to settle into its new format. As ever, listening to the programme will tell you what you need to know.)

The first defining characteristic of the national news bulletins is that they are among the most difficult targets to hit. Assuming you are there for positive reasons and not because something has gone wrong you should regard an appearance on a national radio programme as a significant coup by your communications team. Here again the crucial first step is to listen to the programme. Before you or your team approach national radio, ask yourself if you can imagine that programme covering this story. The answer needs to be 'yes'. By its nature, national radio covers not just national but also international news – so your story about your revolutionary e-commerce move is just as likely to be knocked out by an air crash in Outer Mongolia as a motorway pile-up in Outer London. With such a global agenda, predicting success here is impossible. However, the national news covers more stories from the UK than anywhere else and those items have to come from somewhere – it might be you! So don't give up.

Local radio stations, by contrast, cover a great range of stories – from stories about small local businesses to those concerning multinational corporations based in their patch. Many of them have an extremely parochial mentality, not unlike that exhibited by local newspapers. (When I was on a local paper we had a map showing the exact location where our circulation area ended, and in the two and a half years there I never once stepped over the line. There was no point – we wouldn't run stories about places where people couldn't buy the paper.) Local radio prides itself on being part of the community, and in most places it is fairly easy to build up contacts with the relevant producers. Be aware, however, that much local radio is an incubator for young reporters desperate to move on, so your contacts may not last long before they're on to pastures new. If this happens, ask the person who's leaving to introduce you to their successor.

Generalist and specialist journalists

If you are approached for a radio interview you need to ask who the interviewer will be and what they know about your subject. BBC national and ITN radio both employ specialist as well as general reporters – the specialist correspondents who work for the TV arms of both organizations. If you follow the advice in this book, you or your team will be developing contacts with the specialists in your area of expertise, with all the benefits this presents. The advantages of the bi-media system to you are that you're likely to be interviewed by someone who knows something about your industry (though remember they're not an expert in the same way that you are) and it imposes fewer demands on your time – one interview can get you on to TV and radio across the country.

Local radio stations also employ their own reporters, whose journalistic skills will vary widely. Many of them have been on their stations for years, know all the big issues and personalities and are there because they either come from the area or have settled in it. They will have bags of confidence, good memories and challenge you if you're now announcing something which appears to contradict what you said a few years ago. You need to be mentally on your toes for such interviews, but with the right preparation you can usually give a good account of yourself and the interview will be conducted in a thoroughly professional manner. There is, however, another type of radio reporter who can pose a different threat to you, your company and your story. Local radio is a common starting point for young people trying to build a career in broadcasting or journalism. And like anyone when they're starting out, they may not know very much about what's required. They also may not know much about the area or the background to your story. In addition, being young, they may not have enough confidence to ask you to clarify anything they don't understand, so they just bumble on without being totally clear on potentially a very important point. The onus is on you to ensure that they leave with a proper understanding of your story.

Most errors that occur in local radio, indeed in journalism generally, are the result of genuine mistakes and misunderstandings. With inexperienced local radio reporters particularly, you need to be aware of their potential to misconstrue things. Your own interpersonal skills are your main asset here – you can usually tell if someone hasn't understood something, or is not getting the point. If you suspect this is the case, ask them – but politely, without patronizing them. My own favourite way of doing this is to ask, 'Am I making this clear?' This is not threatening to them and puts the onus on me to explain it better if I receive a negative answer.

Radio resources and operations

Flagship radio programmes are generally well resourced, despite occasional reports to the contrary. 'Resources' here doesn't just mean money. It also includes services such as cuttings libraries and even having enough staff to put out a decent programme. This works in your favour because it increases the general level of professionalism and reduces the risk of mistakes. It means the experience of appearing on radio should go as smoothly as possible within the confines of a fast-moving show. However, the environment of a live radio show is like nowhere else – it can catch you unawares if you're unprepared.

An experience I had with one client will illustrate the situation you might face. She had been booked by Radio 5 Live for a short interview for the breakfast programme one weekday morning. The researcher met us at reception and once we were taken to the newsroom I asked if we could have a copy of the 'cue' – the introduction to be read by the presenter. This is important because it gives you an indication where the presenter might start the interview, and if there are any mistakes or misunderstandings you can correct them then, before they're transmitted. We were given a printout of the 'cue' and a few minutes

later the interviewee was taken into the studio, while I stayed in the control room. To say the least, the studio was daunting to the unfamiliar. It was dominated by a very big studio desk. Ranged around it were the two main presenters, the previous interviewee, the weather presenter, the sports reporter and the financial editor, all in various stages of preparing to go on air or sorting out their papers having come off it. The programme was going out live – and going on around our client. It's very disorientating to be suddenly thrown into a foreign environment like that, especially as the presenters and reporters regard it as normal.

We had been told what time to expect the interview to start (about three minutes after being taken into the studio) but when it did it seemed slightly surprising. One presenter read the 'cue' we'd already seen and asked our client a couple of questions, then the other presenter joined in and started asking different questions, too. It's very easy in such situations to get into an 'us' and 'them' mentality, particularly with the two interviewers and the unfamiliar environment – but my advice is to avoid this at all costs. Just accept that it's going to be disorientating until you've done it several times, then get on with the interview. In my client's case, it all turned out fine as these interviews usually do. Forewarned is forearmed – just remember this set-up has not been designed purposely to make you feel uncomfortable, it just happens that way.

Much local radio, on the other hand, is run on a shoestring. Financial difficulties are a way of life, and multi-skilling is the watchword. One way of looking at this is that it produces a lively, fun environment to work in where the staff have all sorts of opportunities they wouldn't have on a bigger station. Another is that the station seems constantly only one step from disaster, and appears to stay on air in spite of the organization rather than because of it. I have appeared on local radio stations myself where I've been left sitting in reception for an age, then two minutes before I'm due on air a harassed researcher runs in shouting, 'Oh – you're here!' Then I've been led into a studio and told to sit down and speak when the red light comes on – usually within a few seconds. If you ever hear a presenter say something like, 'While you're catching your breath...' that's often what has happened.

As I sat down on one occasion the presenter turned to me in the commercial break before the interview, looked quizzically at my suit, and said, 'Are you the new gardening bloke?' On being told I was in fact there to talk about a breakthrough in treatment for men with prostate cancer he uttered an expletive (off air and under his breath) then said, on air, 'Now, as you've probably heard there's exciting news today for the thousands of British men who suffer from prostate cancer. It really is a terrible disease and up to now there's been little that can be done about it. Now though, that may be about to change. Here to tell us why is John Clare. John – what's the big idea?'

The rest of the interview passed off without incident and nobody would have known that the presenter didn't have a clue what it was supposed to be about. He was a consummate professional and regarded such chaos management as part of his job. Apart from carrying out the interviews he was also playing the cassettes which contained the commercials and timing the whole programme to ensure he hit crucial opt-out points when the station joined up with the network. With this kind of chaos in the studio, it's easy to see why an unprepared executive can be overwhelmed. Now you know what it could be like I hope that for you it's a case of 'forewarned is forearmed'. This flying by the seat of your pants style of radio offers you a great opportunity to drive the interview where you want it to go. Take it. The presenter will be delighted – they need your help to get them through it. The last thing they want is a shrinking violet giving monosyllabic answers.

WHAT RADIO REPORTERS WANT

If you did listen to the radio news this morning, ask yourself this question: 'What was on it?' The chances are you'll recall one or two items – three would be very good. This illustrates an important point about radio. Because it's competing with whatever else the listeners are doing, interviewees – and presenters – have to work even harder to grab the attention of the audience. This means being more lively and energized than

with any other medium. This is the first step to getting good radio coverage – on radio, especially, you need to be 'a good talker'. And here I'm referring to quality, not quantity. Many elements combine to produce a great radio guest, but here are the main ones:

- lively
- articulate
- passionate
- jargon-free
- painting word pictures
- concise and to the point
- memorable.

Think of the best political interviewees – Michael Heseltine, Denis Healey and Kenneth Clarke are the favourites of many interviewers – and you'll see they all have the qualities listed. In essence, whatever your political views they come across as interesting, passionate and engaged with the interviewer. It is interesting to note that they are all now 'elder statesmen' and so are less in awe of the party spin-doctors and not afraid of saying the wrong thing. This leads to another attribute of ideal interviewees – they're relaxed and passionate at the same time. If you've prepared for an interview and are still having to concentrate hard to remember your key messages you're not properly prepared. Your key messages should be second nature so the only mental effort required is to work out how to get from the question to something you want to say. Remember that you're the expert in this subject, and your key messages should be so simple that 'knowing what to say' takes no effort at all. You can, therefore, concentrate on your performance.

TYPES OF PROGRAMMES

Radio producers are inventive and are constantly developing different types of programmes. Here, though, are the main ones you are likely to encounter. All of them can be used to raise your profile and enhance or maintain your image – the central theme of this book.

- news bulletins
- documentaries
- magazine shows
- music programmes with a guest

- round-table discussions
- chat shows
- phone-ins
- consumer/investigative programmes
- debates/witness type programmes

Here are the main points about each of them.

NEWS BULLETINS

Radio provides the fastest news service of all media. A story can break now and be on air within seconds. Because radio is such a low-tech medium, all you need to get on air is a telephone – though reporters and producers usually prefer you in a studio (or a radio car for big-budget stations) to get the best sound quality. Radio news reporters are used to working very fast, so to increase your chances of getting on air you need to take quick decisions about appearing – if you dither they'll move on to someone else. Get all your soundbites and key messages prepared and approved in advance of expected radio news publicity – then you can just concentrate on their delivery.

If you are aiming to seriously raise your profile and you expect this to mean regular appearances, consider having a digital phone line installed to use for interviews. Currently the best standard is ISDN, though there are other technologies in the pipeline.

DOCUMENTARIES

Radio documentaries – in the literal, full-length meaning of the word – are increasingly rare with the current focus on short attention span radio. There are some still made, often by independent production companies on behalf of the big radio stations. You can rarely approach them because there's no systematic way of discovering if anyone is working on one relevant to your area of expertise. If they approach you, be open, honest and helpful and get as much information as you can before deciding whether to take part. If you do appear, make sure you know what main points the reporter is expecting you to make, and how they will fit into the overall picture.

MAGAZINE SHOWS

There are a wide range of programmes under this heading. They include generalist shows such as *Woman's Hour*, and many specialist programmes such as the arts shows *Kaleidoscope* and *Front Row*, and the personal finance show *Money Box*. They are composed mainly of topical features as opposed to news stories (see Chapter 4 on newspapers for a list of the essential differences between news and features – they apply equally to TV and radio). If you have got a novel idea for something which affects people's lives it's always an idea to approach features producers. Features are longer and more detailed than news stories, so if you succeed in getting on air, expect to have to answer more detailed questions about your subject.

MUSIC PROGRAMMES WITH A GUEST

These programmes are modelled on that of the doyen of radio presenters, Jimmy Young. His own style of easy chat while, in between pop records, still asking the hard questions, is much-copied though in my view few of the imitators reach his standard of interviewing. Michael Parkinson, another of the greats, is an exception when he gets back behind a radio microphone. The local radio versions may not come up to JY's standard, but they are still a great draw. These programmes – whether it's the real thing or a local copy – have great potential because the audience are in a receptive mood, as opposed to news audiences who tend to be more cynical. Getting the style and tone right is very important. Listen to the programme in advance (as ever) and as far as possible try to adopt the same style – usually light and chatty, with the right amount of concern. If you sound as you might when faced with John Humphrys you can come over as hectoring and pushy. Be laid back – but make sure you still get your messages in. Practice is the key.

ROUND-TABLE DISCUSSIONS

Start the Week and *Midweek* on Radio 4 are the highest profile examples of this programming genre – essentially it's interesting people sitting around having a chat. On local radio these programmes are popular in mid-morning and at the weekends – often with two presenters plus a number of guests who may drop in and leave before the end of the show. Sometimes the guests will have some common link, on other occasions the only connection will be topicality, that is they've all been in the news recently. This is real 'fireside chat' territory – you're there to be interesting and illuminating, not to plug your corporate message at every opportunity. You've normally been invited because you or your company has done something newsworthy, so you will be allowed an element of pluggery – but don't overdo it. Ask the producer what they're expecting from you. The other danger here is that you become so relaxed you don't sparkle. Remember, a good interview demands an element of performance. Make sure you give it, don't overdo the corporate messages, and you can chalk up another success.

CHAT SHOWS

A chat show is similar to the round table, but you are either the only guest or one of a small number. You're usually there not because of your company, but because of your own personality and achievements. Go through the plans in detail with the producer. The requirement here is to tell anecdotes which make your points come alive. We all love good story-tellers – this is your chance to show your shareholders, employees and the rest of your stakeholders what a rounded person you are.

PHONE-INS

Phone-ins are very popular, particularly on local radio, because they're cheap to produce. In your position you're unlikely to take part in general phone-ins where the presenter talks – usually controversially – to callers about anything in the news. You're more likely to be involved in specialist programmes. The subjects here are only limited by the producer's imagination, but typically include gardening, personal finance, alternative therapies, fitness, new technologies – indeed almost anything. They're very popular with the audience and are one of the elements that make radio accessible – you can't get more accessible than putting the listeners on air.

A word of warning here. Programmes where you handle phone calls from the public can put you in impossible situations, as Margaret Thatcher discovered. The only time she came off worse in a debate during her 11 years in power was on a TV phone-in programme when a caller appeared to know more than she did about the sinking of the Argentine cruiser the *General Belgrano* during the Falklands conflict. It's said that she was so unhappy with the result that she never did another phone-in. These programmes are part of the staple diet of local radio – be careful. Be clear about the topic, and lay down strict guidelines about what you want to talk about. Be very clear as to whether you're appearing alone or with another guest. If there are two of you, you will normally hold opposite views. This is not necessarily a bad thing as long as you're prepared to debate your point of view. Be aware that you need a strong presenter to mediate and step in if callers stray on to areas you want to avoid. These would include anything to do with legal problems, takeover speculation, or anything that might be construed as tipping your own shares.

Having said that, phone-in programmes are about as unmediated as it gets, and are a real opportunity to talk to the public and give a good impression. So don't reject them out of hand – just make sure you, the producer and the presenter are prepared.

CONSUMER/INVESTIGATIVE PROGRAMMES

Programmes dealing with consumer affairs are one of the great growth areas of radio, both national and local. *You and Yours* and *Face the Facts* are two high profile examples. British consumers have started to rise up against what they see as extortion and rip-offs – thanks in no small measure to consumer programmes that claim to expose wrongdoing and make consumers aware of their rights. One problem with these programmes is that they are often more about generating heat than light – they're there for their entertainment value. The producer is unlikely to ring you up with an offer to plug your latest product, so be wary. That doesn't mean, however, that you should reject such overtures out of hand. If you are accused of doing something wrong, investigate the incident before you reject an offer to go on the programme. If you have made a mistake, it might be good to say sorry (with the lawyers' permission, of course). If you've done nothing to be ashamed of, it may be a good opportunity to put the record straight. Ask them to be very specific about the question areas. You can go on to these programmes and win, especially if you're not guilty of whatever crime you're alleged to have committed.

DEBATE/WITNESS TYPE PROGRAMMES

Programmes such as *The Moral Maze* on Radio 4 generally deal with big social issues, but if you're in an area that has an impact on society, you may be called upon to appear. If so, make sure that you listen to some previous examples of the genre – they can be very uncomfortable.

GETTING ON TO THE RADIO

The first step to obtaining radio coverage is effective pitching of the story, using the techniques outlined elsewhere in the book, with particular emphasis on the relevance and suitability of interviewees. Knowing who to approach is very important. The bigger stations have a forward planning desk which sets up stories for the next week or next day. On smaller stations this is the responsibility of the news desk. Aim for the right person – get to know if there's a correspondent in your specialist area, and approach them first. Remember you have more chance of getting your story on if it has an internal champion, which is what the specialist will be if they like it.

Once the station or programme has expressed an interest in your story, you then need to talk it through with the researcher, producer or reporter. Ask them how they see the piece working out, who else will be included and how long they're expecting it to be. In particular you need to know whether you're to feature in a studio interview or a 'package', a pre-recorded piece. As with television, there are advantages to both, and either way you need to know what part you play in the story. If you go 'live' in the studio (or even from another location) your interview will often be heard after a pre-recorded package. If this is the case you should listen to it carefully as it will give you an indication as to the angles they are planning to follow up with you. It will

also allow you to correct any mistakes in the package.

If the reporter wants you to appear in a package, you need to be clear about who else will be included and what part they expect you to play. The benefits to you then are mainly logistical – you can do the interview at a time and place of your choosing, so it causes less disruption to your day. A recorded interview can also usually be redone if you're not totally happy with it. The key to success here is to obtain as much information as possible about the programme and how they view your piece. The main points are:

- know the programme
- know the deadlines
- make your story relevant to the programme
- be clear about what you want to say
- offer case studies
- above all, ensure all suggested interviewees are 'good talkers' – including any case studies
- be available – don't tell them about a story for next week then go off to a conference the day before launch
- be flexible – for logistical reasons you may have to go somewhere else to do the interviews
- if there are any time constraints, for example you won't be available at a particular time, make sure they understand this
- don't badger them
- don't ring to ask if they've got the press release – this is certain to irritate a busy journalist. If you've sent it, properly addressed to the right person, they've got it
- try to build relationships
- be realistic with your expectations.

SUPPLYING YOUR OWN INTERVIEWS

There are two techniques you may consider when you've got a story which you expect to attract a number of different radio stations – a 'radio tour' and a syndicated tape.

RADIO TOURS

This entails you – or the nominated company spokesperson – sitting in a studio and doing a number of interviews with different stations. Typically each station will book a 15-minute slot on the day of the story 'peg'. During the day, therefore, you may find yourself doing a great number of interviews – up to 20 on a good story. There are two challenges here:

- Remembering what you've said in each one, to ensure that you always get your points in. To overcome this, write each key message on a separate piece of card. Before each interview, lay all of the cards on one side of the desk. As you make the points, move the corresponding card to the other side, and put it face down. This way you can see what you've said and the points you still have to make.

- Making the story relevant to a wide range of stations. This is more difficult and the producer will know in advance the extent to which you can localize the story. You can overcome this to a degree by having a wide range of examples to drop into your interview. For example, if I was doing local radio interviews about this book I would aim to talk about the media in the area where the station was based. With radio, you can take brief notes into the studio, so you're not relying on your memory.

SYNDICATED TAPES

As the name implies, this entails producing (or getting a professional to produce) a self-contained radio feature then syndicating it to interested radio stations around the country. It would normally include all the elements radio reporters would expect in their pieces – company spokesperson, case study, third party endorser and so on. The usefulness of this technique is sometimes questioned, so if your advisers suggest you commission a syndicated tape, ask them for persuasive case studies.

TELEPHONE INTERVIEWS

As more companies install digital phone lines, telephone interviews are increasingly accepted. Being in a remote location in this way can be slightly disconcerting because you don't have the feeling of what's going on in the studio. To help you with this, ask the producer if you can hear the station output down the phone for a couple of minutes before your interview. This will give you important information about the tone of the programme (it could be anywhere from serious to flippant) and help you slip into the right frame of mind. As a final part of the radio briefing, here are ten tips for successful telephone interviews:

- don't do it until you're clear about the context and what's expected
- be clear about how long it's going to last and who's interviewing
- don't agree to do it immediately – buy yourself some time
- make notes – but only short ones such as phrases and key words
- prepare your voice – and have a drink of water handy
- choose your ground – ensure that you won't be interrupted or distracted
- don't do it on a mobile phone – you may be cut off and the quality is poor
- listen to the questions – they're generally not as difficult as you think
- remember they can't see you – you have to paint the pictures for them
- stand up! – it eases your breathing.

CHAPTER SUMMARY

- Radio news has great credibility – this can rub off on you.
- The vast majority of radio is exploratory and information-seeking, not confrontational.
- Radio offers many types of opportunities to put your message across.
- People always listen to the radio while they're doing something else, so you need to work very hard to engage them.
- Local radio in particular offers great opportunities for publicity.
- Radio audiences change during the day – you need to understand how they change to target your stories effectively.
- Be sure you are familiar with the tone of the station and programme you're targeting.

- Listen to the programme in advance.
- Find out whether you're in a live interview or a recorded 'package'.
- Local radio employs reporters whose skills vary widely – be careful.
- It is your responsibility to ensure that the journalist understands your story.

- There are two ways to supply your own interviews to radio stations – radio tours and syndicated tapes. Check their effectiveness with your PR consultancy.
- Consider having a digital phone line installed in your offices if you're hoping or expecting to be interviewed regularly.

CHAPTER SIX

Using Public Relations to help put your Message across

When I came into journalism, my job was to write about things that had happened. Now it's increasingly the other way round – things happen so that journalists will write about them. And it works. The people behind the stories are public relations practitioners. According to PR guru Quentin Bell, 80 per cent of stories which appear on the business pages and up to 50 per cent of general news has been produced or influenced by PR practitioners. My own view is that the true figure for general news is even higher if you include PR on behalf of the government, institutions and public bodies. I don't believe this is necessarily a bad thing – if corporations, institutions and even small companies are using communications professionals to help them communicate then that's good news. Just as you wouldn't put an inexperienced amateur in charge of the finance or R&D departments, so you need a professional in charge of your communications. What the public and your key audiences read, hear and see about you are cornerstones of your corporate reputation, which as we have seen is a real corporate asset. The other cornerstone is how you behave, but more on the interdependency of these elements later.

If you are serious about managing your media image, you will need to use public relations in one or more of its various forms. Unfortunately many executives I meet are sceptical about the value of PR and reluctant to invest seriously in it. These same executives wouldn't query the need to invest in advertising in the same way, yet both are an essential part of your marketing mix. This chapter aims to lay out for you the true potential of PR as a powerful management tool which can help to promote a good image of your company and so have a direct effect on the bottom line. If you're a PR sceptic I hope it will improve the image of PR in your own mind, and that you will consider using it in a focused, planned way.

It's ironic that the public relations industry, which focuses entirely on managing reputations, itself gets such a bad press. However, much of this prejudice is based almost entirely on myths and misunderstandings about public relations. In the public mind, and the minds of many senior executives, PR means one thing – employing the services of so-called 'spin doctors', those twenty-first-century alchemists who can turn base stories into golden publicity opportunities. But most public relations practitioners are a world away from the Alastair Campbells, Peter Mandelsons and Max Cliffords whose activities are at the same time devoured and despised by the media. In the real world – and the business community – most PR practitioners themselves are invisible in the news media – only their results are seen. Many of those I work with would run a mile from any personal publicity opportunity. They work behind the scenes and are totally focused on obtaining favourable publicity for their clients or, in a crisis, to reducing the amount of negative publicity or its impact. PR does involve putting the right angle, or positive 'spin' on stories. One cynical definition is 'The truth, nothing but the truth but not necessarily the whole truth.' But it encompasses much more than that. This chapter gives you the whole truth about PR. Most of this book is about putting you in the journalist's place so you can understand what they need. This chapter looks at it from the other side – the PR practitioner, the link between your company and the media.

WHERE DO WE START?

All good PR campaigns begin with benchmarking research, so let's start with some here. To test your current level of PR understanding, answer these questions. What is public relations? How does it differ from advertising, and in what circumstances would you expect the respective disciplines to be most effective? What can it do, and not? When would you hire an outside consultancy and when is your in-house communications department best placed to run a campaign? How can you measure its success? What part does it play in your company's marketing mix? What should you look for in an agency and how would you find the right one for your project?

You probably have a vague idea of the answers, but don't worry if you can't actually articulate them. This chapter aims to answer all those questions and many others concerned with using PR to put your message across in the media. It will enable you to make a valuable contribution to planning your company's PR programmes, assess the quality and strengths of your internal and external PR teams and make informed judgements about their proposals.

WHAT IS PUBLIC RELATIONS?

Let's start by defining the subject. The industry's trade association, the Institute of Public Relations, offers this:

> Public relations is the application of a planned and sustained programme of communications between an organisation and those audiences essential to its success.

The first key phrase here is the idea of 'a sustained programme of communications'. This is a point sometimes not understood by executives whose minds are focused on other aspects of the business. They think they can switch PR on and off like a tap when things are going particularly well or especially badly. You can't. Relationships with journalists are most successful when they're just that – relationships that are nurtured and built up over time. If your company's attitude is that PR is just an occasional tactic to be viewed as the icing on your communications cake it won't work. You'll also find it hard to attract top class practitioners to such an unsatisfying role, so when you do need help you won't

be best prepared anyway. As you can see from this definition, occasional guerrilla-style raids on journalists begging for a few column inches isn't really PR anyway – it's a haphazard and uneconomic way of spending part of your communications budget.

But the main reason why you need a PR campaign rather than occasional 'hits' is that the objective of most communications programmes is either to change behaviour or to change attitudes and so create the conditions for different behaviour. Your objective may be to get people to buy more of your products, or start to feel dissatisfied with the alternatives. To get people to take notice, you have to keep telling them time and again. Once they've got the message, you need to continue telling them until they act on it. To illustrate this trait of human nature, if you have children, consider for a moment how easy it would be if you just said to them once, 'Don't do that' and they did as you asked! They don't. It's the same with adults. Keep saying it. That's how you get noticed. That's why you need a campaign.

The second key point about the definition of PR is the last part – 'those audiences essential to its success'. Just as journalists are very focused on what stories will interest or affect their audiences, you must be equally aware of the converse – which audiences can most affect your product or company?

This starts to get to the heart of public relations and its relationship with the rest of your business. When PR is used well it is a very important contributor to the achievement of your commercial goals. It's also been defined as 'an opportunity to influence key audiences with messages that support your commercial objectives.' I like this second version because it makes very clear that there should be a direct link between your PR activity and what your business wants to achieve. My company spends a lot of time with one foot in the journalistic camp and the other on the PR side of the fence. Unfortunately in my experience the link between PR activity and commercial objectives is not always made. Indeed half the respondents in a survey in *PR Week* in 1999 said that PR was rarely tied to business objectives. One reason is that the overall commercial aims are not always clearly articulated, or not always understood by the people responsible for the PR campaigns.

It's important to differentiate here between your business's *corporate* aims and the specific objectives you have for new or existing products. Product campaigns are in my experience generally very well focused and an integral part of achieving the product's objectives – creating a new market, taking business from existing competitors, taking advantage of a rival's perceived weakness, getting valuable third party endorsers on side and so on. Corporate PR campaigns, however, often suffer from a lack of clarity of thinking. Of course, product and corporate PR are not entirely separate – many companies are very brand focused so there is an overlap because what influences the brand awareness has an effect on the parent company.

FIRST STEPS TO PR SUCCESS

Your own company may be more corporate or brand-focused. It may be changing. Whatever the situation, the first step to a successful PR campaign is clear thinking right at the beginning of the planning stage. In particular you need to answer these questions:

1 What are our objectives for this company or product?
2 Where are we now in relation to those objectives?
3 Who are the key audiences with whom we need to communicate to achieve the objectives?
4 What do we want them to say or think?
5 What communications vehicles will we use in what parts of the journey from here to there (particularly PR and advertising)?

THE COMMUNICATIONS ENVIRONMENT

I assume you have your own ways of identifying your product or corporate objectives and understanding how far you have to go to achieve them. My focus here is the link between that and your communications programme – beginning with how to answer questions 3, 4 and 5. Notice that here I say 'communications programme', of which a PR campaign may be an important part. Other elements may include advertising, direct mail to known interested parties, lobbying, promotions and deployment of a sales force. A very effective starting point, which will initially help you to answer these questions and then provide

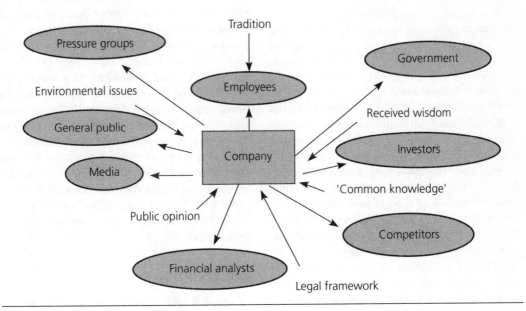

Figure 6.1   A typical communications environment

a longer-term way of analysing your communications needs, is to map your communications environment. You do this by listing all the people or organizations who are likely to talk about you, your product or company, either in public or to each other, where a groundswell of opinion can begin to build. These are your key audiences.

Figure 6.1 illustrates how this may look in principle. All of these audiences can influence each other, so it is important that over time your company monitors what they are all saying. The communications department will play the leading role here, but so will investor relations and possibly your parliamentary lobbyists or whoever is responsible for relations with government. But this watching brief doesn't end there. You should also allow other departments to play their own role. Your sales force, for example, are in contact with your major customers on a regular basis – their feedback is crucial and can act as an early warning system or flag up potential problems or a change of strategy elsewhere in the industry which may affect you or attract media attention to your own plans. For example, if your main competitor decides to reduce prices as part of an aggressive marketing campaign your sales force may hear it first from a customer with whom they have good relations (or whom they just happen to call on the right day). You need the right communications channels in place to ensure that this feedback reaches you quickly so that you can plan your response before your phone rings and it's a journalist asking if you're going to fire the next shot in the newly declared price war.

Of all the key audiences identified on your communications environment map, rarely is any one of them more important than the media. In today's society, where not many of your stakeholders have the opportunity, time or inclination to meet you personally, most of their information about you comes through the media. The media are the gatekeepers to the majority of the other audiences. Yet that's not the whole story. Where a gatekeeper simply acts as a filter and decides who or what (in this case your messages) passes or not, the media also alter the messages as they pass through the gate. The people on the other side of the gate know

this, and are prepared to accept it as a result. Without the time, information or inclination to form an opinion of your messages themselves, the media do this job for them. This is why the stakes in media management are so high.

The communications environment exercise has another benefit. If you look at it as a whole, this is a snapshot of the background noise above which your messages must be heard. It's a snapshot because it only relates to a specific period and will change over time. For example, if you're in an area of activity which in any way can be said to affect the environment then environmental pressure groups will be a central feature, whereas just a few years ago they would have been active only on the margins. Your communications environment is a constantly changing picture and you should repeat the exercise regularly to keep up to date.

There is one more element to the exercise which will return us to the five questions and allow you to measure the progress of your communications campaign. Having identified your key audiences you can plot them on a scale from negative to positive in terms of how they view you. This will give you a good picture of your current image and standing. Having measured it you can then decide how you want it to change and monitor it over time. It is likely that a key objective will be to move as many of them as possible towards the plus sign. Doing this requires a 'horses for courses' approach – for which different types of PR activity are ideally suited. For some audiences, like third party opinion leaders, an element of your PR plan may be to organize occasional seminars or newsletters to keep them informed about what you are doing so they understand what's happening. So in the example quoted in Chapter 2, the launch of a device for tracking down stolen vehicles, important third parties would be the motoring organizations, who will be the first port of call for journalists wanting comments about its usefulness.

THE ADOPTION PROCESS

Question 5 asks what communications vehicles you would use in what parts of the journey from where you are now to meeting your commercial objectives. I am thinking particularly here of PR, the focus of this chapter, and advertising, with which it is often compared and sometimes confused. They both have strengths and weaknesses, and to make an informed decision as to when to use which discipline you need to understand what psychologists call the process of adoption. This is the thought process through which people typically travel from never having heard of something to deciding they can't live without it. From your point of view, this is the process your communications programme is driving when you set out to create a market for a new product or company:

Unaware – Aware – Comprehend –
Convinced – Action

All communications campaigns, whether to cancel third world debt, sell Pot Noodles or anything in between, are based on this process. In many cases the 'big picture' – in your case buying your products – is made up of the same process repeated time and again with your key audiences. Depending on the audiences, different communications vehicles will be more successful at taking you on different parts of the journey. If you're in healthcare, for example, one of your key audiences is physicians. They are not likely to be totally convinced about your new product based on the advertising alone. But if your claims are backed up by peer-reviewed scientific trials published in respected scientific journals then you will start to influence the audience. So taking your key opinion leaders on the journey above will get you to first base on the big campaign to persuade the public and sell more products. In this instance you would also be meeting the regulatory authorities to discuss what advertising claims you can make and making the case to politicians in charge of healthcare budgets to include your products.

PR v. ADVERTISING

Here I want to look briefly at one of the other communications tools – advertising – as an understanding of the differences between it and public relations is crucial to using PR successfully. Here are the essential differences:

Advertising	Public Relations
Clearly comes from the company	Includes third party endorsement so appears more distant from company
Top-line only	More depth and detail
Mainly broadcast medium, i.e. widespread audience	Can be targeted to specific audiences
Conveys your messages exactly as as you want	Messages filtered and edited by journalists
Conveys your messages when, where and however often your budget will permit	Each communication is a 'one-off'. No guarantee your messages will appear in target media – or anywhere

Let's look at the differences in more depth and explore their pros and cons. Advertising clearly comes from the company so everybody who sees it is aware that this message is occupying this slot in print, radio, TV or on a poster only because the company concerned has paid for it. This is great for high profile campaigns and can get you huge recognition. The downside is that the audience will always retain an element of scepticism, a reaction along the lines of 'They would say that, wouldn't they?' PR, on the other hand, appears generally in the editorial columns and slots and therefore seems more distant from the company. It's also been written by somebody unconnected with the company – usually a journalist, though sometimes an independent opinion leader – so there is a tacit acknowledgement that somebody else (outside the company) agrees with it. It often involves the endorsement of others because the journalist will usually canvas the views of other knowledgeable people and quote them in the piece. If your messages can stand up to this much scrutiny then your company or product must be very robust. The public have a tacit understanding of this endorsement process, and are therefore less sceptical of editorial messages – though they have to be backed up with the right actions.

It is easier to target PR than advertising. For

example, if you are launching a new range of computers you may target new adult users with claims about their ease of use, business users with the portability and power of the laptops and children with the speed of the processor and its resulting ability to handle high grade computer games. In theory you can do the same with advertising, but producing ads for each sector is very expensive. With PR you just give your press release and pitch calls to journalists a different angle depending on their readership or audience, and change the slant of the interviews.

The next difference lies at the heart of the power of advertising – its beauty lies in its simplicity. It is often said that the commercials are the best thing on television today because they're clever and simple at the same time. Think of a poster ad – it's a brilliant encapsulation of one idea. That's where it differs from PR. Each advertisement has just one big idea, whereas PR is ideally suited to communicating nuances and slight differences. However, because your messages are filtered by journalists PR is a much less certain medium than advertising. Your message can fall at the first fence and never reach anyone, however good your targeting is and however well you study the lessons of this book. Another downside is that every PR 'hit' is a one-off. You can't repeat it (at least not for some considerable time). You can't say, 'That survey about computer use got us lots of publicity for our new range last week – we'll do it again next week.' The nature of news rules it out. But you can, of course, buy more advertising slots. So although it will cost you much more to get your advertisements developed and produced, they can be used repeatedly for as long as you or your agency think suitable and for as long as your budget will stand it.

PR and advertising each suit a particular type of message. For example, if you're looking for broad awareness of your new range of baked beans then advertising is great. You don't need PR because everyone knows what baked beans are. If, however, your main selling point is the health benefits of the revolutionary new formula baked beans, then advertising alone won't do it. You will need pieces in the editorial columns with quotes from nutritionists and doctors about the health benefits.

Let's take another example – digital versatile discs (DVDs), touted as the high quality picture and sound replacement for videotapes within a few years. Before anyone had heard of DVDs, you would not have sold a single one if all you had done was bought advertising space. The first step was to create a market for them, to create an awareness of their benefits (and existence). This is where PR scores heavily. It is ideally suited to creating a market by the appearance of news stories and features about the benefits of the new format and its advantages over video tapes. Once you have created a market you can then use advertising and other measures to drop your product into it. This is what we mean by the 'marketing mix' – a mixture of different methods which will create awareness and increase understanding of your product or company, with each technique supporting the other. If you look at them in the round, your communications campaigns will be more effective than many – assuming you have followed the first rule of this chapter and forged a strong link between your commercial objectives and how these can be supported by your PR campaign. Too often this does not happen. Executives often appear to get their advertising, direct mail, sales force and lobbying programme sorted out, then try to 'bolt on a bit of PR' – this approach doesn't work. PR needs to be an integral part of the marketing mix.

It would be a mistake, however, to believe that PR is only useful when you are creating a market for a new product. It plays other very different – and equally important – roles in your company. For example, it can very effectively support or reposition mature products, defend products or even the company when it is encountering public problems, and build corporate image. I will return to these other benefits of PR later in this chapter. But for now, here are the crucial points in the early stages of planning a PR campaign.

SUMMARY OF THE FIRST STEPS

- good PR starts with clarity of thought
- good PR starts from linking it to your commercial objectives

- involve the PR team as early as possible
- map out your communications environment
- decide which communications vehicles fit the changing requirements
- assess the role of PR within the marketing mix.

WHAT PR CAN DO

Many senior executives I meet are suspicious about PR because they're not clear about what it can do. Others are sceptical because they expected wonders from a small investment and were disappointed. Put another way, either they don't believe PR can achieve anything, or they have unrealistic expectations. This section deals with the reality of what PR can achieve, and looks at the circumstances in which you can use it most effectively. Let's start with a basic statement about the power of PR:

> PR cannot change reality. It can, however, help to change perceptions.

This is the nub of all the arguments about the effectiveness of public relations, so let's examine it in detail and see how it affects you as a senior executive. PR can't change reality, so if you would like your company to be known as warm, caring and cuddly, yet your decision-making is all ruthlessly business-driven, then these two positions are inconsistent and cannot exist together. PR can't change your business philosophy. But it can make more of what you're doing anyway, and ensure that it gets noticed and that you get the credit for it.

In the words of a highly experienced PR consultant: 'We're jugglers, not conjurors.'

PR practitioners can't make a bad product good, make something work if it doesn't or increase the capacity of your server so nobody will have problems accessing your new e-commerce site. They can't make a company which treats its employees, the community or the environment badly look very good. They can do it once in an article, but such a position cannot be sustained. If every decision you take is motivated by profit then successful PR may lead to positive pieces in the business pages about your growth, results or achievements, or single you

out as an example of how to ⌐
trend. Or if you really do beh
feely, cuddly way, then it can ⌐
the credit for it. This is another rⅇₐ⌐
successful PR campaign is always linked ⌐
commercial aims – the two must be consis⌐
Underlying all the advice in this chapter is the
assumption that your corporate behaviour is
consistent with the messages being transmitted.
US PR guru Arthur Page put it succinctly:

> Public perception of an organization is
> determined 90 per cent by doing and
> 10 per cent by talking.

So unless you're doing the right things you can't sustain an image, but if you are doing the right things you can certainly increase people's appreciation of that through public relations. As an example take a successful company at the extreme end of the 'cuddly image' scale – Virgin. The company, and in particular Chief Executive Richard Branson, had used PR brilliantly for years with devastatingly positive results. When Virgin entered the financial services business Branson's personal reputation was so high that the picture on the launch brochure cover was his smiling face. The clear implication was 'You know me – I'm the man who wants to run a non-profit making lottery, took on BA over their monopoly on routes, and made huge donations to AIDS awareness campaigns – you know you can trust me with your money.'

The doing fitted the talking and vice versa, and everything in the garden seemed rosy. Then Virgin diversified into trains – and what a PR disaster it was. No amount of 'cuddly Richard' stories could gloss over the fact that the trains didn't run on time. Even Virgin's PR, excellent as it was, couldn't change the reality. The way to improve the image of Virgin Trains was to improve the service first, then use PR to tell people about it.

Journalists are cynical by nature, and whenever they receive anything from a PR practitioner their initial reaction is to ask themselves how the perception squares with the reality. The next time you are involved in planning or commissioning a PR campaign, ask yourself the same question. If there is an inconsistency between

and deeds, the solution is simple – you
change one of them.

WHERE PR CAN HELP – AND HOW

Having looked at what PR can and cannot do in
principle, I now want to turn to the areas where it
can help in practice, then move on to examine
the way it gets results. Earlier I talked about how
PR can help to create a market for a new product
or company. But that's only the start of the story
– literally. PR has great benefits post-launch in so
many ways that the range and subtlety may
surprise you. Indeed, the only limitations on
where you can use PR are you or your agency's
imagination. As a guide, however, here are some
of the common occasions when PR is typically
most effective:

- product launch
- repositioning a mature product
- differentiating a product in the marketplace
- raising/creating interest in a product-related
  topic
- building corporate image in a way that sup-
  ports the product
- defending a product which is encountering
  negative publicity
- managing issues.

We can look at these in terms of the product's
lifecycle as follows:

Pre-launch	Preparing the market
Launch	Announcing availability
Post-launch	Maintaining interest
	Expanding the market
	Publicizing new uses
	Creating brand loyalty
	Managing decline

You will be aware which of these stages relate to
your products and your company. Over time it is
likely that most of them will be relevant. Once
you've decided to use PR in any of these circumstances your discussions with your communications department or agency (or both) will turn to
the ways in which you may achieve your objectives. PR practitioners have a wide variety of
tools at their disposal and creative PR people are
constantly developing new techniques. Your PR
budget will be spent most effectively if you are
aware of what the tools are. Unfortunately this
wide understanding is quite rare, and this leads
us to another common misconception – many
executives still believe that PR is about column
inches in newspapers. Many journalists believe
that too, and it was only after I started Lion's Den
and began working with PR practitioners on a
regular basis that I really understood what else
they do. This is why some journalists still have a
poor impression of PR practitioners. In reality
counting column inches is perfectly valid as one
measure of success in some circumstances.
However, most of the time it will only give you
part of the picture.

The view that PR is entirely about column
inches is damaging on several counts. First, it's
wrong. Second, you can have loads of column
inches but they may not say what you want – any
measurement of success must include a qualita-
tive, as well as a quantitative element. Third, if
you force your PR team to concentrate on
column inches you run the risk of not benefiting
from their other, wider skills, with consequent
reduced return on your investment. In particular, while phoning journalists and trying to persuade them to write about you is an important
part of PR, there are other techniques which
attempt to attract publicity in a less obvious way
– and that is what I want to explore now. I have
divided PR tools into two groups: those directly
focused on journalists, and others that have
another primary purpose but also offer great
opportunities for media publicity.

Direct media focus
Press releases
Press conferences
One-on-one briefings
Editorial interviews
Backgrounders
Photocalls
Feature articles
Advertorials
Facility trips for journalists
Provision of case histories
Provision of third party views
Videos, CD-ROMs and DVDs

Broadcast footage
Video news releases

Publicity vehicles
Conferences and seminars
Event press support
Newsletters and publications
Special events, e.g. round tables
Surveys
Awareness days or weeks
Campaigns
Promotional items

You may find some aspects of the list surprising and even find that some are undertaken by other agencies or consultants outside the PR discipline. For example, the production of videos or CD-ROMs may be done by a video company and promotional items such as hats, pens and T-shirts may be provided by a promotions specialist. Both activities, however, may well be managed by your PR consultancy. Each situation will differ slightly depending on the brief and the people involved. The reason is that different PR consultancies have different skills sets, partly depending on the background of their own personnel. Former journalists, for example, naturally veer towards placing stories, while those who've had any contact with Parliament usually stress the benefits of getting politicians on side. In scientific and medical fields, many PR practitioners have come from a conference and exhibition organizing background, so they will be keen on developing relationships with opinion leaders. All of these are perfectly acceptable views in the right circumstances. You must beware, however, the one-trick agency whose 'one size fits all' philosophy may not be appropriate to your specific needs. Remember – if your only tool is a hammer you're likely to suggest that the answer to all problems is a nail!

It is not necessary for you to understand the details of how these different approaches work, but a broad understanding will help you to evaluate the quality and appropriateness of PR plans being developed in your company's name. Here, then, is a brief outline of each, beginning with the group directly focused on journalists.

DIRECT MEDIA FOCUS

Press releases

These are the basic tools of PR and the bugbear of every journalist. A well-targeted, short and well-written press release is a joy to receive. Unfortunately the majority of press releases are irrelevant to the recipient, too long and terribly written. Poor PRs measure their output by counting the number of releases sent, however inappropriate. Too many executives and product managers spoil good press releases by editing them and disrupting the flow and style. Invariably they make them longer. My guidance here is simple – leave the writing to people who can write. I sometimes ask a correspondent on a national newspaper to save his mail for me at the end of a day. I then put it into a binliner and tip it on to the floor as the opener to a presentation about successful PR. The number and variety of the releases is quite a shock to the audience. The stunt makes two points – the irrelevance of the majority of releases, and the amount of competition. With this much chaff to wade through before you get to the wheat, it's also not surprising that sometimes things get missed, which is why you need a stronger relationship with a journalist than just having their address.

As one senior US PR man said to me, 'I can go on writing press releases as long as the client continues writing cheques – but it's not a course I'd recommend.' Bombarding journalists with inappropriate releases is counter-productive as it only encourages the 'groan factor' when they see the same logo popping out of the fax machine or in the post. As in so many things in media relations, less is more. Good PRs know this – so should you.

Press conferences

A press conference is a very blunt PR tool. It's not very targeted, everybody gets most of what they want but nobody gets anything extra. Most journalists with a different angle – or even a novel question – will discuss it on a one-to-one basis over the wine and nibbles after the scrum is over – no point in letting your competitors have the benefit of your creative powers. However, sometimes a blunt instrument is just what you need. A well-organized and conducted press conference gives you a rare opportunity to convey your messages direct to a large section of one of your key audiences – the media.

On this subject, journalists and PR practitioners display a rare unity of opinion – neither of them are very keen on press conferences (even though the alternative is still not apparent, but might be once the Web's bandwidth becomes greater and real-time video can be transmitted to journalists' desks). There are exceptions but many journalists don't favour them because they impose someone else's timetable on a busy schedule and generally the most they will come back with is the same story as everyone else – which as we've seen previously is OK as a back-covering exercise but not much incentive to travel halfway across town in bad traffic and awful weather. Organizing a press conference can reduce many PR practitioners to a bag of nerves because they're always worried that nobody will turn up – or at least, not many journalists (clients tend to show up mob-handed, licking their lips in anticipation).

Most press conferences are completed successfully from both viewpoints, but there is one downside for you – a 'pack mentality' can occasionally develop. This usually happens when one journalist takes exception to one of your claims (or has been a thorn in your side in advance) and starts an argument. Other journalists see the weakness in your argument and join in (sometimes they join in just for the sport) and before you know it you feel like a mass murderer in the witness box at the Old Bailey. The way to avoid it is to rehearse the main arguments as part of your media training programme and make sure the conference has a strong, independent chairman known to some of the journalists. He or she can then let the argument run for two or three questions, then say 'We have got a lot of ground to cover, so we must move on, but if you want to continue this line of questioning later, I'm sure that will be fine.' Be warned, however, that this approach will not work if you really have been overclaiming or misbehaving.

One-on-one briefings

These usually involve a senior PR practitioner briefing a key journalist (usually a specialist correspondent). You'll have a good chance of success if you can a) get the journalist to do it, and they're not diverted to another story on the day, and b) you've been honest about the strength and relevance of the story in advance – no journalist wants to feel they've been misled, whether deliberately or accidentally. If you have both these factors in your favour, journalists are often keen on this technique because it allows them to pursue their own angle on the story and get something different from the competition. Individual briefings also offer the opportunity to go into the issue in depth. Because of the speed at which news happens, briefings are often more suitable for feature articles, although they are excellent for raising awareness of a need (also known as preparing the market for launch). The journalist will want many of the other elements mentioned earlier, such as case studies and background material. The downside for you is that one-on-one briefings make great demands on your time.

Editorial interviews

Such interviews offer a virtual guarantee of success. If you can entice a journalist into a face-to-face interview your interviewee has to be boring in the extreme for the reporter not to make something out of it. The challenge is to entice the journalist into doing it. Editorial interviews are suitable for a wide range of news stories and features, but are a particular favourite with journalists on the business pages and profile writers. If you are asked to take part in an interview, success from your point of view depends on being very clear in advance about what the journalist is expecting and ensuring that they have all the background information necessary. Is it a profile piece, a straight commentary on your results or an explanation of the synergy between your company and your takeover target? Be sure you know what type of journalist you will be meeting. A news interview will be fairly straightforward, but there are some feature writers who specialize in old-fashioned hatchet jobs. If you're meeting a feature writer with any kind of reputation, ask to see previous examples of their work. If they seem to dip their pens only in vitriol it doesn't mean you should avoid them – just be prepared.

Backgrounders

A short backgrounder is an essential element of any press pack. It can be written either as a list of key points, or as a features article as outlined in Chapter 4.

Photocalls

Today's newspapers make more use of visuals than ever before and a good picture will greatly enhance your chances of coverage, particularly in the broadsheets. The key, as ever, is in the planning – and creativity is rewarded. For television, as we have seen, pictures are everything. Celebrity endorsers are ideal for photocalls.

Feature articles

You can commission feature articles by freelance journalists and pay to have them distributed by a PR features agency. The tone of the article needs to be right. It must sound like an independent piece, as opposed to an advertisement or advertorial, though of course it can be entirely favourable to your company or product. The main features agency in the UK is a subsidiary of the Press Association, which is itself an old, highly regarded 'genuine' news agency. They employ journalists who will write the piece for you and ensure that the tone is suitably journalistic. The features are then syndicated throughout the UK and are likely to appear in small regional or local newspapers.

Advertorials

These are a cross between an advertisement and an editorial. The difference between an advertorial and most other PR tools is that it has obviously been sponsored by the company and so loses the extra credibility which accrues to articles filtered through the normal journalistic selection procedure.

Facility trips for journalists

A look 'behind the scenes' can sometimes be a sufficiently tempting carrot for a journalist to write about you – as long as the scenes and the

look are interesting and relevant to the readership or audience. Ideally, both content and pictures need to offer something different or unusual. If you have a good story the content is usually easy enough. The challenge with so many businesses today is that they're not very visual, and a picture of 'people in an office working at screens' is not going to excite the picture editor. This means the content needs to be even more exciting to compensate, or you need to work harder on the visual element. However, a state of the art plant, lab or design studio may offer many opportunities. Visits to sites or plants in other countries can be even more tempting to journalists, particularly those from the regional press based in areas of the UK where you are also a leading employer.

Remember that most journalism is based on a time-related peg, so be alert to specific dates or events which make site visits particularly relevant. For example, you may have a new type of plant in another country, and the time when you've announced that the same style of operation is coming to the UK is a good time to offer journalists a facility trip. (Be careful though that this can't be tied in to a story about you cutting jobs as a result.) For example, when Wal-Mart bid for ASDA, many journalists were keen to visit a Wal-Mart store to see how it differed from UK stores and to paint a picture of the 'shape of things to come'. In this instance, of course, they were able to just turn up. In most cases it is preferable that you do the organizing and hosting, so that you have more chance of controlling what they see, if not say.

Provision of case histories

Relevant case histories convert good ideas into reality. 'Ordinary people' are also more convincing to journalists than company spokespeople. The key is to find a persuasive case study which will strike a chord with the journalist's readership or audience and immediately clear the 'What does this mean to our readers?' barrier. For maximum impact you should produce the case histories in person for interviews, as opposed to simply supplying contact details. Having the case studies attend a press conference can be a powerful way of enhancing your chances of publicity. Companies are sometimes reluctant to expose 'ordinary people' to the glare of media publicity in this way, but in my experience you have little to fear. In these circumstances journalists will not be as critical of them as they are of you and your colleagues. They regard the case studies as 'amateur' rather than 'professional' interviewees. Bear in mind, however, that the most powerful case studies are extremes, as discussed in Chapters 2 and 3, so you need to work hard to find good examples.

Provision of third party views

This technique needs sensitive handling. You run the risk of your opinion leaders losing their 'third party' status if they are seen to be too close to the company, yet independent endorsement is crucial to your success. Then when you do offer them as potential interviewees, some journalists will prefer to find their own opinion leaders. So when is a third party not a third party? The key to success here lies in the selection of the opinion leaders – go for those with the highest possible reputation among journalists. If you get a real top-notch person to endorse you, don't worry if they won't shout about it from the rooftops – they're not part of your sales force. I know some opinion leaders in the medical field, for example, who can attract more headlines if they describe a new treatment as 'interesting' than others who say 'this is a major breakthrough'. Knowing the leading opinion leaders is an important element of what your PR team bring to you – if you're looking to appoint a new team, you should press them on this.

Videos and CD-ROMs

Videos and CD-ROMs can bring the world into the newsroom – or to your press conference. They're also a powerful way of making a case if they're produced professionally with the right audience in mind. It is important to avoid the over-produced, commercial-style video which is more suited to your sales conference. Think about a short piece in the style of *Channel 4 News* or *Newsnight* – serious in tone, short on razzmatazz but addressing the key questions. If you brief your production company at the start of the project they can, with the right experience,

produce a version in the right tone to be played at the press conference.

Broadcast footage

If TV programmes are going to cover your story, make sure they've got the right pictures to illustrate it. This means your factories, labs or offices looking as clean, tidy and efficient as possible, with everyone wearing the correct clothing and headgear for the job, and the current logo subtly in shot. The way to ensure this is to supply it yourself. Get a production company to produce the footage for you. But make the images interesting (see Chapter 3 on television for more on this).

Video news releases

These are based on the same idea as broadcast footage, but pegged to a specific story on a particular day. A VNR will include footage allowing the journalist to tell the story, backed up by relevant third party and case study interviews. The interviews need to be specific to the story and so are only relevant on the day in question. The supporting pictures, however, will have a longer shelf life if they look like broadcast footage – no 'artyness' or special effects – and can be used to illustrate stories about you or your sector time and again. The key to a successful VNR is to get it professionally produced by ex-TV journalists with a background in news, as opposed to any other form of television. A good VNR should be indistinguishable from a TV news piece.

PUBLICITY VEHICLES

I now want to address the wider remit of PR practitioners – the organization of events that have their own primary objective, usually educational or relationship-building, but will also attract media publicity.

Conferences and seminars

Look through the papers, or turn on the TV or radio news and check how often you hear or read phrases like, 'A conference today heard ...'. The conference industry is big business – you probably attend or speak at a fair number yourself. A conference or seminar (which in this sense is a very small conference) gives you several bites at the same cherry. First, it allows you to bring together a number of the leading experts in your field and bring them up to date and enthuse them about your products, plans or company. This will enable you to forge relationships with some of them, and spot those who are most likely to be sympathetic to your point of view. This is often an important part of your pre-launch strategy. Second, you can invite journalists to the conference and expect coverage. There are also other publicity opportunities for pre- and post-conference stories and interviews.

The key to a successful conference is the right combination of topic, content, speakers and venue. Topical topics can be a big draw, particularly if they are backed up by big name or controversial speakers whose views are likely to attract publicity themselves. The venue is a tricky subject. Although in an ideal world all but the most fanatical hair-shirt mentality journalists would love to spend a few days at your expense in some exotic location, in reality most of their schedules don't allow it. In addition, some newspapers and broadcast organizations ban foreign travel sponsored by companies who are likely to be the subject of the resulting report. For the delegates themselves, however, it may be a different matter entirely. They may be more tempted by a conference in Barcelona or the south of France than closer to home. So inevitably you compromise and, budgets permitting, go for the exotic location because without the delegates, you don't have a story at all.

However, back in the journalist camp, all is not lost. You just need to adopt different tactics. This is where the importance of pre- and post-conference interviews becomes apparent, as the conference may provide a strong news peg for stories based around it, enabling journalists to write about the conference without actually attending. This means they will write about the content, speakers and topic, which were your key publicity objectives anyway, so with the right planning and topic you may still achieve your goals. You need to ensure that your PR team put a lot of effort into organizing the pre- and post-conference interviews.

The very big events with thousands of delegates are organized by specialist companies, but increasingly PR consultancies are setting up and running small to medium size events. With the larger ones, a PR team will be responsible for handling media publicity and running the press office for the event. As with so much PR activity the key to success lies in the planning – get the PR team involved early on so they can contribute their own ideas and spot the opportunities. Some conference organizing companies now have PR consultancies or departments within their organization. Though this may sound like a great idea, it can be a double-edged sword. Such a PR team is likely to know their way around the subject area, but their PR skills may not be up to the standard of a consultancy whose core skill is public relations. Hiring the 'one stop shop' may appear to make sound financial sense but may not give you the best chance of maximizing the publicity opportunities.

Event press support

A common complaint from journalists attending large conferences is the difficulty in finding information, contacting speakers and checking facts or statistics used in presentations. They also need somewhere to work from, with telephones, fax machines, modem points and ideally computer terminals with a printer. Your PR team are best placed to organize all this, and should be the first port of call for all journalistic inquiries about the conference itself. Make sure they have their background material and copies of all presentations in advance, to enable journalists to plan their own stories. The easier you make it for reporters to get what they need, the more likely that you will get what you want. However, never forget that a pleasant face and efficient manner will not get you into the paper if the story is not strong enough.

Newsletters and publications

These are often produced after conferences and seminars, but can also be a regular or occasional event, published with a frequency depending on what information you want to communicate. The target audience can be opinion leaders, customers, shareholders or any of the key audiences identified in the 'communications environment' exercise (p. 81).

Special events

Such events are suitable for situations where respected people in the same industry hold differing views or can offer different perspectives. The agenda can be as creative as you and your PR team can make it, but must underpin your overall communication objectives, for example raising awareness of a subject or issue. The topic usually has a futuristic and controversial feel such as 'Why should the NHS pay for lifestyle drugs?', 'On-line shopping – opportunity or threat to high street retailers?', 'Tackling traffic – is the car industry shirking its responsibilities?' These may be sponsored by a pharmaceutical company, a large retailer and a car manufacturer and offer smaller scale versions of the benefits of conferences – relationship-building with opinion leaders, amplification of views and editorial publicity – given the right subject and contributions. They are also a rare opportunity to encourage participants and the audience to think differently about a subject. Keep such events short – 90 minutes is about right – and hold them at breakfast time with free coffee and croissants.

Surveys

If anyone ever researched the most common words in the introductions of news stories, 'survey' would surely come at or close to the top. To journalists, they provide a ready-made peg, 'A survey *today* claims …' and the relevance to the audience is easy to discern. Having made those points, now the downside – surveys are so common that your own effort is certain to come up against very tough competition. Despite their success rate, many surveys are greeted with cynicism by journalists who can spot the difference between a real survey and a thinly disguised product plug a mile away. (Some product plugs still get in, however, as long as they're cleverly done.)

The key is to commission the survey from a respected polling organization, and ask questions to which we care about the answers. Take advice from your PR and media advisers on this, and remember the first question a journalist asks, 'What does this mean to my readers, listeners or viewers?'

Awareness days or weeks

This tactic was very successful until like all good ideas it was copied and then flogged to death. I saw one report which claimed that there are on average four 'awareness days' for every actual day of the year. They do still work in the right circumstances, however, for example awareness weeks sponsored by charities and medical pressure groups still attract media attention. The key to success is the same as with surveys – your corporate intentions need to take a backseat, and you need to find something different or interesting to say. One other tip – celebrities are a good way of raising awareness but only if they have some real connection with the cause. As one senior journalist said to me, 'I'm always suspicious that the celeb's main interest is in the fee they're getting for attending the photocall.' If this really is the case, save your money. Awareness weeks arranged by genuine third parties can offer good opportunities for sponsorship, which itself may attract media publicity.

Campaigns

Compaigns are a tactic best suited to organizations whose activities appear in some way socially beneficial, and if that's the area you're in they can be very successful indeed. The key to success lies in getting one or more media organizations on your side, so start by briefing your specialist correspondents on an individual basis. A campaign is like an awareness week that carries on as long as necessary but with one crucial difference: it must have a measurable objective, so when you reach it you can say, 'Great. We've won.' Without this, it is in danger of just fizzling out. For example, a campaign for more paths for ramblers will never succeed because ramblers will never say 'We've got enough paths now.' Whereas a campaign to open specific paths across a particular area has a definable endpoint, and may well succeed.

Promotional items

Baseball caps, T-shirts or bumper stickers bearing your logo won't get you into the media on their own, but they will increase awareness of your brand or company. Depending on your field of activity and the particular media opportunities, your spokespeople may be able to wear them and plug the company – but don't dress them up like a Formula One driver, plastered in sponsors' logos!

I hope this discussion has given you an idea of the enormous range of possibilities open to you if you use public relations in a focused, considered manner. So how do you choose a PR team to do it for you? That's the question I now want to address.

CHOOSING A PR CONSULTANCY

An important question here is to ask yourself whether you need an outside consultancy at all. The answer depends on a number of factors, the first one being whether you have an in-house department or person and, if so, whether they have the expertise, time and resources to run the planned PR campaign. Most organizations of any size do have an in-house communications capability, so the question then is simple – 'Can they handle what we have in mind?' The biggest obstacle may be the time they have available to take on more work. If you're putting a high-profile PR programme in place it will put considerable strain on an existing department which probably already has a full in-tray. So if, for example, you plan a high intensity programme three times a year it may suit you to use an outside consultancy for those projects. They can supply the extra resource when you need it and you won't have people sitting around less than fully occupied for the rest of the year.

With the current trend against increasing headcount in favour of outsourcing, it is likely that you will decide an outside agency does have a role to play, if only on a project basis. Before you start shopping around for one you need to be very clear about what you want them to do. This is an important consideration because you don't want to pay for expertise you already have, but you do want to buy in skills and contacts which will complement your existing capabilities.

As outlined at the start of this chapter, you need to be clear about your objectives and how they support your marketing efforts. For example, if you're a UK company planning a UK programme, you may not need an international PR consultancy whose charges may be higher. You also need to consider whether you want people to think strategically and help you with problem-solving or whether you want to devise the strategy in-house and are just looking for tacticians. You may need to bolster your in-house media contact skills, or build relationships with opinion leaders. Once you've identified your needs and objectives for the PR programme you are then in a position to start your search for an agency.

FINDING THE RIGHT AGENCY FOR YOU

First, draw up a list of potential candidates. By all means use reference books, but also ask around. Consult colleagues and friends working in the same industry – ask who they've used and what the agency's strengths are. Also inquire about their ways of working and how they relate to the client. I recommend that you draw up a list of about five potential candidates. You should ask them all to come in and give you a capabilities presentation. This will be more or less off the shelf though obviously tailored to make it relevant to what they think you need. The point here is that you're not asking them to invest a huge amount of time and effort at this stage – you're asking them to come and showcase their agency.

As you sit through the presentations, ask yourself two questions:

● Can they deliver what we need?
● Do I like them?

To answer the first one, measure your needs against their demonstrated capabilities and experience. For example, you may need a campaign which will rely heavily on contacts with journalists in one sector such as specialist or national press, TV or local radio. Have the agency demonstrated these kinds of contacts, and the ability to get results? Alternatively you may be about to embark on a market preparation campaign which will focus heavily on getting third party opinion leaders on your side, in advance of approaching journalists. Has the agency demonstrated a reliability here? If your campaign is an international one, does the agency have a reliable international network? Draw up a score card against each of your requirements.

Having answered the objective question about their capabilities, you also need to address the subjective one – do you like them? This really is very important, because if you don't get on, there's no point in taking it any further. It is impossible to overestimate the importance of the right chemistry between the client and the agency. The road you are setting out on will be very pressured at times and the relationship will come under strain. If there are simmering personality differences they are bound to surface when you most need to present a united front.

This exercise should reduce the field to two or three candidates who you decide to brief in detail. They will then come back with a considered proposal for what you want them to do. At this point you are asking them to expend a considerable amount of time and commitment. The time spent will often run into tens of thousands of pounds – a point not always understood by executives who sit on the other side of the table listening to the resulting pitches.

WHAT GOES INTO THE BRIEF?

The brief to the agencies is a vital document and needs to be well thought out. Although the candidate agencies will talk to you or other people about it, their proposals will primarily be based on your written brief. It is therefore the most important signpost to your objectives. But it is more than that. It says a lot about you and the clarity of your thinking, which is where this chapter started. A good brief is welcomed by PR consultancies and generates enthusiasm and excitement in the team who will work on it. It demonstrates that you and your colleagues have put a lot of effort into thinking about it – just the sort of clients agencies want.

Unfortunately briefs are often poor or nonexistent. A poor brief is usually a clear sign that the executives have not thought hard enough about what they really want the PR agency to do

for them. It often means that an agency spends a lot of time responding to the half-baked ideas they thought the client wanted and the end result is not what the client had in mind at all. The client then goes back to the drawing board with a clearer view, the agency feels it has invested a lot in helping the client distil their thoughts and everyone ends up dissatisfied. To cap it all, the agency which helped the distillation process is sometimes not even invited to re-pitch.

To avoid this chapter of accidents, here is a checklist of what should go into a PR brief:

- company background, including relevant experience
- market information
- product characteristics
- business objectives
- PR programme objectives
- SWOT analysis
- competitor analysis
- key audiences
- key issues
- other marketing support
- budget
- details of presentation (time, scope and audience).

Most of this list is self-explanatory so I will simply go through the key points. The starting point is a good review of the current situation. You have a lot of background information about your company, the product and the market, so why make it difficult for somebody else to find it? You should share at least enough to give an outline of the size of the market, and the percentage share your company or product currently enjoys (or expects to). You should also outline the main issues in the industry or product area, and the 'unique selling proposition' of your offering. Expect them to be keen enough to add to what you've given them to demonstrate the dedication and thoroughness they would bring to the project. Next, tell them about your commercial objectives for the product and how the PR programme's objectives support that. It's also important to spell out what other marketing support will be available – TV or newspaper advertisements, direct mail, sales force? The budget is a very important consideration, as this will allow the agency to cut its cloth accordingly.

Finally you need to outline the pitch presentation – when and where, who will be on the selection team, how long the pitch will last and what you're expecting from them.

EVALUATING THE SUCCESS OF A PR PROGRAMME

Evaluating the success of public relations programmes is a fast-developing science. It's also becoming an increasingly common and necessary part of a PR programme – the Public Relations Consultants Association has demanded that all members include measurement and evaluation of PR programmes by the end of 2000. In the first instance, measurement and evaluation will enable you to say whether your PR budget was well spent, and to justify budgets or suggest changes for the following year. But evaluation is far more than just a financial issue – if public relations is tied closely to the strategic and business aims of an organization, and if it is truly accountable, it will have earned its higher place in your company's decision-making process. Evaluation and measurement will tell you whether this is the case. Evaluation also helps with future planning because it will tell you what worked well and what was less successful. It is, therefore, an important planning tool as well as a method of post-rationalization.

In public relations terms evaluation has been a thorny topic for some years. This has partly happened because companies generally spend a lot less on PR than on advertising, yet the kind of investment required to fund a research programme to measure success would cost about the same. With most PR and advertising you are aiming to change attitudes or behaviour – measuring the change accurately is equally expensive whatever tools you've employed. Proportionally, therefore, evaluation of PR programmes seems prohibitively expensive. However, this cannot alter the fact that the most accurate evaluation starts with benchmarking research, that is asking what your key audiences think about you or your product at the start of

the programme. There are several ways to keep costs to a minimum. Tapping into existing research to obtain your benchmark and sharing costs of endpoint research, either between PR agencies or with ad agencies, will go some way. Obtaining a clear answer to the question 'Where are we now?' in this way has wider benefits and will help with your objective-setting.

Measurement is becoming an increasingly sophisticated business and new evaluation techniques are constantly being developed. Any decent communications agency should have a number of tools at their disposal – ask them as part of the pitching process how they will evaluate success. The main techniques are:

- 'before and after' research
- output and outcomes research
- media placement targets
- audience reach
- advertising value equivalent
- content analysis.

'BEFORE AND AFTER' RESEARCH

With a communications programme you are trying to produce change in attitude or behaviour. To measure the change you need to gain an accurate picture of your starting point. Surveys, omnibus research, focus groups and one-to-one interviews are effective ways of achieving this if they are conducted by reputable, independent organizations.

OUTPUT AND OUTCOME

Both output and outcome are important, but be clear about the difference. You should agree targets for both at the start of the programme. An output is a measure such as column inches, number of broadcast items, or the number of sales calls requested. An outcome is what happens as a result, for example an increase in sales or spontaneous awareness of your company or product. It may be that you can only accurately measure output because you have taken other action which will affect outcomes, such as increasing your sales force. This is perfectly acceptable as long as you know what you are aiming for.

MEDIA PLACEMENT TARGETS

At the start of a campaign you should agree targets for different media outlets with the agency. This will usually mean a specific number of pieces in the trade press, regional and national press, TV and radio.

AUDIENCE REACH

This is what the ad agencies call OTS – opportunities to see. It is based on circulation and audience figures of the media which publicized your campaign, how many people have had the opportunity to see, hear or read about you...

ADVERTISING VALUE EQUIVALENT

... and how much it would have cost to buy advertising which would achieve the same reach. Remember that editorial coverage is far more credible than advertisements, so you are getting considerable added value.

CONTENT ANALYSIS

Counting column inches alone is not enough. You need the content of the columns analysed to see how many of your key messages are included compared with other messages, for example those of your competitors or detractors.

CHAPTER SUMMARY

- At least 50 per cent of the stories which appear as general news have been influenced by PR practitioners.
- Many executives misunderstand PR and confuse it with 'spin-doctoring'.
- PR is a sustained programme of communications aimed at changing attitudes or behaviour.
- PR focuses on essential audiences.
- Mapping your communications environment will help identify the audiences.
- The media are a crucial audience because they are gatekeepers to so many others.
- Advertising and PR have different functions and techniques – do not confuse them.
- PR cannot change reality, but it can change perceptions – but it must be backed up by actions.
- PR is about more than column inches in the papers or seconds of airtime – it encompasses a wide range of tools.
- You need to decide whether and when you need an outside PR consultancy.
- The first step to having a good relationship with an agency is to brief the candidates carefully.
- Evaluating the success of PR programmes is increasingly possible – and important. Ask your agency about measurement.

CHAPTER SEVEN

Crises and Issues Management – the Media's Role

I spent much of my journalistic career covering things nobody expected to happen. Unexpected events for those concerned. Good stories for us. Crises for the companies involved. Plane, train and bus crashes; BSE-infected beef, salmonella-infected eggs; contaminated Perrier and Coca-Cola; dangerous drug side effects; disasters at football matches and on ferries; financial crashes; mass job losses; plant closures – these types of stories all march straight on to page one. There are many elements of a crisis which attract the media. It could be the size of the numbers involved, the scale of the event or the relevance to ordinary people, which fits the story neatly into the 'news is anything that makes people think, "That could be me"' category. It may be the simple element of surprise which fits the most basic definition of news, 'news is something that makes people say "Gee Whiz"'. It might be that a particular event encapsulates a wider fear or controversy. The safety fears over genetically modified crops are an example of a wider fear of the unknown and mistrust of science which non-specialists don't understand and specialists find difficult to communicate.

Many potential crises can be spotted in advance and averted. Identifying some before they occur would demand the powers of a clairvoyant. Others are caused because lifestyles change or by the actions of third parties, acting not out of malice, but in their own commercial interests. For example, when Camelot launched the UK National Lottery it didn't care whether people continued to do the football pools as long as they bought lottery tickets as well. In the event, Littlewoods Pools, which had been a dominant force in the industry for decades, soon found itself in crisis, and having to lay off nearly 3000 of its 4000 strong workforce. Some crises are caused by criminal actions, some by incompetence, others by sheer bad luck. When a toxic leak at chemical giant Sandoz polluted the Rhine, it transpired the incident was triggered by rats chewing through cables and causing a short circuit.

The many causes of crises, however, share one common element – media attention, either actual or planned. The media define a crisis, and can either fan the flames or help fight the fire. At the time of writing the future of Sellafield as a nuclear fuel reprocessing plant is in doubt after a number of scandals over safety received huge media attention. Customers began cancelling orders when the bad publicity was followed by a critical report from the authorities. It isn't only large multinational concerns that are at risk of a crisis. Any company of any size can find itself blinking in the harsh light of fierce media criticism. The scale may vary but the effect on the company will be the same – a crisis is always a defining moment for a company's reputation. The way it's handled and its outcome will colour the views of all the company's key audiences for years to come – assuming the company survives. There are many examples of serious implications: PanAm never recovered from the Lockerbie disaster, Ratners was sold off after the furore over the quality of one of its products, research into GM foods has been set back years and although many companies have survived because of their sheer size, they have seen the effects of a crisis on their balance sheets and profit and loss accounts.

The keys to successful crisis handling are preparation and planning. To start that process effectively you must believe that it could happen to you. This realization is becoming increasingly common, but unfortunately there are still too many executives who don't accept it. They still think a crisis is something that happens to someone else. Two famous advertising slogans sum up my advice as to how you should view this. The first comes from the National Lottery: 'It could be you.' The second has been the strapline for Martini ads for decades – 'Anytime, anyplace, anywhere'. That could mean today, tomorrow or on Friday evening at the start of a holiday weekend. Whatever the reasons behind the event which brings the media circus to your front desk, it's not only your corporate reputation that's at risk – your personal standing could also be on the line. Handling a crisis is a guaranteed way of getting noticed internally and externally – for better or worse. For example, the reputation of British Midland Chairman Michael Bishop was considerably enhanced by the way he handled the crash of one of his aeroplanes at Kegworth in 1989. On the other hand, one of the first business stories of 2000 was the removal of Coca-Cola chief Doug Ivester following criticism over his handling of the contamination crisis in France and Belgium in 1999. You can see how high the stakes are.

One challenge for most senior executives is that crises in most companies are extremely rare so their personal exposure to crisis handling is limited. Yet when a crisis hits, they're expected to deal with it as though they do it every day. Another worry is that as a senior executive it is unusual for you to be taken outside your comfort zone and to feel that you're not in control. This feeling of unfamiliarity can be the first destabilizing influence on your normal surefootedness and confident decision-making. Add to this your understandable nervousness at the speed with which events unfold, and a growing feeling that the media seem to know more than you and are constantly coming up with new dimensions, and you can see why the spotlight is so uncomfortable. Before you know it, not only is the crisis grabbing headlines, but so is your handling of it, and the chairman's on the phone.

I have some good news. It doesn't have to be like that. Many crises can be foreseen and they can all be managed. This chapter tells you how. My objective is to give you the tools to help you identify potential problems before they become crises, and if this process fails, to show you how to handle an actual crisis. I aim to achieve this by answering four key questions:

1 What is a crisis?
2 Can crises be averted?
3 What can you expect from the media in a crisis?
4 What should you do if a crisis strikes?

WHAT IS A CRISIS?

Crisis is an overused word in many companies. Just as some people claim to have the flu when they've really got nothing worse than a bad cold, some executives claim to have a crisis when they're just having a difficult day at the office. For example, I was in a meeting with the MD of a large company one day when he was called away 'to sort out a crisis'. It transpired that some Balkan refugees had stowed away in one of the company's delivery vehicles. A potential problem, and a sad state of affairs for the frightened family found huddled in a truck, but hardly a crisis. On another occasion I was with the directors of a large travel company when news came through that a Turkish extremist group had declared European holidaymakers 'legitimate targets' for attack. The company had bookings to take more than 100 000 Britons to Turkey that summer. That was certainly a potential crisis which could have had a substantial effect on their business had the threat been more serious.

So what is a crisis, and what is just a bad day? There are a number of good definitions of a crisis, but this one summarizes the essential points:

> A serious incident or series of events
> which affects human safety, the
> environment and/or product or
> corporate reputation and which has
> received or is threatened by adverse
> publicity.

You need all three of these elements – the incident(s), the threat to reputation and media publicity – to be experiencing a crisis. The last one is in many ways the most important, because without media attention the threat to your reputation is considerably reduced. If you can keep the story out of the media then handling the problem becomes an internal issue, where external forces are less likely to wrest control of the situation from you. Be careful, though, that the media does not become the sole focus of your efforts to the detriment of sorting out the problem which precipitated the crisis. The media will be gone next week but you will still have a business to run and want it functioning normally again as quickly as possible.

Some crises build up over time while others just arrive out of the blue – a crash is an example of the latter, while a trickle of reports about side effects of a new drug falls into the former category. These two types of crises offer you very different opportunities to prepare your strategy and tactics, but if you take on board the advice in this chapter you should be as well prepared as possible for either.

CAN CRISES BE AVERTED?

The simple answer is 'very often, yes'. If not averted completely, the impact of many crises could be minimized by preparation and prompt action. This section looks at how to do that. Almost all crises develop from one (or more) of four categories:

● disasters
● an issue which has escalated out of control
● serious financial problems
● criminal activities.

Of these, criminal activities, such as extortion, kidnap or sabotage, are the most difficult to avert, but even here you can increase security and take heed of warnings. The likelihood of a disaster happening on your patch can often be reduced by identifying weaknesses in your operation and putting them right by replacing out-of-date, worn-out plant and machinery, for example, or by investing more in training. Issues can be identified in advance and appropriate action taken to manage them before they escalate, and avoiding financial problems is part of your normal responsibility. The key to successful crisis management – and where possible, preventing or minimizing the effects of the crisis – is in *contingency planning*. This takes two forms:

● issues management
● preparedness planning.

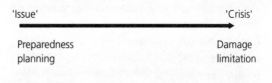

'Issue'	'Crisis'
Preparedness planning	Damage limitation

Figure 7.1   The issue–crisis continuum

ISSUES MANAGEMENT

This involves identifying all the issues that may pose problems for you and taking appropriate steps to either prevent them or minimize their effect. The link between issues and crises is an important one to understand. An unmanaged issue is a crisis waiting to happen. The two exist on a continuum, as illustrated in Figure 7.1. The position you occupy on that scale dictates your options, from prevention to damage limitation.

An *issue* is something that may affect you in the future – next week, next year or even further ahead. A *crisis* is a problem that is here now, preventing 'business as usual'. I think of an issue as a speck on the horizon which may be a tornado. If you spot it early enough and recognize it for what it is, you can take evasive action – that's issue management. However, if the tornado hits and you find yourself repairing the damage and clearing up the mess while attempting to operate normally, that's crisis management. Increasingly large companies set great store by tornado-spotting. The main objective of issue management is to prevent an issue developing into a crisis. For example, the number of reports claiming that mobile telephones might cause brain damage is an issue for you if you're in that sector. It takes time for a groundswell of opinion to build up and if you use that time to prepare counter arguments you will have a good chance of avoiding the type of crisis which has hit the genetically modified food industry as a result of other scientific reports.

Horizon-scanning

I now want to introduce some tools for identifying potential issues for your company, calculating where your business is at risk and prioritizing the action you need to take. In recognition of the tornado analogy we call these horizon-scanning exercises. Here I am going to concentrate on three:

- the nightmare scenario
- PESTLE analysis
- quadrant analysis.

The nightmare scenario

This simple exercise is designed to get all potential issues out in the open. It involves getting the senior executives and managers together in one room and asking the question: 'What part of the business which comes under your responsibility gives you most concern?' The answers can be illuminating – and some of them may horrify you. It is not uncommon to find companies sailing close to the wind with some specific problem which has been swept under the carpet, ignored for financial reasons or mentally filed away under 'too hard'. The reason these sessions are so useful is that it is rare that anyone specifically asks this question and looks at the whole situation in the round. When you do, you may find several ticking time bombs which could go off at any time. Once they are brought out into the open you can start making plans to defuse them. Which brings me to the next exercise.

PESTLE analysis

PESTLE is an acronym which will provide you with a framework for identifying issues which, if not managed, could turn into crises for your company:

P	Political
E	Economic
S	Social/sociological
T	Technological
L	Legal
E	Environmental.

(This used to be called a pest analysis – the addition of legal and environmental concerns illustrates how corporate life has changed in recent years.) As a normal business practice you will always be on the lookout for potential issues. The advantage of the PESTLE analysis is that it acts as an *aide-mémoire,* a checklist of where to look. Almost all of your issues can be grouped under these six headings. The point of the exercise is to identify them. Again this should be carried out by your senior executives and managers gathered in one room to encourage free-flowing discussion. Your own list will be specific to your company and industry sector, but here are the types of issues often identified by a pestle analysis.

Political

Impending legislation, whether from European, UK or Scottish Parliaments, the Welsh or Northern Ireland Assemblies or other forms of devolved UK government, for example the London Mayor and Assembly, can adversely impact your business. If you are running a restaurant or retail chain, for example, minimum pay and working hours directives may throw up new challenges for you. Restrictions on advertising (for example to children) may curtail some of your activities, and proposals for taxes and levies could have far-reaching effects on your business. Don't forget to analyse potential issues thrown up by your local authorities, for example changes in planning policy.

Economic

Some economic issues are provoked by political decisions, for example a strong pound or high interest rates. Others are a combination of political and economic. For example, the differing tax rates on levied new cars in Europe and the availability of dealers who help customers buy and import a new car from abroad have been a growing threat to the UK car industry. Your results, interims, share price, dividends and the rest of the tools of analysis are also of constant interest to the business media – and any hint of poor performance can knock confidence and soon affect the rest of your business. Directors' pay and share options will also come under this heading.

Sociological

Personnel issues are mainly identified under this heading. Job losses and other aspects of headcount are obvious ones, as are claims for unfair dismissal. You may also find yourself coming under fire for the working conditions of your contractors (about which you may know very little). In 1999 some big names attracted adverse publicity when it was claimed some of their subcontractors were employing child labour in India and the Far East to make clothes and sporting goods. Other conditions such as maternity (and paternity) leave could pose problems here, as can arguments over pensions.

Technological

Charles Darwin's theory of evolution – adapt or die – is back in fashion with the dominance of information technology. The biggest issue here is simple – 'How will the Internet affect our business?' With surveys forecasting the end of the high street as we know it, more music moving to the Web and online dealing democratizing stockbroking, the question is not whether your company will be affected, but in what way and to what extent. There are then the industry-specific questions. Is the whole technological basis of your industry about to change (consider the inroads DVDs appear to be making into the video cassette market)? If so, what's your position? Enthusiastic embrace, or dyed-in-the-wool Luddite?

This heading should also prompt you to consider the older technology on which parts of your business depend, and which may provoke an immediate crisis if it goes wrong or breaks down. Is all your crucial equipment up to date, working efficiently and safely? Have you put off some capital expenditure for two or three years, so some piece of kit is now reaching a critical point of efficiency or safety?

Legal

The world is becoming more litigious. Increasingly you will be asked to justify corporate decisions and actions in a legal environment, whether courts, councils or committees. You probably already consult your corporate lawyers far more frequently than even five years ago – and this graph is on a steep upward curve. If any of your actions are in any way controversial, ask yourself this question, 'How will it look at the inquest?' (I use inquest here in a non-literal sense, though tragically this will not always be the case.) Legal issues not only provoke crises in the media, but can also be a severe drain on your corporate purse.

Environmental

Probably the fastest-growing area of potential problems for businesses is the environment. Unwanted emissions; stricter anti-pollution controls; the effects of traffic fumes leading to anti-company car measures; increasing concern about the habitats of rare birds and animals which may scupper your building plans; and very media-savvy environmental campaigners always ready to tell their side of the story to eager journalists – usually backed up by emotive pictures, these issues provide very fertile ground for crises.

Quadrant analysis

So you've carried out the two exercises outlined above, and now have a page full of issues. Each one is a potential crisis, and it's not uncommon at this stage for you to be surprised how many there are. You may feel that if you endeavoured to put them all right you wouldn't have any budget left for anything else! That's where the final exercise is useful. A quadrant analysis is a way of prioritizing the relative importance of all your issues. Every issue can be assessed in terms of risk and exposure, that is how likely is it to happen, and if it does, how exposed will you be on a number of fronts, principally media, legal and financial? A quadrant analysis as illustrated in Figure 7.2 allows you prioritize your issues.

If you plot your issues on this graph you will see that the most threatening issues are those

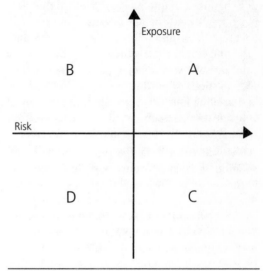

Figure 7.2   Prioritizing your issues using quadrant analysis

with a high likelihood of happening coupled with almost certain high exposure – those in quadrant A. Your next task is to take steps to move them out of this quadrant. In many cases you can achieve this by changing the practice or piece of equipment causing concern. For example, if your manufacturing plant uses flammable chemicals and you're worried about the crisis potential of a fire, you can upgrade your fire alarms or increase security. If you're worried about new employees handling the dangerous chemicals you can invest more in training. If you're running a railway you can decrease the likelihood of collisions by upgrading the signalling equipment. In these cases you are buying your way from quadrant A to B. You will still attract adverse publicity if an accident happens, but you have reduced the likelihood of such an event.

In some cases you can reduce the risk of negative media coverage by preparing the ground in advance. This usually means putting the situation into context, so that journalists write their stories based on the full picture, rather than those parts provided by a range of sources from 'common knowledge' (which may be wrong) to the 'other side' in a high profile dispute. This technique is useful when you are faced with the start of an unjustified campaign, for example over environmental issues or allegations of unsafe or unethical practices. If the campaign takes hold the allegations could damage your reputation and will consume large amounts of management time. Much better to take the wind out of the campaigners' sails before they pick up speed by putting the matter into context and briefing journalists on the true position as you see it. The issues would then move from quadrants A to C. This technique, however, only works if you really are the innocent victims of unjustified allegations. If you're guilty you will only succeed in drawing more attention to yourself.

As an example of how briefing journalists may avert a crisis, take the process of xenotransplantation, or using pigs' organs for human transplants. If we all woke up one morning to find, with no previous warning, that a man or woman had been given a pig's heart our reactions may vary from disgust to horror and fear of what pig illnesses may be transmitted into the human race. If, on the other hand, the first operation had been preceded by much open debate in the media, with leading scientists, pressure groups and people waiting for transplants all putting their points of view, much of the reaction would be different. You can see, I hope, that the ways of moving an issue out of quadrant A are a matter for you and your company, but buying or briefing your way out are the most common.

Over time your objective will be to move as many issues as possible towards quadrant D. There will always be some issues which remain in quadrant A – they are your priority, where you need to be best prepared.

An important point to realize is that your horizon is constantly changing. New specks appear frequently so you need to carry out these scanning exercises regularly to remain prepared. Even then, there will always be the occasional problem which is impossible to predict. The farsightedness of some issues managers, however, is truly impressive. For example, when the BSE problems first came to light in the UK, one pharmaceutical company realized that the gelatine coating of some of their tablets came from British cows. The risk from it was so minute it was impossible to calculate. However, as media publicity is about impression as much as reality, the company decided to change the coating. They had the new coating in place before anyone thought to ask about it so there was no problem.

PREPAREDNESS PLANNING

Identifying and managing the potential issues is only half the story. The other half is preparing for what to do if any of them blows up into a crisis. In reality there are some overlaps between issues management and preparedness planning. Where this is the case, the manner and order in which you carry out the recommended tasks is less important than the fact that you do them.

There are several ways of preparing your company to handle a crisis. I prefer a structured approach which minimizes the chances of missing anything. When I am called into a company to advise on their crisis preparedness (ideally well in advance of having to use the back door to avoid the media pack at the front), I adopt a four stage procedure:

- audit
- prepare
- test
- refine.

Let's examine each of these steps in turn.

Audit

This is an audit of vulnerabilities, and aims to identify where you are at risk in terms of your crisis preparedness. Depending on the business you are in, there will be some areas where you are better prepared than others. For example, if you are in oil or chemicals and your business involves transporting dangerous substances around the world, you will probably be very well prepared for an accident or toxic spillage (though the way some companies have dealt with such events in recent years suggests otherwise). A vulnerabilities audit will check how prepared you are for these types of events, and also measure your level of preparedness for other events which are much less likely, but will also attract huge media publicity if they do transpire. The audit should provide a snapshot of your crisis preparedness. It can be divided into two parts: the processes and the content. To provide an outline of what should be included in a crisis audit, let's go through a rough audit of your own company's crisis preparedness.

To check your processes, ask yourself these questions:

- Do you have a crisis management plan?
- When was it last reviewed? (Any more than six months ago and you're living on borrowed time.)
- Do you have a crisis management team, and do they all know their roles in the plan?
- Can they all be contacted quickly in an emergency?
- Do they all have deputies to cover for holidays and sickness?
- Do the switchboard and reception staff know how to cope with a deluge of media calls?

- Do they know where media calls should be referred, and what to say to journalists?
- Would the plan work over a holiday weekend, or while most of the country is partying over Christmas and New Year?
- Do you have a room which would be used as a control centre for media calls?

So much for the logistics – now let's consider the content.

- Have you carried out the exercises explained earlier and identified likely issues which could become crises?
- Have you done all you can to minimize the risk?
- Do you have spokespeople media trained and ready to give interviews?
- Are your key messages co-ordinated and accessible to relevant personnel?
- Are they up to date?
- Do you have background briefing materials on all your products and services?
- Do you know (or can you find out quickly) when the last fire drills and Health and Safety Executive checks were conducted?
- Are you confident that independent opinion leaders will be supportive if the media contacts them?

The more times you answer 'yes' to these questions, the higher your state of crisis preparedness. With both the logistics and content in place if a crisis does break you will be free to concentrate on the unfolding events and changing picture.

Prepare

How did you do? Whether you scored high or low, you now know where you stand. Your next task is to fill in the gaps revealed by the audit. It may mean going to an outside firm of crisis consultants to develop a crisis management plan, or updating the contact numbers in the plan. It may mean upgrading to newer technology which will enable you to contact key personnel quickly in an emergency. Your audit might have revealed that your key messages for some important products are out of date. Another possibility is that contacts with independent third party opinion leaders may not be as strong as you'd like. You can remedy this by launching (or re-launching) a programme of opinion leader development. This part of the four-stage procedure is crucial – I recommend that you brief a senior person to take it on as a project, and set a date for completion and regular reporting back.

Test

You now need to test your crisis management plan. Parts of this process are simple, some are very sophisticated. You can also do it in stages. As a start you should test your crisis management team callout procedures. This is simple – you just arrange for them to be called at an inconvenient time, say 9 p.m. on a Saturday, and see how many respond to the call, and how quickly. At this stage you may want to just log the fact that they've called in, and end the test there. Or you may want to go so far as calling them together into the crisis room, making sure it's accessible and all the communications are working. In this case, you may not want to do it at such an inconvenient time, and some companies give a warning that 'there will be a test sometime within this week'. This minimizes the disruption to normal business, while still retaining an element of surprise.

The next step in testing is a desktop exercise. This is usually done during office hours, and normally involves an outside crisis consultancy. You need to brief them fully on the type of crisis which may hit your business, and allow them to come up with a realistic scenario, usually based on a 'worst case' hypothesis. You may tell the crisis management team in advance that there's going to be a test during a particular week, or even on a specific day (though not the specifics of what it may entail). The team will gather in a large meeting room, or sometimes in the crisis control room, and be put through their paces by the crisis consultancy. Different consultancies will run the session in their own way. My method is to start with a fake TV or radio broadcast which immediately plunges the company into a crisis which gets worse as the exercise progresses. Other aspects unfold as the day goes on, designed to put different parts of the crisis man-

agement plan under pressure, for example customers, regulators, ex-employees, opinion leaders, politicians and pressure groups will all play a part in making life difficult for the crisis team. Throughout it all, the media are putting pressure on and ensuring that the team are trying to hit a moving target. If you are an international business you can complicate the exercise by running it across different time zones which will replicate the extra problems your geographic spread could pose in a real crisis.

Once the session is over you need to look at what went well and what didn't work, then make recommendations for improvement.

The most extreme form of testing is a full crisis simulation. This involves a substantial financial outlay and can be as detailed and realistic as your budget allows. The aim here is to simulate a real crisis as far as possible (without going so far as real deaths or injuries!). In some industries the exercises are required by law – airports, for example, have to run them regularly. They work with the emergency services (police, fire and ambulance) to make the exercises as realistic as possible, even hiring 'extras' to play the parts of dead and injured passengers. How far you go down this line depends on your line of business, and your resources.

Refine

The final element of preparedness planning is to learn the lessons from the previous parts, and build them into your processes. In particular it is likely that the tests will have shown up deficiencies. Based on these, you will need to refine your crisis management plan. The plan should always be evolving – it just changes more dramatically after the exercises (or after a real crisis) than during normal business.

WHAT CAN YOU EXPECT FROM THE MEDIA?

Given the theme of this book you may have been surprised by the lack of focus on the media so far in this chapter. That's because you need to get all the preparatory work done behind the scenes in advance of the crisis breaking – well before the media arrive. Once the crisis breaks all of your backstage preparations may be examined – if you've carried them out properly you have a great chance of surviving the crisis intact. In a crisis there is virtually nothing which reporters regard as off-limits if they feel it is relevant to the problem. Your actions and procedures relating to the cause (or potential causes) of the crisis will come under intense media scrutiny – that's why it is worth investing properly in the preparation. Safety drills, equipment checks, training of personnel, evacuation procedures, prior warnings about potential problems – they're all the subject of media inquiries, and that's why you need to check them before the media do.

So, the media define a crisis by their presence, and are the driving force in developing it, forcing you to respond to an unfamiliar and changing situation. Executives who've been through a crisis often speak of 'hitting a moving target' or 'finding the goalposts have moved'. Much of that is due to media pressure, so handling the media is a crucial part of successful crisis management – in some circumstances, the major part. If you follow the advice here you will maximize your chances of meeting your objectives.

A word first on that very point – objective-setting. As so often, identifying what you hope to achieve at the start of a programme will give you the greatest chance of doing so. It is the same in a crisis – you need to set objectives at the very first meeting of the crisis management team. In this situation, being realistic is the key – and that can be very difficult when viewed from the inside. In most crises your company – or someone on its behalf – has done something wrong. This means that in relation to this incident your corporate image is starting in the negative area of the scale. Success may mean restoring it to neutral for the time being – achieving a healthy positive position may well take longer. You are unlikely to come up smelling of roses. If you realize this you will be able to set realistic, attainable objectives for the outcome of the crisis and the longer term.

If you've identified your troublesome issues correctly and set about managing them, you really do have time to plan your strategy and get your defences organized. Use this time wisely for your internal preparation and external

briefings with journalists and a range of opinion leaders.

The philosophy of crisis planning can be summarized as, 'Hope for the best but prepare for the worst'. For example, if there is a memo in existence expressing worries about an aspect of your operation which subsequently proves correct, expect it to surface. Even worse, expect to find someone waving it on the TV news. If you start with this attitude, most developments won't match up to that scale of disaster, so at least your worst nightmares won't be coming true.

So what can you expect from the media? In Chapter 2 on the journalist's role I attempted to put you in the minds of journalists going about their normal day-to-day business. In a crisis, media behaviour changes. In a nutshell all the elements of a reporter's role – the speed, pressure and competitiveness – become even more extreme. Their personal views, which tend to be in favour of the underdog, may also become apparent and find their outlet in scepticism, cynicism and suspicion of the corporate world. They may take a 'David versus Goliath' stance. Bearing in mind that in most crises you are starting from a position where something has gone wrong and innocent people have been aggrieved, hurt or even killed, this view is not always surprising. In the emotionally charged atmosphere of a crisis, emotion and sympathy for the victims may be the natural reaction of the readers – and journalists, as we have seen, are usually fully in touch with the feelings of the readers.

In 'normal' circumstances journalists often share the following traits:

- sceptical of simple explanations
- cynical of corporate objectives
- curious and resourceful in seeking information
- confident in demanding answers of senior people unused to being questioned
- on the side of the underdog
- belief that 'people have a right to know'.

In the extreme environment of a crisis these feelings can increase, and lead to a more extreme set of perceptions:

Individual	Corporate
Small	Big
Weak	Strong
Poor	Rich
Truthful	'Economical with truth'
Victim	Villain
= innocent	= guilty

This picture is certainly not the view of all journalists, but it is likely that there will be some reporters covering your crisis who hold these views, so you should be prepared.

The extent to which these exaggerated perceptions apply to you will depend on a number of factors. The most important one by far is how the journalist regards you just before the crisis hits. It is impossible to over-emphasize the importance of relationship-building in advance of a crisis. If the first time a journalist hears from you is when you've got a problem, you have a mountain to climb in terms of your corporate credibility. Conversely, if the journalist knows and respects you and your company you have every chance of emerging from the situation as positively as possible given the caveats mentioned earlier. Relationships with journalists are even more important in times of crises than in normal situations because of this simple but often overlooked fact:

> Nobody wants to lend you an umbrella
> in the rain.

Crises caused by criminal activity tend to be viewed differently by the media because in these cases you are the victim and are likely to get a more sympathetic hearing. For example, privatized water companies have come in for severe media criticism over profits and alleged 'fat cat' salaries. Yet when there was a blackmail plot to poison water supplies in England by an Irish terrorist organization the water companies were portrayed as victims and the coverage was very much in their favour. There is one important proviso even here – you must have been seen to take all reasonable precautions to prevent the criminal activity. For example, if there was a terrorist or kidnap threat against your employees but you chose to ignore it, you can expect to come under fire if they are then kidnapped or harmed.

Media relationships, then, can have quite a bearing on the reporting of crises. However, even if you have an excellent relationship with a journalist, you cannot expect them to pull any punches if you've done something wrong or neglectful. If there has been an accident and people have been killed or injured and you hadn't taken the right precautions then you will quite justifiably find yourself facing difficult questions. Remember, as with all journalistic interactions, this is not a personal vendetta – the journalist's role is to ask the questions anyone would ask if they had the opportunity. In a crisis, this includes the aggrieved, the victims and their families.

JUDGING THE IMPACT

If you know you may have a problem coming up, you will want to estimate the likely impact and coverage. This is only feasible up to a point because news forecasting is more art than science and cannot be done in isolation. As already discussed, it depends on so many factors including what other stories are around. My advice is to prepare for the worst however much publicity you think you may attract. Expect much work done in crisis preparation to be wasted, and regard this as a sign that you are ahead of the game. However, I can give some general guidance which will help you to judge the likely impact of your story on the news schedules. To interest the media and become a crisis, most problems feature all the following elements:

- something is at stake
- someone finds out
- someone is to blame
- it concerns or affects the readers or audience.

The considerations for journalist are the same as for any normal news story (it just scores more points on a mythical 'news value' scale):

- What happened?   An explosion? A sex scandal? A financial crash? How unusual (or sometimes how common) is it?
- What else is around?   Quiet or busy newsday? Does this story fit naturally with another one today?

• Who is affected?	Babies? Children? Famous companies or brands? A celebrity?
• How many affected?	The more people affected the stronger the story.
• When did it happen?	Is it new or at least being brought to light?
• Why did it happen?	Apparent negligence? Management incompetence? Sheer bad luck? Crazy employee?
• Other factors	Easy to cover – is there a crew nearby? Is this the editor's favourite topic?
• Linkage	Can it be linked to another similar problem? Does it illustrate a trend?

Assuming the story survives this inquisition, the amount of coverage then depends on factors such as:

• how big are you?
• how good is your reputation?
• luck
• fashion.

If you consider your particular problem in this way you will get a rough idea of its likely impact. However, prepare as though you were heading for the lead story on the BBC News – and remember that Lady Luck always plays a role.

WHAT SHOULD YOU DO IF CRISIS STRIKES?

However well prepared you are, events will sometimes overtake you, and I now want to turn to what to do when that happens. When crisis strikes the eye of the storm, that calm region in the centre, is the best place to be. With the right preparation, that should describe the atmosphere in your crisis control room. Assuming you have a well-developed crisis management plan and are well prepared in terms of your background materials, key messages and available internal spokespeople and third party opinion leaders, the first important point is that you and your team face two distinct challenges:

• managing the problem
• managing the media.

It is important that these two tasks are delegated to different teams and handled separately. As the crisis unfolds and media pressure becomes more intense it is easy to divert too many resources to handling the media to the exclusion of sorting out the problem. The only person who should play a role in both of these teams is the chairman of the crisis management team. He or she must be a very senior executive with sufficient authority to make decisions and ensure that they are carried through. The chief executive, site manager or general manager is usually the best choice.

Once the crisis management team have been called together, you need to quickly define the problem you are facing and set objectives for the outcome. I recommend that you set up three flipcharts in the crisis control room. On one, list what you know. On the second, what you don't know. During the crisis some elements will move from 'don't know' to 'know' as the picture becomes clearer. Most people find this some level of comfort – it's a psychological boost that you are making progress. Other questions will crop up and ensure that the 'don't know' chart is always full but you should treat them in the same way. The third chart is for the schedule of media interviews. This should include name of spokesperson, identity of journalist, time and location. The three charts together focus the team on what needs to be done – in terms of the problem and the media – and are a handy snapshot of the situation at any moment. This can be helpful for team members who have to leave the control room to deal with another aspect of the problem, or to do interviews.

While the people responsible for logistics are unlocking the control room and setting it up, your senior team members, led by the chief executive, should be deciding on the strategy and setting objectives. You may decide to come out with guns blazing or to lie low. Whether you decide to adopt a high or low profile partly depends on your corporate culture – one approach or the other will usually 'feel right' for you. You also need to consider whether there are other organizations around who could take the first blast of heat. For example, when a Ministry of Agriculture report claimed that 'gender-bending' chemicals had been found in nine leading brands of baby milk, the leading manufacturers decided to put the industry body forward as spokespeople, rather than individual companies. This allowed the industry to present a united front. You can see the same in other sectors where there is a strong and reputable trade group – the Association of British Travel Agents or the Society of Motor Manufacturers and Traders for example.

This leads to an important decision which needs to be taken early in a crisis – who will be your spokesperson? Your choice says a lot about how seriously you are treating the situation – choosing the CEO or executive chairman sends a clear signal that your company are giving this the highest priority and this will normally gain you credibility. However, there are two potential downsides. First, the CEO might not be the best communicator or may not convey the right image. In most crises you need to show concern and sympathy and if your company is in the wrong a touch of humility. These qualities are not always in evidence in the kind of people who reach such dizzy heights! Emotions often run high in crises, and people of that seniority often tend to respond on a purely intellectual and analytical basis. Rather than taking the heat out of the situation this can fan the flames. One example was the Railtrack executive who condemned the 'hysteria' surrounding the Paddington disaster in 1999. Intellectually his view that 'My company is being pilloried because somebody else's driver went through one of our lights which was working perfectly' was correct. Emotionally though it sounded like an attack on the victims' families, and grabbed its own share of the headlines the next day.

Second, if you do field your top person and the situation gets even worse, you don't have anyone more senior to bring in for the next stage of the battle. You've deployed your biggest gun and it's not won the war. In reality, with the right preparation and forethought, this should not happen. In addition, CEOs usually have extra credibility because of their position which will carry them through most difficult circumstances as long as they behave in a dignified, courteous manner. Credibility can, however, be a fragile thing, as the British Gas Chairman Cedric Brown found when he locked himself in his office to try and avoid pursuing journalists questioning his remuneration package – avoid this type of behaviour at all costs!

HANDLING THE MEDIA

Once the story's out, you've got your spokesperson and there's a media scrum at the front gate you will come under intense pressure to play the game by the journalists' rules. For example, they will demand interviews to suit their timetable. Be as helpful and prompt as possible, but don't rush into anything if you're not ready. It is not uncommon for a TV news crew to arrive with a live links truck almost without warning. You may then receive a call from the reporter saying 'We're going live in five minutes from outside your building – we really want to put your case and we need someone to do it.' In most cases you should refuse a request at such short notice and in such a location. Tell the reporter you would be happy to be interviewed but five minutes is not enough notice. Arrange an appointment for a more suitable time and place – say, in your office or a conference room in 45 minutes (depending on their deadline).

It is important to be responsive to journalists' needs and deadlines, but not at the expense of your own credibility and preparation. To make the best of interviews you should only give them on your terms. This means when your spokesperson is ready, not when the reporters want it. You should, however, do all you can to ensure that your spokesperson is ready as soon as possible, and always be alert to the possibility that your timescale may not fit theirs perfectly. The earlier you say something the more opportunity for your views to be circulated at the same time as those of your critics (there are always critics in a crisis) rather than afterwards. If you leave it too long you risk your critics making all the running and setting the agenda, and may find yourself always struggling to catch up. Given the importance of the early strike, how do you make sure your views are heard, without exposing an unprepared spokesperson to a potentially difficult interview? The answer is by issuing a holding statement.

Holding statements

In the early stages of a crisis journalists want to know the answers to just three questions:

1 What has happened?
2 Whose fault was it?
3 What are you doing to prevent a recurrence?

At this stage it may not be possible to answer these questions fully. A holding statement is a way of buying time until you can release more information. It ensures that your view is heard against the background noise, and gives the journalists something to include in their report. Most holding statements can be written to the CAP formula: concern, action, perspective, that is express concern, say what you're doing, and put the incident into perspective. In more detail, it involves making the following points:

● the company is/is not aware
● express concern (not liability)
● working to establish facts
● fuller statement later
● positive experience to date.

In the majority of cases you will be aware of what has happened, so a holding statement after a fatal fire and explosion in a factory, for example, may read:

> Bloggs Electronics sincerely regrets the loss of life and injuries caused by this morning's incident and we send our heartfelt sympathy to the families of those affected. We are working to establish exactly what happened and will issue a further statement as soon as we have anything to add or by 12 noon today at the latest. In the meantime the whole site has been closed and all non-essential staff have been sent home on full pay. Bloggs have been on the Any-town site since 1956, and this is the first serious accident in all that time. For further information please contact Ivor Storey on 02028 123 456.

That's it. Keep it short because most reporters will only use one or two lines from it. Save the detail for later. It is important to tell the media when to expect more details, as this helps their planning and logistics. It is even more important to end on a positive note because it helps to put the incident into perspective – if you don't do that, nobody else will.

After the first report of a crisis journalists' demands for information start to widen and deepen. They will want more details to add to the basic questions outlined earlier. This is where the advantage of separate teams for the media and the problem start to pay off. While your media team have been fielding initial inquiries and ensuring everyone has the holding statement your problem team have been finding out more answers to feed the media team for the next round of inquiries. The process should advance on parallel tracks in this way throughout the crisis.

News in a crisis

The way that 'news' is produced in a crisis can easily catch out the unprepared executive. The first challenge is the speed with which events unfold. The speed of news catches out many executives on ordinary stories – in a crisis it happens even faster. In the late 1990s a story broke involving a hospital in Wales where a pregnant woman prisoner had given birth while shackled to a bed. The story first appeared in a local paper at 11.30 a.m. and caused outrage. By lunchtime – just 90 minutes later – every national newspaper had contacted the hospital, the spokesperson had given five radio interviews and was preparing to go live on the BBC and ITN lunchtime news programmes. One definition of news is 'history written in a hurry'. In a crisis the slogan of a popular radio news bulletin is more appropriate – 'News at the speed of sound'. This is why you need to do as much preparation as possible in advance – this is no time to start looking for information for background briefings.

Another element that distinguishes a crisis from a 'normal' news story is the identity and type of reporter who turns up to cover it. Crises are often covered by the 'hard news' reporters sent by the news desk in place of your specialist contacts. In the trade they're known as 'firemen' (though in reality many are women – political correctness has some way to go in newsrooms). This can alter the normal atmosphere of your interviews and press conferences dramatically – hard news reporters have no relationship with you and are unlikely to see you again once the crisis is over. As individuals most of them are interesting, witty company with a fund of amusing stories. As a bunch though, they're hard-nosed, cynical hacks with a natural suspicion of 'big business' and one clear aim in mind – getting the story at almost any cost. The cosy media briefings you've enjoyed in the past as you've unveiled your new products to specialists are a far cry from this situation. This is one reason why crisis training is essential for all companies of any decent size – it will give you a taste of what's to come.

Yet here executives often miss a trick. Because the specialist correspondents are not in the media scrum, they assume they have no role in the story. This is a mistake. Next time you see a newspaper report of a crisis, look at the bylines, or the names of the reporters who've covered the story. You will always see the specialist correspondents as well as the 'firemen'. The correspondent back at the office has a crucial role. He or she usually has a better grasp of the context and has the luxury of seeing a fuller picture, thanks to the different angles coming from numerous sources, including the news agencies and reporters at the scene. The correspondent's job is to add context and insight to the straight reporting. Very often they actually write the story from the screens of copy produced by the others. This gives you a great opportunity. If you know them, ring them and put your side of the story. Too many companies ignore this valuable route into the heart of the newspaper, radio or TV station. Make sure you're not one of them.

What to expect

Time, speed, volume and aggression are common elements of reporters' behaviour in most crises. And there are many other facets of crisis reporting, which if you know about them you can take in your stride.

Expect initial reports to be confused, inaccu-

rate and sometimes wildly speculative. Journalists initially have little to go on, and have a duty to report what they can. Very often this means unreliable and inconsistent eyewitnesses. You have a chance to correct inaccuracy once you have established the facts and started talking to the media. Correcting mistakes and damping down speculation is another reason for saying something – even if that just means issuing a holding statement – as soon as you reasonably can.

At some times during the crisis expect journalists to know more than you do. This can be disconcerting but may not be anything to worry about. The rules here are, with every new allegation, hold your nerve and check the facts, and never comment on speculation. The fact that you are temporarily trailing in the information stakes doesn't necessarily mean your lines of communication have broken down. It may just be that one of the other parties involved in the crisis has given a news conference, and the reporters are faithfully reporting it back to you for your reaction. Or …

… the rumour mill works overtime with a media pack. Hanging around outside a company HQ waiting for something to happen encourages feverish speculation which can quickly become accepted as fact by others in the press pack. Journalists live in terror of missing an angle and seeing it turn up on a rival front page. In addition, desk-bound news editors sometimes seem to harbour grudges against reporters who have the freedom of the road. One way of getting their own back is to constantly demand that increasingly ridiculous angles are checked out. Having been in this position my first reaction (when I was sure it was only wild speculation) was to check out the angle with one or two friends in the press pack. Every time the rumour is passed on to a new person or group it becomes more and more true. Then you get the call.

The bigger the number, the bigger the story. Journalists never 'round down' numbers. So any figure over £9 million becomes 'nearly £10 million' and so on. Most journalists – even those on respectable broadsheet newspapers – will use the biggest numbers possible. This makes it very important that you don't allow yourself to be pushed into speculating or mentioning any numbers at all unless you are absolutely sure. Stick to the facts and continue to quote only what you know.

Journalists' contact books are full of 'experts' who appear as though someone's rubbed a lamp whenever a crisis breaks. They are chosen for a variety of reasons ranging from expertise to availability. There is a range of views in most industries so it's perfectly reasonable for journalists to contact people whose opinion differs from yours. In addition, they will usually go to another source to get their reaction to your side of the story – a perfectly acceptable part of the job. On some occasions the 'experts' quoted may have been thorns in your corporate side for some time and you will know how to deal with them. Sometimes they're axe-grinders in disguise. It's very difficult for a news editor, TV or radio producer to resist when someone calls the news desk and says 'I'm professor of such and such at so and so university. I've studied accidents like this for 20 years and I have a pretty clear view as to how it could have been avoided.' Reporting the views of someone in that position is part of our responsibility as journalists. After all, who knows, they may be proved right.

The expert's views can lead to a rash of uninformed speculative stories as to the causes of your crisis. Don't be 'bounced' into reactions which you may regret later, whatever the provocation. Stick to what your own inquiry has established. If it's too early to talk about causes, say so. If you can easily rebut their claims about what you should have done to avert the crisis, say that too. However, don't spend too much time on this. Expert opinions are like buses – there'll be another one along in a minute, in all likelihood with a different destination. What you should avoid is being forced into a reactive role where you spend most of your effort and executive time responding to journalists' inquiries. If you allow this to happen the media will be in the driving seat. You want to be in charge. This is where your relationships with third party opinion leaders can be a trump card. Their opinions can carry significant weight as long as they are regarded as reputable and independent.

In nearly every crisis someone will say 'This was a disaster waiting to happen.' Journalists will always report it because occasionally it's true – and it's usually impossible to prove it's false until the inquiry reports. We don't find out the truth, however, until long after the crisis is over. If the crisis has involved members of the public, the full facts won't normally come out until the inquiry report which may be months or years later. As part of your crisis handling you will normally be rebutting such remarks by talking about the steps you had taken to avoid such a disaster.

HANDLING THE CRISIS

Another early task is to map out your communications environment as illustrated in Chapter 6 on public relations. This will allow you to identify key audiences. In particular you need to answer these questions:

Who and what has been affected by this crisis?

If there has been an accident this will include victims and families, but also neighbours, customers, shareholders, possibly the environment and your own staff.

Who can affect us?

This question often leads to a misunderstanding because executives feel that the first answer is the media. The media can affect you, but this usually takes a few hours as they take their cue from others. The people who can really take control of the situation from you are the regulatory authorities, police and fire brigade, who can take over very quickly. If there has been a fire or explosion, for example, they can come in, seal off the site and leave you and your team out in the street. (There is always the possibility that an explosion would render your premises unusable anyway, so you do need an alternative HQ.) They are more likely to do this if they feel you're not in control. It is crucial, therefore, that you communicate with them early, so they know you're handling the situation. The Health and Safety Executive, local MPs and the local authority should also be kept informed if relevant.

Who needs to know?

Anyone affected, as in the earlier list, needs to know, plus those likely to be affected over time.

Depending on the type of crisis this might include customers whose orders will be disrupted, shareholders, the Stock Exchange in extreme cases and subcontractors. In most businesses there is another group of people who have a connection with the company and need to be kept informed. These include your non-executive directors and any high profile people associated with your company, such as royalty or celebrities who hold honorary positions. These people are often overlooked, but wherever possible you should ensure that they hear the news from you, not a reporter calling for a reaction.

HANDLING INTERVIEWS

In 1963 a famous study at the University of Los Angeles attempted to identify what elements were most important in how people receive messages from an interviewee or someone making a presentation. The results were surprising. They showed that only 7 per cent of the message comes from the content, while 38 per cent comes from the non-verbal communication, that is the way you look and sound, and 55 per cent is received from body language. The exact percentages have been disputed since, but the main fact remains – the way you say it and the way you seem when you say it are often more important than what you say. This is particularly true in crisis media interviews especially in the early stages when there may not be much that you can say.

Some of these rules for media interviews have already emerged during the discussion, but here are the main points:

- you, or your spokesperson, need to appear as honest, human and communicative as possible
- remember that if things have gone wrong you're probably starting from a negative position, so a touch of humility may not go amiss
- express concern or regret (but not liability, without agreeing it with the lawyers)
- be reassuring and appear in control
- resist combat even with the most aggressive interviewers. If you wrestle with a pig you both get dirty, and the pig loves it!

- be polite and don't bully the interviewer
- listen to the question – it may not be as bad as you fear
- never speculate
- choose your ground and avoid 'doorstep' interviews (they make you look guilty)
- don't read company statements – look at the audience
- be wary of press conferences – they can go wrong
- keep up to date with what the media are saying about you, and ask for the very latest information before you start your interview
- be clear about your key messages.

... AND FINALLY

The phones have stopped ringing. The media circus has moved on. Some other company is on the news digging itself out of a hole. The pub is in sight. But wait. You have two more questions to answer.

What have we learned from this?

This is the best chance you'll get to discover whether your crisis management plan (CMP) actually works and where, if any, the weaknesses are. Get someone to write a report on it, and interview the main participants about what went well and badly. Do it now while it's still fresh in everyone's mind, or tomorrow at the latest. This is the hardest part, when everyone wants to get back to their 'proper jobs', but you must use your authority to push it through. Your crisis consultants can help to draw up the report. Later you can refine the CMP based on what you've learned.

Will the publicity return, and when?

While you're mentally going back to your day job, the forward planning editors on TV, radio and newspapers are making a note in the news diary to check the next stage of the story. This may be the inquest or report of the inquiry, the victims announcing legal moves, or even the anniversary of the crisis (journalists love anniversaries). You need to prepare for that, too.

CHAPTER SUMMARY

- The first step to crisis management is to accept that it can happen to you.
- A crisis involves actual or threatened media attention, an incident and a threat to your corporate or product reputation.
- Many crises can be averted and all can be managed.
- The key to successful crisis management is contingency planning, which consists of issues management and preparedness planning.
- Horizon-scanning exercises provide a framework for identifying potentially dangerous issues which could develop into crises – but remember the horizon is constantly changing.
- Preparedness planning is a four-step process: audit, prepare, test, refine.
- Reporters' normal attributes – cynicism, scepticism and sympathy for the underdog – are exaggerated in a crisis.
- The way reporters react to your crisis can be significantly influenced by their prior relationship with you.
- Building relationships with reporters in advance is very important – nobody will want to lend you an umbrella in the rain.
- 'Hope for the best but prepare for the worst' is the watchword of crisis management.
- When you're in a crisis, set clear objectives at the start.
- In a crisis, separate managing the problem from managing the media.
- Use the CAP formula for drafting holding statements – concern, action, perspective.
- Don't be 'bounced' into reacting to every allegation – stay in control.
- When it's over, ask yourself what you have learned – and when will the publicity return.

CHAPTER EIGHT

Putting it all together

This final chapter provides the last two pieces in the media handling jigsaw – how to prepare for an interview and techniques to ensure that you get your messages across during it. As success in an interview is so dependent on knowing what journalists want and how to take advantage of it, it will also pull together some of the main strands of the book. The chapter will therefore serve as a refresher and as a stand-alone guide to media interviews. First, here are my seven steps for successful interviews:

1 Take confidence from the fact that you are the expert. That's why they've come to you.
2 Remember it's not personal. A reporter's job is to ask questions, and nearly all of them will be perfectly reasonable.
3 Be clear about why you're doing the interview, and what you want to get out of it.
4 Find out what part you play in the story, and what the journalist is expecting from your contribution.
5 Prepare and practise thoroughly – this could be 'make or break time' for you, your company or career.
6 In the interview, be determined to get your key messages in as often as possible – use the bridging technique to keep getting back on track.
7 When it's over, review your performance against your objectives – and learn from it.

STEP 1: BE CONFIDENT

Journalists only ever play home games. However big a beast you are in your own organizational jungle, when you go in front of a journalist you are stepping into someone else's territory. It isn't necessarily hostile territory and with the right reconnaissance you're unlikely to be ambushed. However, the interview process can still be unfamiliar and daunting. Whether the reporter has a notebook, tape recorder or camera – or even if they're on the end of a telephone line – they are full of confidence (or at least it appears that way). Wherever the interview is physically taking place, mentally journalists are at home. There are many aspects of an interview which even senior executives can find off-putting – and a loss of confidence is often the result. Don't let it happen to you. As a confidence-booster, keep this thought in your mind: 'I know more about this than they do – that's why they've come to me.'

To help your mental confidence-building process, and to ensure that as little as possible comes as a surprise, here are some of the confidence-sapping events which often surround different types of media interviews.

If a TV crew come to your office they may ask if they can move the furniture around to get a more interesting background, then ask you to sit in an unfamiliar position. They might also ask you to change your tie (if it's 'strobing' or flaring) and alter the angle of your glasses or take them off to avoid reflections. Even with today's lightweight equipment it will seem there's a lot of it around your office, the lights shine in your eyes, they've disconnected your phone and asked you to turn off your mobile and pager – then they ask you to relax! It's not surprising you don't feel at home anymore. You have several options here: you don't have to do anything you don't want to, though they are trying to help you look your best, so you may reach a compromise based on the time you have available. Another option is to do the interview in another office, or a conference room. Then your communications executive can look after the crew while they set up the equipment and you are adding the finishing touches to your preparation in your own office. You just turn up at the interview room for a quick chat with the reporter, do the interview and go back. This is a great time-saving technique, though some reporters may want to interview you *in situ*.

If you go to the studio you may well feel you're entering the lions' den. The only people who feel confident in TV studios are the people who work there. It can be the most intimidating place and the way you're treated may compound this feeling. It's not unusual for an interviewee to be ushered into the studio while one item is playing out and the presenter is taking instructions in his or her earpiece from the programme producer. To you, it feels like you're being ignored. Then you hear your introduction being read by the same presenter, they turn to you and you're on! It can all happen so fast that it is unsettling. The way to minimize this discomfort is to do all your preparation before you are led into the studio. You will often sit in the 'Green Room' or hospitality suite where you can see the programme being broadcast. Look at the set and familiarize yourself with it. Ask the researcher where you will be sitting and who will be doing the interview. Your PR person should ask for a copy of the introduction, so you can respond to it. You should also check the facts you established before you agreed to appear, such as how long the piece will be (this may have changed in the last few minutes) and whether you will be the first or second speaker. All of this should increase your confidence level to the extent that all that's unfamiliar when you're in the studio is the harsh lighting.

Radio reporters carry far less kit than their TV colleagues and usually come armed with just a very small tape recorder. However, it is surprising how intimidating a small hand-held microphone can be. The intimidation comes from the way reporters move the mike between the two of you – they can take away your power to be heard with no notice. They don't set out to snatch the mike away in the middle of an answer, and it generally only happens as a result of your answering technique, that is when they think you've finished but then you unexpectedly carry on. The way to avoid this is to adopt a clear, definite way of speaking, be brief and don't ramble, so it's obvious when you have more to say.

During fast-moving news programmes such as the breakfast, lunchtime or drivetime shows, a radio studio is a very busy place. In fact to the unfamiliar outsider it seems like chaos. In among the weather and traffic reporters, financial editor, sports presenter and another interviewee, not to mention the two main presenters, it can feel like it's all going on around you and nobody knows you're there. Relax. Follow the same routine as for TV, and find out as much as you can about the format before you go into the studio. When you're in, ignore the chaos and stay focused on the reason you're there – your story, your company, your messages. As with TV, you'll suddenly hear the 'intro' to your story then you're on. Some radio stations encourage both presenters to chip in with questions – be prepared.

The confidence-draining aspect of print interviews is that the journalists have so much scope for telling the story in a way they want it. Your interview is the meat in the sandwich – they bake, slice and use the bread to suit the tastes of the readers. Don't be put off by this. Just be confident and stick to the subject. Worrying about every nuance and aspect of their questions and your answers is a sure way to an ulcer. You will have identified the best angles in advance, so all you have to do is stay focused. A print interview usually lasts longer than a broadcast interview, so your first challenge is to stay alert for longer, and be prepared to give much more detail in your answers. Avoid letting journalists put words in your mouth, and at the end ask them if they've got what they wanted. Also ask what they regard as the best angle – they'll often tell you. If it's not what you expected, go over your key messages again.

Increasingly, media interviews take place by telephone. So much business also happens by phone that this will probably be your most comfortable mode of being interviewed. The lack of facial response can be restricting as you can't always tell how well your remarks are going down. Adopt a technique of recapping your main points at appropriate stages in the interview. If you're not being recorded and you have a good soundbite or phrase you're pleased with, repeat it to ensure the journalist got it. Shorthand is a dying skill among many reporters, and they may be trying to write down your previous comment when you offer them your finely crafted *bon mot*. I once interviewed a scientist who was trying to dampen what he felt was unsubstantiated hype in the national press over scientific breakthroughs. As an example he referred to a recent story about the cloning of a monkey. The newspapers had claimed that this procedure, carried out by a multinational company in Switzerland, brought human cloning a step closer. 'Saying that is like claiming that a "buy one get one free" food offer in Tescos is addressing the problem of world famine. It's just ridiculous' he said. Then later in the interview he repeated it – leaving no chance that I hadn't got it. Quite right – it was a very good quote and made the introduction to my piece.

STEP 2: REMEMBER IT'S NOT PERSONAL

In some companies the higher you climb on the corporate ladder the more appropriate becomes the story of the emperor's new clothes. I meet many executives who are just not used to having their views questioned. Indeed there was one chief executive of a huge multinational whose local operatives asked his staff if they should wash the sheep in a neighbouring field before his visit! In these cases being challenged by journalists, or by anyone, can come as a bit of a shock. Some senior executives think they're being attacked personally. In the majority of cases they're wrong. The way to avoid the surprise is to undergo a media training session before you step into the media spotlight. This will prepare you for the unfamiliar experience of being questioned as well as identifying your strong and weak points. Whether you're used to being questioned or not, the way you respond to questions can affect the way you're portrayed. Even if you're used to being challenged by colleagues, when outsiders (journalists) do it about a subject close to your heart it is only human to react defensively. Human, but wrong. I have worked for some of the world's largest, most successful companies across a wide range of sectors, and many of them feel they're singled out for unfair treatment. This is a misunderstanding of the journalist's role.

Reporters are very clear about their place in the world: their role is to ask the questions anyone else would ask if they had the opportunity. That's all they're doing. Good reporters will show respect but not deferment. From our first days in the job we've grown used to interviewing important people and if necessary asking uncomfortable questions. Journalists are gatekeepers to your customers, and as such are asking questions legitimately. In reality, it is quite rare that journalists ask a question you couldn't have foreseen – your sales reps probably get more difficult, detailed questions on their pitch calls to potential customers.

So don't take it personally. Listen to the questions, let the reporters have their say, and answer – politely but clearly. Don't be patronizing – reporters hate being 'talked down to'. Remember that the reporter is doing his or her job, just as you are. In answering, remember my earlier advice: never underestimate their intelligence, and always underestimate their understanding.

STEP 3: BE CLEAR ABOUT YOUR MOTIVES

Most of the executives who undergo the admittedly dreadful experience of a bad interview are guilty of the same crime: they didn't have a clear objective, and didn't know what the journalist expected. To begin with the first part, when you are approached for an interview, ask yourself these questions:

- Why me?
- Why now?
- Why am I being asked to do this interview?
- Why is my company being asked?
- Do we have key messages and can I reasonably expect to convey them successfully?
- Am I the right person to do the interview?
- Can I make things better by doing the interview than by not doing it?

The last question is the crucial one. Anything less than an unequivocal 'yes' and you may be committing professional suicide. The question is a summary of the main points raised by the others. Let's take a moment to examine it by shifting the emphasis, starting with a point often missed: 'Can *I* make things better?' It is very flattering to be asked to give an interview – to the extent that many executives don't ask the basic question, 'Why me?' The process which leads a journalist to an interviewee is a haphazard one, and can just as easily work for you as against you. If I'm sitting in the newsroom and want an interviewee or a quote on a subject, I may just ask around my colleagues to see if anyone knows 'a good talker'. It may happen that someone mentions your name in connection with a story which sounds similar to one they've covered previously. Of course, your number is in the contact system, so within moments I've got you on the line.

If the call is not intercepted by your own PR department, you may be caught slightly off-guard when you pick up the phone, and agree to talk without really understanding the line of questioning. If it's not really your bag, say so at the outset – it saves time on both our parts, and if you start expressing an opinion I might quote you. So ask yourself, 'Why me, and why not somebody else?' It may be that the subject of my call is right up your company's street, but you're not the person to drive it there. If this is the case, you'll gain many more brownie points by saying so than by busking it. I have stressed the importance of corporate reputation throughout the book, so I hope that by now you wouldn't want to trust it to amateurs – including yourself – however well intentioned. Explain to the journalist that you're not the right person, but you can put them in touch with someone who is. Then do it! Keeping your promises to journalists is very important. If you tell me you can get me someone I start to relax – and I won't leave you alone till you've delivered them to me (at least via telephone).

Let's get back to the question. 'Can I *make things better*?' 'Making things better can mean many things, depending on your starting point. In a crisis, or just during a difficult day at the office, it may mean making things less bad, or explaining a previously misunderstood point of view. It may mean coming out smelling of roses, and enhancing your career in the process. With the right preparation, my view is that most of the time you can indeed 'make things better' than if you didn't talk.

Timing plays an important role in the answer, and underlines the relevance of another crucial question above – 'Why now?' I have talked elsewhere about the role of topicality in the journalistic decision-making process. There is always something which leads a journalist to your company *today* as opposed to yesterday or tomorrow. You need to know what it is. It may be a report or a publicity vehicle put out by your own PR consultancy – or one put out by your main competitors which raises specific shortcomings or failings in your company or product range. Whatever the reason for the approach, you need to understand it. This will give you a very good chance of understanding the journalist's agenda, and provide a guide as to the approach they may take in the interview.

The answer to the remaining question about your key messages should have been sorted out long before the journalist rings, as outlined in the chapter in using public relations to get your message across. So they are the main questions to ask yourself. Now let's turn to the other, equally important, part of the preparation equation.

STEP 4: FIND OUT WHAT PART YOU ARE EXPECTED TO PLAY

A big failing on the part of many executives who're approached for interviews is that they don't ask the journalist enough questions – indeed many of those I meet hardly seem to ask any questions at all. You can't make an informed decision about whether to take part until you know the full picture. The questions you should ask can be divided into content-related and logistical.

Here are the basic content-related questions:

- Who are you and whom do you represent?
- What exactly do you want to know?
- Who else are you talking to?
- Where do you expect me to fit in?
- Who (if not you) will be doing the interview?

The first question is obvious, but unfortunately the answer may be less so. There are so many media outlets that nobody could be expected to know them all. If you've never heard of the newspaper, magazine, TV or radio programme the journalist represents, say so – politely of course. In particular, ask them about the target audience because this will play a crucial part in deciding how to pitch your messages. The answer to the 'Who are you?' question should also tell you a little about the journalist, specifically whether they are a specialist or general reporter, or maybe a freelance (in which case ask if they have a commission for the article – if they don't you may be wasting your time).

Most people will ask the journalist what they're asking about. This is a good start but in many cases doesn't go far enough. They might reply, 'The government's recommendations for regulating e-commerce' – which doesn't take you much further. However, if you ask, 'What exactly do you want to know' you may get the answer, 'I'm calling about the government's recommendations for regulating e-commerce. I'm talking to a number of major corporations like yours who've moved a lot of their business on to the Internet. I'd like to know your views, in particular about whether the proposals would put UK businesses at a disadvantage.' Immediately you have a clearer picture.

If you follow this up by asking who else will be interviewed and what part the journalist expects you to play you will then have a very good idea of what the piece is about – and can make a decision in principle as to whether you want to take part. The response to the query about other interviewees is also useful in another respect – it will give you an idea as to the strength of the opposing view (remember journalists very rarely just talk to one side). The last question is important in dealing with TV and radio calls, when the caller may not be the interviewer. Many times I have spoken to polite, almost fawning researchers at the BBC, who when I asked who would be doing the interview have said, 'John Humphrys' – the most feared man on the radio! As so often in media handling, forewarned is forearmed.

So you've got a good understanding of what the piece is about, and quite possibly are on the point of agreeing to take part. Before you do, there are a few other points to be clarified. These are the logistical questions:

- When do you want to do it?
- How long will you need?
- How long will the piece be?

- For TV or radio – is it recorded or live?
- When is the deadline?

There is often some flexibility in these matters. For example, if you are the first person I've called on a story you will have more choice as to when we do the interview than if I've already got two interviews set up for the morning. You are also allowed more flexibility the more I want you. So if you're the crucial element in a piece, I will bend over backwards to accommodate you – even to the extent of re-scheduling the other interviewees. If you're just a bit-part player, a 'nice to have' then I won't be so accommodating. This time consideration applies to TV and to a degree to radio reporters. The concept is slightly foreign to many newspaper reporters where most interviews take place over the phone. Here, if I get you on the line, my expectation is that we're doing the interview. (It's what I do for a job – why else would I be ringing?)

Sometimes executives don't realize they're being interviewed until they're halfway through a call. When this happens, they sometimes complain of subterfuge. In fact, this is almost certainly mistaken. As a newspaper reporter I believe there's an implicit understanding that if I start to ask you questions then I'm taking note of what you say and may use it in my piece. This should not be any cause for concern on your part – you're a senior executive and I assume you are entitled to speak. It's also very likely in your position that your calls will be screened so you're unlikely to be caught on the hop. Nevertheless, it may happen – if you've given your direct line number to a journalist you met at a conference, for example.

If you know me – or if you're well known and respected in your field – you can prevent this by offering to talk on a 'for background' basis right at the start of the call. This is a common practice but does require careful handling and a level of sophistication in your media skills. In particular, you should never risk going off the record with sensitive information which would embarrass you or your company if it appeared with your name on it. This is particularly true with journalists you don't know. However, filling them in with background information which helps the piece, but making it clear you don't want to be quoted by name, can work very well in some circumstances, particularly if you're very knowledgeable and I'm tempted to come back for more on another day. You may decide to do this if you are aiming to summarize a complicated situation, to put something into context, or if you realize that the reporter has misunderstood an important element of the story – not that uncommon considering that journalists are generalists and you're a specialist. The reason for doing it is to help them write an accurate story. The reason for keeping your name out is that you don't want your company to be seen commenting on the matter.

The next step in your decision-making process is dependent on your diary and theirs. Whatever answer you receive to the question, 'How long will you need?' you can either be firm and set a time limit on your commitment, or add about 50 per cent to their estimate. Journalists of all types suffer from anxiety which often manifests itself in a lack of confidence that they've got everything they need, so they hang around far longer than necessary, asking increasingly detailed (and sometimes trivial) questions. They're often secretly relieved if you set the time limit, so go ahead and do it.

The next question, 'How long will the piece be?' is easier for broadcast journalists to answer than their print colleagues. This is partly because the newspaper or magazine production process involves so many people after a story has left the reporter that the final length is difficult to foretell. TV and radio news programmes, on the other hand, usually have an 'average' length per item, say one and a half minutes, or one minute 45 seconds. The importance of this answer is that it is an indication of how long you've got to tell your story. If I'm at ITN and I've told you in answer to an earlier question that I'm talking to you, your biggest rival and a junior government minister, and my piece is one and a half minutes long, you're not going to get more than 15 seconds each. The extra time is eaten up by my commentary, possibly some explanatory graphics and my final summarizing 'piece to camera'.

There are several reasons why it's important to know whether a broadcast interview is live or recorded. First, if it's recorded you can usually stop and do it again, which is clearly not possible with a live interview. But there are other reasons – the experience of going live can be daunting for even very experienced executives, so this will put extra pressure on you. In addition, your answers must reach a level of clarity, brevity and memorability in a live interview which can be achieved through editing if the encounter is recorded. The live interview has advantages, however, if you can achieve the above. In particular your remarks will go out unedited for the live transmission, though they will usually be recorded and edited for later news bulletins. Another advantage of 'going live' is that you usually then have the opportunity to respond to the edited report, so you are reacting to the very latest position. This can be a big advantage in a fast-changing situation. Many experienced broadcasters are keen to exploit this advantage and so request to go live wherever possible. A word of caution, however: don't take a request for a recorded interview as a sign that your words are going to be edited and taken out of context – many programmes are structured in such a way that they don't have any 'live' interviews at all, except with their own reporters.

A central theme of this book has been the time-sensitive nature of news journalism. This is so extreme that for many journalists, for example those working for Sky News or CNN, one deadline merges into another. The effect is that they live on the deadline – 'I need it now!' is their reaction to any question about a deadline. However, most will give you a reasonable answer if you persist. Try saying something like, 'Well if you're really asking me can I do an interview right now, the answer's no. But I could talk to you briefly at such and such a time.' As long as that time is not too far away you've just turned into a 'bird in the hand' – which any reporter will prefer to two in the bush. Be reasonable and flexible and put yourself out a bit and you can usually reach some mutually satisfactory arrangement.

OK. You've decided to take part in an interview. Let's raise the stakes and say it's high profile. It's on the chairman's pet project and you're going live on national television – and you know he'll be watching at home. How are you going to spend the time between now and then? By following rule number 5.

STEP 5: PREPARE AND PRACTISE THOROUGHLY

PREPARATION

Failure to prepare is preparation for failure.

During the oil crisis of the 1970s the price of oil was rising at a terrifying rate, with an alarming effect on petrol prices in the industrialized west. The Saudi Oil Minister Sheikh Yamani, whose country held most of the cards in the negotiations, was asked by an interviewer, 'What's the right price for a barrel of oil?' He thought for a moment then said, 'Whatever people can afford – plus 10 per cent.' The (possibly apocryphal) story illustrates how you should approach the amount of time you allow for preparation – whatever you can afford, plus a bit more. It is understandable when corporate life is lived at such a frenetic pace that you may feel you can't afford much time to prepare for a media interview. Understandable but wrong. However well you know the subject, you must prepare for the specific interview. You need to take into account the interviewer, the audience, the specific situation pertaining today, the other interviewees and the time you have to make your points. Anyone who takes the attitude 'I know this subject so I don't need to prepare' is heading for a fall. Here is a framework to help you prepare fully:

M   Message
A   Audience
L   Language
E   Examples
S   Soundbites

First, the message. It is so important that your message is concise and clear – and here's a technique for developing it. We call it the elevator test, and it works like this. Imagine you're alone on the ground floor in an elevator (or a lift as we still call it in the UK). As the doors close someone else squeezes in. They just happen to be the only person in the world who can turn your pet project into a global success and give you what you want professionally. They're only going up one floor so you have about 20 seconds to summarize your point. What are you going to say? Once you've identified that, you have your key message. You can then develop secondary and third-level messages and so on, but they all flow from the elevator message.

Hand in hand with your message is your consideration of the audience. Every audience has a level of understanding about you, your product or company. They may know a lot, or a little. They may be labouring under some pitiful delusion about you based on ignorance or misunderstanding. This is their starting point – let's call it A. You need an objective for your interview, which is generally to move them to point B at the other end of a straight line. Point B may be where they think positively about you, or feel they want to try your new product, or realize your competitors are wrong. Whatever it is, you need to be clear about it. Then you can set about moving them from A to B. The way you achieve that is by the other letters of the mnemomic.

Language is the first vehicle. All large corporations have their own language, often based on 'management consultantspeak', verbal shorthand and acronyms. The first step to choosing the right language is to ditch the jargon and speak English. This need not be intellectually difficult, but in many cases executives are so steeped in the jargon they don't realize when they're using it. One way to avoid this pitfall is to turn to external media training consultants, who rate jargon-busting as a core skill. The second aspect of language is that it must strike a chord with the audiences. You hear people praising executives with phrases like, 'He speaks our language.' This is what communication is about – using the right words to the best effect. Work on it.

Examples translate abstract into concrete. They answer the silent question we all ask whenever we see, read or hear a news story – 'What does this mean to me?' Journalists are excellent at answering this question – it's another case of making it relevant, the key to so much successful media handling. Think of the news stories which surround the Budget. The Chancellor says tax is going up or down a penny, and the news pages and programmes spell out what that means to people on different incomes and levels of income tax. They also increasingly tell us what the extra taxation will buy. These are very good illustrations of using examples to underline a point.

Once you've sorted out your examples, you have one last point to work on before you start your practice – the soundbite. A soundbite is a short way of summarizing a larger, complicated picture. It is the part that represents the whole. It should be short, memorable and vivid. The best soundbites paint word pictures, which is the best way of being memorable. My favourite sound-bites include Richard Branson criticizing British Airways with the words, 'Calling yourself "The world's favourite airline" because you carry more passengers than anyone else is like calling the M25 the world's favourite motorway' and Archbishop Desmond Tutu's criticism of the Mandela government in South Africa, 'This government stopped the gravy train just long enough to get on it.' These not only provided excellent broadcast soundbites, they also pro-vided great newspaper headlines. With the right forethought, you can do the same.

This leads to a second point about successful soundbites – they must be worked out in advance. Because they're so memorable, if you make them up on the spot you may find you're digging yourself into a deeper hole. You should also avoid trying to be too clever – a sin commit-ted by a spokeswoman criticizing a government initiative with the phrase, 'It can't go on like this – the situation's completely out of hand. It's become a Frankenstein's monster and now they'll never get it back in the bottle.' Memo-rable, certainly. But did it enhance her personal standing with the audience? Probably not.

PRACTICE

> '*Lucky b**tard*' – voice in the crowd to golfer Gary Player after he'd sunk a long putt.
> '*D'you know? The more I practise, the luckier I get.*' – Player's response.

Handling media interviews successfully is a skill. Like learning a sport, it requires technique and practice. I will come on to some techniques in a

moment, but for now let's consider the practice. The final part of your preparation is to undergo a practice interview which is as realistic as possible to the high profile, career-changing one your chairman will watch this evening. If you were expecting publicity on a particular issue you will have called in outside consultants to put you through a media training session. If there's no time for that, don't despair. You can usually do some practice with them on the phone to get you into the flow of the likely questions, then get your own internal communications team to run you through likely points.

STEP 6: GET YOUR KEY MESSAGES IN AS OFTEN AS POSSIBLE

This step strikes at the heart of the main objec-tive for most executives who need to prepare for an interview: how to ensure that you get your message across. This section shows you how. The first step is to realize why you're taking part in the interview at all – because you have a point of view to communicate. It follows, therefore, that an interview is not like a normal conversa-tion, which has ebb and flow and turn-taking. Your responsibility is to grab the steering wheel and drive it on to your agenda. There are three steps to doing this:

- be very clear what you want to say
- jump to conclusions
- use the bridging technique.

HAVE A CLEAR MESSAGE

'Being clear about what you want to say' needs some explanation. It is more specific than 'Knowing what you want to talk about'. For example, I once interviewed a senior executive from a oil company which is a partner in a huge project to develop hydrogen-powered cars. In the future they may eradicate fossil fuels and reduce the risk of global warming. His company was involved in making the hydrogen power technology work in a car engine, and developing the delivery technology and infrastructure – the filling stations. However, he spent the entire interview talking about the cars of the future and the attractions of hydrogen as a power source.

He painted a vivid picture of how they were virtually silent and had no emissions yet could go as fast as cars do today. At the end I said, 'Thank you for that great plug for your car-making partners in the project – if we invite you back maybe you'll tell us what your own company is doing.' He was horrified – he'd thrown away a great chance for plugging his own company to millions of viewers. In fact, as it was a training session he was able to do the interview again, and he never repeated that mistake.

Another example was a senior scientist from a company who'd developed a new kind of nico-tine replacement therapy. My first question was, 'Do you think some people have an addictive personality so they'll always find it more difficult to stop smoking than others?' His answer took up most of the three minutes allowed for the interview – it ranged from heroin addiction to substance abuse, touched on compulsive shopping disorder, and talked about how nicotine was more addictive than heroin. It was fascinating and anyone watching would be struck by his impressive knowledge of the subject matter. But that wasn't why he was there. He hadn't mentioned his company once, nor told us that their

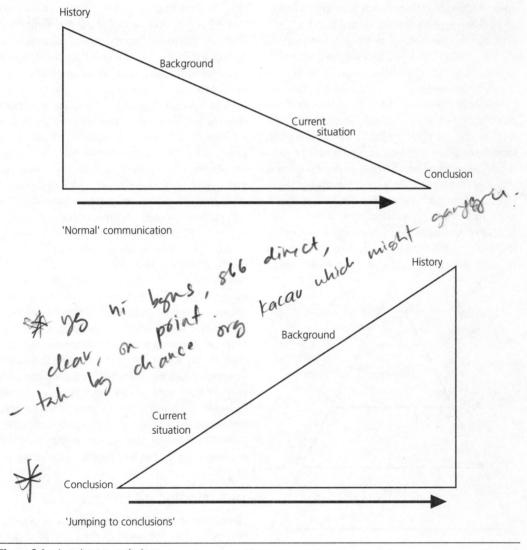

Figure 8.1   Jumping to conclusions

method of quitting smoking was better – let alone why!

These two executives made the same mistake. They were both very clear about *what they wanted to talk about* but not at all clear about *what they wanted to say*. Use the elevator test outlined earlier to help you define it.

JUMPING TO CONCLUSIONS

The second step to getting your point across concerns the way you answer questions. Figure 8.1 illustrates the technique which I call 'jumping to conclusions'. The first graph shows how many people answer questions or conduct other communications efforts, such as writing a report or making a presentation. They build a case, starting with the history, moving onto the background, bringing us up to date on the current situation then reaching a conclusion. I call this the scenic route, and it's fine with many audiences, particularly if they won't interrupt you, and you can keep their attention. With journalists, however, neither of these things apply. You should, therefore, answer questions the other way round. Start with the conclusion, because this is your key message. Then if you have time you can take us through the supporting evidence, but if not, you've made your point anyway.

There are three main reasons for adopting the 'jumping to conclusions' technique. The first is because it reflects the way journalists write news stories. Figure 8.2 illustrates this. We start with the intro, which is your conclusion. We then move to the main facts, fill in the details and tie up the loose ends. Check this yourself with any newspaper you have to hand. We write stories in this way because the intro is the exciting part – it's what's new. It also acts as a shop window, enticing the readers to come inside and look further. This triangle shape arranges the facts in descending order of importance or interest, so the story can be cut from the bottom without losing any of the best parts. This makes it easier for the sub-editor to cut the story to make it fit any available size of space. The importance of this to you is that the more you can give us stories in the way that we would use them, the more likely we are to use them. Press releases need to be written in the same way – they need to grab our attention at the start, before we throw them in the bin.

The second reason for jumping to conclusions is that if you take the scenic route of Figure 8.1 I might interrupt you before you get to the point. You then find yourself on a slip road, wondering how you get back on the motorway. You only need this to happen twice and you can find yourself a long way from your intended destination. If you jump to the conclusion, however, you get your point in first. Then if I interrupt you, you've still made your point.

To illustrate the third reason for using this technique, consider how you listen to interviews on the radio. You will probably find that your attention level starts high, then drops off. Then it rises again with each new question which provides another voice, area of discussion, or some conflict between the interviewer and interviewee. In general, then, the audience are mentally 'tuning back in' to the interview at each question. That is the point where you want your key messages – when people are paying attention. If you take the scenic route your key messages are in the low points of the attention graph.

THE 'BRIDGING' TECHNIQUE

So you know what your messages are, and you're determined to put them at the front of all your answers. But you don't get the right questions.

Figure 8.2   The structure of a typical news story

So what do you do? You bridge. This means taking a word from the question and using it as a bridge to one of your key messages. Let's illustrate it by using the two executives discussed earlier who didn't get their points across. The first question to the oil company executive was, 'Hydrogen-powered cars ... sounds amazing. What will they look like?' This question is right in the area he doesn't want to spend much time on – remember he wants to talk about how his own company is making the technology work. So he builds a bridge. He might reply, 'They'll look just like the cars out there today with a crucial difference – what's under the bonnet. At ABC Oil we're working on developing the hydrogen-powered engine and you're right – it's amazing. It will be almost silent, and the only emission will be a few drops of waste water. We're one of the world's leading experts in making energy work and we're into this in a big way. We've just fitted the prototype hydrogen engine to the first car. . . .' You can see here how effective the bridging technique is. Within a few seconds he's in his own territory of expertise and plugging his company.

Let's consider the second example: the nicotine replacement therapy scientist. Again, the first question is unpromising to say the least, 'Do you think some people have an addictive personality so they'll always find it more difficult to stop smoking than others?' The problem here is that it's such a wide topic he can spend hours on it without plugging his own company. The answer is to narrow it down – and the bridging technique is perfect for this. Such a wide-ranging opening question offers a wide range of bridging opportunities. Here's one: 'There's some research to suggest they might – but it's only a matter of degree. Just about everyone finds quitting difficult and it's accepted now that some kind of help will increase your chances. What our trials have shown is that our new quit packs increase your chances even more ...' Here's another: 'Well, nicotine is so addictive that even people with strong willpower in every other respect get hooked very quickly. It's because smoking is an addiction that they need help to come off it – and our trials have shown that our new quit packs do that more successfully than the old type of nicotine replacement therapy.'

With a little thought and practise on the technique you can almost always bridge back to your key messages. But to build a bridge you need two secure anchor points – and sometimes the question doesn't offer you that. There are times when all the words in the question are negative. For example, 'So your profits are down, sales have slumped and you've had three chief executives in as many years. Are you really expecting the City to take the new management team seriously with that kind of track record?' In cases like this you need a fallback position. That's where generic bridging phrases come in. They are phrases such as:

The real issue here is ...
The fact of the matter is ...
That doesn't alter the main fact
You say that, but what our customers (people) tell me is ...
Let's not forget that ...
But ...
However ...

So in the example above, the answer might begin, 'Everyone knows the company's been through a difficult period. The real issue now is whether we have the right management team in place to put that behind us and tackle the challenges of the future – and the answer is that we do. Today's announcement shows that . . .'

When we introduce executives to the bridging technique they are sometimes wary, fearful it will make them sound like a politician who refuses to answer the question. The thought may have occurred to you too. Let me reassure you that you won't – for several reasons. First, you will be able to answer many questions straight on. Second, on most occasions when you use the bridging technique you will be using words from the question as in the examples on hydrogen and quitting smoking. Third, and most importantly, bridging is a three-stage process. It's actually quite simple and we call it ABC, for acknowledge – bridge – communicate. The acknowledgement of the question is the crucial element here. Without it, you sound like you're not answering the question. With it, you're dealing with the question briefly then moving onto your own agenda.

Your advisers can help you to work out the

best ABCs for you depending on the questions you're likely to be asked, but here are some generic ones to illustrate the technique:

> That's right ... but more important ...
> key message
> No, that's not right ... the position is ...
> key message
> I don't know that ... what I do know is
> ... key message
> I'd expect them to say that ... but the
> main fact is ... key message

There are two other important points to note about the bridging technique. First, the acknowledgement can often be a brief answer to the question, as in the example about addictive personalities, 'There is some evidence that they might...' Sometimes interviewees become locked in a mindset which says, 'If I answer the question I'll be driven onto his or her agenda, so I won't answer any questions at all.' This is as much a mistake as those who take the opposite tack and slavishly answer all the questions and wait for the subject to come round to their own message.

Second, be sparing with this technique. Don't let your whole interview become a bridge-building exercise. The best interviews lie somewhere between the extremes quoted above, neither being 'on message' to the point of incredulity (as some politicians are) nor answering every question however irrelevant. Aim to answer as many questions as you can, to acknowledge all the questions, and to get at least one of your key messages into every answer. People, that is the audience or readers, are not stupid. They can tell if you're being evasive. An interview entirely composed of bridging and not answering the question is like a football match ruined by professional fouls, or a tennis game between two heavy-hitting serve and volley merchants – not good for the spectators. Try to bring a little open play into your game – you can still score and you're more likely to be asked back!

STEP 7: REVIEW YOUR PERFORMANCE AGAINST YOUR OBJECTIVES

This is the rule most often ignored – and follow-ing it may not bring such bad news. Many executives on our courses come out of the TV or radio studio, or indeed finish a mock print interview, convinced they've made a real hash of it. This is rarely the case. Once they've seen themselves on the video they are usually pleasantly surprised and agree that it was nowhere near as bad as they thought at the time. The same is probably true of your own media interviews. If this is the case, it's important that you look back at them so you can get a realistic view of your performance. If it's not the case then you need to learn from your mistakes. Start the review by restating your objectives and key messages. Then examine the interview(s) to see if you successfully communicated them. Ask your PR advisers to help you with this, but also involve media training consultants – their external view is more likely to be objective than that of your subordinates who will have one eye on their career.

WHAT JOURNALISTS WANT

In this final section I want to summarize the key themes of the book in terms of what journalists want and how to take advantage of it, and to underline what I consider to be the most important tips and techniques for improving your chances of obtaining media publicity. You may remember from earlier that we can summarize a journalist's wish list in four lines:

> Headline – to grab their attention
> Deadline – they're getting shorter all
> the time, and it's vital you know them
> Good line – a memorable phrase,
> quote or a soundbite
> Bottom line – summarize your story in
> a few seconds for the pitch.

When executives ask me what is the most common mistake that people make in dealing with journalists, my answer is simple: assuming too much knowledge. Journalists are great bluffers. Their job involves going into any situation and giving the impression of being in control. This leads many interviewees to believe the journalist knows more than they do. Remember – a journalist's knowledge is 'a mile wide and an inch deep'. As an expert, your knowledge is the opposite – 'a mile deep and an inch wide'. Figure 2.3 (p. 27) illustrates this point. It's clear from this that to make the most of discussions, interviews or conversations with journalists you must start in the common ground – in the inch by inch square at the top. You can then take them some way into your knowledge base.

An important element of starting in the common ground is that you must know where it is. The answer will depend in part on what type of journalist they are, either a specialist or a generalist. Don't be afraid to ask them how much they know about a subject. In my view, potential interviewees don't ask enough questions of journalists. Start with the questions earlier in this chapter. Also remember that wherever your story starts, it will swim around the media pond, and as it does so its nature will change to fit the audiences. Don't be surprised by this – journalists are excellent at finding the right angles for their audiences. You can, of course, help them when you write press releases by producing several, targeted at different groups.

If assuming too much knowledge is the most common mistake, the second is not understanding this acronym: FAB – features and benefits. This is a simple acronym used in selling and marketing. To sell somebody something you need to persuade them of the benefits. It's the same with stories – journalists put themselves in the position of the readers, viewers or listeners and ask 'What does this mean to me?' Selling the benefits gets over this problem. If you fail to answer the question then the audience – or the journalist on their behalf – asks the question in another way, 'So what?' Avoiding 'So what?' is a key to successful story pitching and interviewing. That's where FAB comes in. Too many people, particularly experts, get hung up on the features of a story, rather than the benefits. To return to the hydrogen-powered car example quoted earlier, the benefit is a powerful engine which has all the advantages of petrol engines in terms of safety and reliability but none of the drawbacks – it's almost silent and causes no pollution so will cut down global warming. The feature is how the chemical reaction involving the hydrogen powers the car – interesting to engineers and chemists, but not to the public.

The interviewee has usually spent some time, sometimes years, working on the features, so it's not surprising if this is the area on which they concentrate. But when dealing with journalists, put the benefits first, then explain the features if you're asked.

Some people are confused about the difference between features and benefits, so let me illustrate it by way of three examples:

1 My car has a driver's airbag (feature) which means that if I'm in a crash I'm less likely to be injured (benefit).
2 This computer has a remote mouse (feature) which means that when I use it to make presentations I can walk around the stage and I'm not limited by having to touch the computer (benefit).
3 Many modern drugs have far fewer side effects than older ones (feature) which means that patients will continue to take them until they're successfully treated (benefit).

You can see from this that the key to the difference is the phrase 'which means that...'. Use this phrase yourself to identify the benefit. If whatever you say can be followed by the phrase 'which means that...' then whatever comes after it is the benefit. If you listen to the radio news you will often hear the interviewers ask, 'What's the point?' The FAB technique answers the question.

My next mnemonic is EST. All journalists' favourite words end in these three letters – biggest, smallest, fastest, slowest, dearest, cheapest, richest, poorest and so on. Sometimes they only end in -ST, as in first, last or worst. The concept behind this is very important to understanding what journalists want. They like absolutes because absolutes cannot be beaten. Either a new drug is the first cure for the common cold or it isn't, your new car or computer is either the fastest available or it isn't. Journalists love this type of clarity. The word 'first' is a very interesting journalistic concept because it addresses the concept that 'news is change' – if something is the first, then something has changed. As a general rule, the more EST words you can get into your stories and press releases the better their chances.

TLA is my final acronym. It stands for Three Letter Abbreviations. Avoid them – they're probably not understandable to people outside your industry. Some modern corporations use virtually their own language, completely foreign to outsiders. I clearly remember being called into one multinational corporation which had an issue about to break. To help them prepare their messages I asked for copies of the internal memos relating to the issue. I sat down to read them and 15 minutes later I rang the director who'd called me in. 'Have you got a DOA?' I asked. 'What's that?' he said. 'A Dictionary Of Acronyms' I replied. He got the point. The memos were impenetrable without translation into something approaching English. Internally the verbal shorthand was very useful. Externally it didn't make any sense.

The point about language was made earlier in this chapter, but it is so important I make no apologies for repeating it. Avoid TLAs, and avoid jargon – if you don't I will translate it for you into language my readers will understand, and there's a great risk that I won't understand it either, so then you really are in trouble.

CONCLUSIONS

Throughout this book I have urged you to be very clear about your key messages. My own key messages have, I hope, shone through many of its pages. They are, first, that positive media coverage is there for the asking if you know what you're doing. Second is that to handle the media successfully you need to understand what the reporter wants, and that their primary thought is 'What does this mean to the readers?' The third point concerns your mindset – be positive, be clear and be concise. If you follow the advice in this book you will find your encounters with journalists to be mainly positive and satisfying.

I wish you the best of luck in exploiting the connection between the media headline and your corporate bottom line.

CHAPTER SUMMARY

- Remember that a journalist has come to you because you're the expert.
- Preparation is the key to success – get your communications team to find out all they can about what the journalist wants out of the interview.
- Decide what you want out of the interview.
- Remember that it's a reporter's job to ask questions – it's not personal and they're not attacking you.
- The crucial question is: 'Can I make things better by doing this interview than by not doing it?' The answer must be a resounding 'yes'.
- Ask yourself, or find out, why the journalist has chosen to come to you today.
- Most people don't ask journalists enough questions – make sure you do.
- There is no such thing as 'off the record'.
- The journalist is always thinking, 'What does this mean to my readers or audience?' You must make the answer very clear.
- Handling media interviews is a skill – you can improve with practice.
- In an interview, use the 'jumping to conclusions' and 'bridging' techniques to get back to your agenda.
- Remember to sell the benefits, not just the features.
- When dealing with journalists, never underestimate their intelligence, always underestimate their understanding.
- A journalist's knowledge is 'a mile wide and an inch deep'. Your knowledge is 'a mile deep and an inch wide'. You must start with the common ground.

A Word on the Web

The Internet is revolutionizing the way we work and play – and the media business is changing as much as any other. All the advice in this book about pitching to journalists remains relevant to any delivery medium, including the Internet. However, the Internet will affect your media image and handling in a number of ways.

Newspapers, magazines, TV and radio have recognized the threats and opportunities the Web represents, so have embraced 'New Media' with enthusiasm. All national newspapers, TV and radio stations have had Web sites for some time and by the beginning of January 2000, 85 per cent of regional newspapers also had a Web presence. It is likely that this figure will rise. The effect of this is that your news can be disseminated more quickly and widely than previously. This can be good or bad for you, depending on the nature of the news being spread. The Web is monitored by journalists and Web authors put a lot of effort into ensuring that stories on their sites are picked up. As I write there are two stories which started on Web sites that are receiving a lot of publicity – allegations that Foreign Secretary Robin Cook knew of a plot to assassinate Libyan leader Colonel Gaddafi, and a claim that John Lennon was an IRA supporter. The biggest story to hit US politics for 20 years – the Clinton/Lewinsky affair – broke first on a Web site within minutes of the author hearing about it. Although you are unlikely to be involved in stories like this, these examples do illustrate how powerful the Web has become over a short time.

It also means that news about you is now available to the public for as long as it remains on Web sites – another nail in the coffin of the argument that 'today's news is tomorrow's fish and chips wrapper'. In a sense, the vast information resources on the Web mirror those which were previously only available to journalists through cuttings libraries. This, coupled with the Web's global reach, is a very strong reason to work hard to ensure that your company is portrayed accurately.

Another effect of the Web-based media is that it gives you or your communications team yet another media monitoring task. It is now vital that you keep up with what's being said about you on major Web sites. Keeping track of the entire World Wide Web is an impossible job, but you should monitor the main news sites. For UK stories they are BBC <http//news.bbc.co.uk> and ITN online <http//itn.co.uk>, Sky News <http//sky.com/news>, the Press Association <http//www.pa.press.net> and primarily the broadsheet papers. For company news the *Financial Times* Web site <http://news.ft.com> is one of the best sites around on any subject, and the *Guardian* <http//www.guardian.co.uk> and *Telegraph* <http//telegraph.co.uk> Web sites are also very highly regarded. For international news, start with CNN <http//cnn.com>. The mid-market and popular papers are starting to take their Web presence more seriously, so over time you will find that you or your communications team have as many Web sites as newspapers to check in the morning. The Web-searching task is made easy of course by keyword searches – you can be in and out of a Web site in a couple of minutes if you're just searching for your company name.

There is another important difference between Web stories and those which appear about you in the traditional media. If you find a serious inaccuracy about you or your company, you should ring the Web editor responsible and point it out. If it really is inaccurate and not just a matter of interpretation, he or she may decide to change it, something which can never happen with traditional media outlets, where your only recourse is a correction or (rarely) an apology after the event. This is another reason for adding the Web to your media monitoring list.

One important advantage of the Web is that because space is infinite, it allows online journalists to go into stories in much more detail. This starts to address the accusation that newspaper coverage of stories is 'a mile wide and an inch deep'. With the Web, in theory it can be a mile wide and a mile deep. In practice what are sometimes regarded as explanatory 'sidebar' pieces (so-called because they often run down the side of the page in a single column) in newspapers become quite detailed 'shoulder' pieces on news Web sites offering more detail or background on the main story. A criticism of news is that it takes things out of context, with the Web this doesn't have to be true. It also illustrates just how much space is required to put the whole context back in!

This leads to a question increasingly asked by executives and communications specialists – should you try and pitch your stories directly to Web editors? There is no easy answer to this because online journalism is changing so quickly. When news Web sites were first developed they tended to just carry the material included in their traditional parent. We are already starting to see, however, Web stories that are not replicated in the traditional outlets. As online journalism becomes more accepted, this trend will become very important and some Web sites will start to become powerful outlets in their own right. My advice, therefore, is to keep an eye on the major sites, and if you feel like pitching directly to the online team, have a go. It certainly won't do any harm.

THE WEB AS A SOURCE

So much for the end product of online journalism. But what about the other side of the coin – using the Web as an information resource? Let's look at this from two points of view and see how they might affect you or your company's image. First, how do journalists use the Web? In many different ways. There are technophiles and technophobes in journalism as there are in every other profession. Some of them – the technophiles – absolutely love the power the Web gives them. I was recently on the phone to a journalist trying to sell him a story, and while we were talking he turned up some relevant Web sites. 'How does your story compare with what was reported

here last month?' he asked. So the Web is another reason to be on your toes when you're pitching stories! In time, clearly, all journalists will begin to use the Web as a resource. The importance of this to you is that there are now many other points of view easily available to journalists, some of them opposing your own. So you need to be prepared. The actual views should not surprise you, because I assume you always know what critics are saying about you. The effect of the Web is to make those views instantly available to any journalist working on your story.

But please don't start to believe that the Web is necessarily bad news for you. It isn't – it can be a great help to you as you strive to communicate your messages to a wider audience. Communicating via the Web is a huge subject in its own right, but here I want to touch on two elements which affect your media handling strategy. The first concerns the way you communicate with journalists themselves, the second relates to how you talk to other interested parties.

Large corporations are now using the Web to communicate with journalists. Many of them have a Web site page called 'Press Room' or something similar. Many of them put their press releases on the Web, and leave them there indefinitely. This is a great idea and one which most journalists heartily encourage as it saves time. I agree with one proviso – it should not replace efforts at building relationships with journalists, and talking to them to explain matters. You can also find out who's been in to look at what's going on, which can be helpful in targeting interested journalists. You can occasionally use journalists as a means of intelligence-gathering. Once you have established a relationship with a particular journalist, it's always worth asking them which Web sites they rate, and which ones they look at for an opposing view. You should have this information anyway, but new Web sites spring up so quickly – and fold just as fast – that this might tip you off about a new site which may pose you problems.

The other great change brought about by the Internet is that it allows you to communicate with interested parties without having your communication mediated by journalists. This is why the Internet has been described as a 'media bypass'. This is true but any unmediated communication direct from the company is always going to be less trusted than something scrutinized by journalists fulfilling their role as gatekeepers. Using the Internet generally (rather than just the Web) will allow you to enter into dialogue with consumer groups and check out their reaction to your initiatives. Always remember, though, the Web leaves a very clear trail – so don't put anything on it you may regret.

In practice you should aim for a twin track strategy: approach journalists in the manner detailed throughout this book, while at the same time using the Web to communicate directly with key audiences. The key is to ensure that your messages are consistent.

One other point – because there are huge variations in the extent to which journalists use the Web (and even e-mail) don't assume they've seen something just because it's there. As a rule of thumb, assume they have seen the bad news about you, but missed the good news, and you won't go far wrong. Finally – keep your Web site up to date. It really makes you look amateurish if this is not done, and will frustrate journalists who have begun to rely on it.

SUMMARY

- Almost all newspapers, TV news programmes and magazines now have Web sites.
- The Web means that your story can be disseminated more quickly and widely than previously.
- The Internet can be a great help in communicating your message to the public.
- Web stories are available to the public worldwide for a long time, so you need to work hard to ensure that you get the right kind of coverage.
- Build a 'press room' area for journalists on your Web site.
- Monitoring important Web sites is a key task for your communications team or media monitoring company.
- If you find a serious inaccuracy, ring the editor and ask for it to be changed.
- Online journalism can go into more detail than any other type. You should regard this as an opportunity and be ready to supply detailed information about your company and products quickly – and remember, they'll want it electronically.
- Pitching directly to Web sites will become commonplace.
- Journalists use the Web as a source, but don't assume they've seen it, especially if it's good news.

Index